William Shakespeare

ALL'S WELL THAT ENDS WELL

Edited with a Commentary by Barbara Everett
Introduced by Janette Dillon

PENGUIN BOOKS

PENGUIN BOOKS

Published by the Penguin Group
Penguin Books Ltd, 80 Strand, London WC2R ORL, England
Penguin Group (USA) Inc., 375 Hudson Street, New York, New York 10014, USA
Penguin Group (Canada), 10 Alcorn Avenue, Toronto, Ontario, Canada M4V 3B2
(a division of Pearson Penguin Canada Inc.)
Penguin Ireland, 25 St Stephen's Green, Dublin 2, Ireland (a division of Penguin Books Ltd)
Penguin Group (Australia), 250 Camberwell Road, Camberwell, Victoria 3124, Australia
(a division of Pearson Australia Group Pty Ltd)
Penguin Books India Pvt Ltd, 11 Community Centre, Panchsheel Park, New Delhi – 110 017, India
Penguin Group (NZ), cnr Airborne and Rosedale Roads, Albany, Auckland 1310, New Zealand
(a division of Pearson New Zealand Ltd)
Penguin Books (South Africa) (Pty) Ltd, 24 Sturdee Avenue, Rosebank 2196, South Africa

Penguin Books Ltd, Registered Offices: 80 Strand, London WC2R ORL, England

www.penguin.com

This edition first published in Penguin Books 1970
Reprinted with revised Further Reading 1998
Reissued in the Penguin Shakespeare series 2005

1

This edition copyright © Penguin Books, 1970
Account of the Text and Commentary copyright © Barbara Everett, 1970
Further Reading copyright © Michael Taylor, 1998
General Introduction and Chronology copyright © Stanley Wells, 2005
Introduction, The Play in Performance and revised Further Reading copyright © Janette Dillon, 2005

Set in 11.5/12.5 PostScript Monotype Fournier
Typeset by Palimpsest Book Production Limited, Polmont, Stirlingshire
Printed in England by Clays Ltd, St Ives plc

Contents

General Introduction vii
The Chronology of
   Shakespeare's Works xvii
Introduction xxi
The Play in Performance lix
Further Reading lxxiii

ALL'S WELL
THAT ENDS WELL 1

An Account of the Text 107
Commentary 121

General Introduction

Every play by Shakespeare is unique. This is part of his greatness. A restless and indefatigable experimenter, he moved with a rare amalgamation of artistic integrity and dedicated professionalism from one kind of drama to another. Never shackled by convention, he offered his actors the alternation between serious and comic modes from play to play, and often also within the plays themselves, that the repertory system within which he worked demanded, and which provided an invaluable stimulus to his imagination. Introductions to individual works in this series attempt to define their individuality. But there are common factors that underpin Shakespeare's career.

Nothing in his heredity offers clues to the origins of his genius. His upbringing in Stratford-upon-Avon, where he was born in 1564, was unexceptional. His mother, born Mary Arden, came from a prosperous farming family. Her father chose her as his executor over her eight sisters and his four stepchildren when she was only in her late teens, which suggests that she was of more than average practical ability. Her husband John, a glover, apparently unable to write, was nevertheless a capable businessman and loyal townsfellow, who seems to have fallen on relatively hard times in later life. He would have been brought up as a Catholic, and may have retained

Catholic sympathies, but his son subscribed publicly to Anglicanism throughout his life.

The most important formative influence on Shakespeare was his school. As the son of an alderman who became bailiff (or mayor) in 1568, he had the right to attend the town's grammar school. Here he would have received an education grounded in classical rhetoric and oratory, studying authors such as Ovid, Cicero and Quintilian, and would have been required to read, speak, write and even think in Latin from his early years. This classical education permeates Shakespeare's work from the beginning to the end of his career. It is apparent in the self-conscious classicism of plays of the early 1590s such as the tragedy of *Titus Andronicus*, *The Comedy of Errors*, and the narrative poems *Venus and Adonis* (1592–3) and *The Rape of Lucrece* (1593–4), and is still evident in his latest plays, informing the dream visions of *Pericles* and *Cymbeline* and the masque in *The Tempest*, written between 1607 and 1611. It inflects his literary style throughout his career. In his earliest writings the verse, based on the ten-syllabled, five-beat iambic pentameter, is highly patterned. Rhetorical devices deriving from classical literature, such as alliteration and antithesis, extended similes and elaborate wordplay, abound. Often, as in *Love's Labour's Lost* and *A Midsummer Night's Dream*, he uses rhyming patterns associated with lyric poetry, each line self-contained in sense, the prose as well as the verse employing elaborate figures of speech. Writing at a time of linguistic ferment, Shakespeare frequently imports Latinisms into English, coining words such as abstemious, addiction, incarnadine and adjunct. He was also heavily influenced by the eloquent translations of the Bible in both the Bishops' and the Geneva versions. As his experience grows, his verse and prose become more supple, the patterning less apparent, more ready to accommodate the rhythms of ordinary speech, more colloquial in diction, as in the speeches of the Nurse in *Romeo and Juliet*, the characterful prose of Falstaff and Hamlet's soliloquies. The effect is of increasing psychological realism, reaching its greatest heights in *Hamlet*, *Othello*, *King Lear*, *Macbeth* and *Antony and Cleopatra*. Gradually he discovered ways of adapting the regular beat of the pentameter to make it an infinitely flexible instrument for matching thought with feeling. Towards the end of his career, in plays such as *The Winter's Tale*, *Cymbeline* and *The Tempest*, he adopts a more highly mannered style, in keeping with the more overtly symbolical and emblematical mode in which he is writing.

So far as we know, Shakespeare lived in Stratford till after his marriage to Anne Hathaway, eight years his senior, in 1582. They had three children: a daughter, Susanna, born in 1583 within six months of their marriage, and twins, Hamnet and Judith, born in 1585. The next seven years of Shakespeare's life are virtually a blank. Theories that he may have been, for instance, a schoolmaster, or a lawyer, or a soldier, or a sailor, lack evidence to support them. The first reference to him in print, in Robert Greene's pamphlet *Greene's Groatsworth of Wit* of 1592, parodies a line from *Henry VI, Part III*, implying that Shakespeare was already an established playwright. It seems likely that at some unknown point after the birth of his twins he joined a theatre company and gained experience as both actor and writer in the provinces and London. The London theatres closed because of plague in 1593 and 1594; and during these years, perhaps recognizing the need for an alternative career, he wrote and published the narrative poems *Venus and Adonis* and *The Rape of Lucrece*. These are the only works we can be certain that Shakespeare himself was responsible for putting into print. Each bears the author's dedication to Henry Wriothesley, Earl of Southampton (1573–1624), the second in warmer terms than the first. Southampton, younger than Shakespeare by ten years, is the only person to whom he personally dedicated works. The Earl may have been a close friend, perhaps even the beautiful and adored young man whom Shakespeare celebrates in his *Sonnets*.

The resumption of playing after the plague years saw the founding of the Lord Chamberlain's Men, a company to which Shakespeare was to belong for the rest of his career, as actor, shareholder and playwright. No other dramatist of the period had so stable a relationship with a single company. Shakespeare knew the actors for whom he was writing and the conditions in which they performed. The permanent company was made up of around twelve to fourteen players, but one actor often played more than one role in a play and additional actors were hired as needed. Led by the tragedian Richard Burbage (1568–1619) and, initially, the comic actor Will Kemp (d. 1603), they rapidly achieved a high reputation, and when King James I succeeded Queen Elizabeth I in 1603 they were renamed as the King's Men. All the women's parts were played by boys; there is no evidence that any female role was ever played by a male actor over the age of about eighteen. Shakespeare had enough confidence in his boys to write for them long and demanding roles such as Rosalind (who, like other heroines of the romantic comedies, is disguised as a boy for much of the action) in *As You Like It*, Lady Macbeth and Cleopatra. But there are far more fathers than mothers, sons than daughters, in his plays, few if any of which require more than the company's normal complement of three or four boys.

The company played primarily in London's public playhouses – there were almost none that we know of in the rest of the country – initially in the Theatre, built in Shoreditch in 1576, and from 1599 in the Globe, on Bankside. These were wooden, more or less circular structures, open to the air, with a thrust stage surmounted by a canopy and jutting into the area where spectators who paid one penny stood, and surrounded by galleries where it was possible to be seated on payment of an additional penny. Though properties such as cauldrons, stocks, artificial trees or beds could indicate locality, there was no representational scenery. Sound effects such as flourishes of trumpets, music both martial and amorous, and accompaniments to songs were provided by the company's musicians. Actors entered through doors in the back wall of the stage. Above it was a balconied area that could represent the walls of a town (as in *King John*), or a castle (as in *Richard II*), and indeed a balcony (as in *Romeo and Juliet*). In 1609 the company also acquired the use of the Blackfriars, a smaller, indoor theatre to which admission was more expensive, and which permitted the use of more spectacular stage effects such as the descent of Jupiter on an eagle in *Cymbeline* and of goddesses in *The Tempest*. And they would frequently perform before the court in royal residences and, on their regular tours into the provinces, in non-theatrical spaces such as inns, guildhalls and the great halls of country houses.

Early in his career Shakespeare may have worked in collaboration, perhaps with Thomas Nashe (1567–c. 1601) in *Henry VI, Part I* and with George Peele (1556–96) in *Titus Andronicus*. And towards the end he collaborated with George Wilkins (*fl.* 1604–8) in *Pericles*, and with his younger colleagues Thomas Middleton (1580–1627), in *Timon of Athens*, and John Fletcher (1579–1625), in *Henry*

VIII, *The Two Noble Kinsmen* and the lost play *Cardenio*. Shakespeare's output dwindled in his last years, and he died in 1616 in Stratford, where he owned a fine house, New Place, and much land. His only son had died at the age of eleven, in 1596, and his last descendant died in 1670. New Place was destroyed in the eighteenth century but the other Stratford houses associated with his life are maintained and displayed to the public by the Shakespeare Birthplace Trust.

One of the most remarkable features of Shakespeare's plays is their intellectual and emotional scope. They span a great range from the lightest of comedies, such as *The Two Gentlemen of Verona* and *The Comedy of Errors*, to the profoundest of tragedies, such as *King Lear* and *Macbeth*. He maintained an output of around two plays a year, ringing the changes between comic and serious. All his comedies have serious elements: Shylock, in *The Merchant of Venice*, almost reaches tragic dimensions, and *Measure for Measure* is profoundly serious in its examination of moral problems. Equally, none of his tragedies is without humour: Hamlet is as witty as any of his comic heroes, *Macbeth* has its Porter, and *King Lear* its Fool. His greatest comic character, Falstaff, inhabits the history plays and *Henry V* ends with a marriage, while *Henry VI, Part III*, *Richard II* and *Richard III* culminate in the tragic deaths of their protagonists.

Although in performance Shakespeare's characters can give the impression of a superabundant reality, he is not a naturalistic dramatist. None of his plays is explicitly set in his own time. The action of few of them (except for the English histories) is set even partly in England (exceptions are *The Merry Wives of Windsor* and the Induction to *The Taming of the Shrew*). Italy is his favoured location. Most of his principal story-lines derive from printed writings; but the structuring and translation of these narratives into dramatic terms is Shakespeare's own, and he invents much additional material. Most of the plays contain elements of myth and legend, and many derive from ancient or more recent history or from romantic tales of ancient times and faraway places. All reflect his reading, often in close detail. Holinshed's *Chronicles* (1577, revised 1587), a great compendium of English, Scottish and Irish history, provided material for his English history plays. The *Lives of the Noble Grecians and Romans* by the Greek writer Plutarch, finely translated into English from the French by Sir Thomas North in 1579, provided much of the narrative material, and also a mass of verbal detail, for his plays about Roman history. Some plays are closely based on shorter individual works: *As You Like It*, for instance, on the novel *Rosalynde* (1590) by his near-contemporary Thomas Lodge (1558–1625), *The Winter's Tale* on *Pandosto* (1588) by his old rival Robert Greene (1558–92) and *Othello* on a story by the Italian Giraldi Cinthio (1504–73). And the language of his plays is permeated by the Bible, the Book of Common Prayer and the proverbial sayings of his day.

Shakespeare was popular with his contemporaries, but his commitment to the theatre and to the plays in performance is demonstrated by the fact that only about half of his plays appeared in print in his lifetime, in slim paperback volumes known as quartos, so called because they were made from printers' sheets folded twice to form four leaves (eight pages). None of them shows any sign that he was involved in their publication. For him, performance was the primary means of publication. The most frequently reprinted of his works were the non-dramatic poems – the erotic *Venus and Adonis* and the more moralistic *The Rape of Lucrece*. The *Sonnets*, which appeared in 1609, under his name but possibly without his consent, were less successful, perhaps because the vogue for sonnet sequences, which peaked in the 1590s, had passed by then. They were not reprinted until 1640, and then only in garbled form along with poems by other writers. Happily, in 1623, seven years after he died, his colleagues John Heminges (1556–1630) and Henry Condell (d. 1627) published his collected plays, including eighteen that had not previously appeared in print, in the first Folio, whose name derives from the fact that the printers' sheets were folded only once to produce two leaves (four pages). Some of the quarto editions are badly printed, and the fact that some plays exist in two, or even three, early versions creates problems for editors. These are discussed in the Account of the Text in each volume of this series.

Shakespeare's plays continued in the repertoire until the Puritans closed the theatres in 1642. When performances resumed after the Restoration of the monarchy in 1660 many of the plays were not to the taste of the times, especially because their mingling of genres and failure to meet the requirements of poetic justice offended against the dictates of neoclassicism. Some, such as *The Tempest* (changed by John Dryden and William Davenant in 1667 to suit contemporary taste), *King Lear* (to which Nahum Tate gave a happy ending in 1681) and *Richard III* (heavily adapted by Colley Cibber in 1700 as a vehicle for his own talents), were extensively rewritten; others fell into neglect. Slowly they regained their place in the repertoire, and they continued to be reprinted, but it was not until the great actor David Garrick (1717–79) organized a spectacular jubilee in Stratford in 1769 that Shakespeare began to be regarded as a transcendental genius. Garrick's idolatry prefigured the enthusiasm of critics such as Samuel Taylor Coleridge (1772–1834) and William Hazlitt (1778–1830). Gradually Shakespeare's reputation spread abroad, to Germany, America, France and to other European countries.

During the nineteenth century, though the plays were generally still performed in heavily adapted or abbreviated versions, a large body of scholarship and criticism began to amass. Partly as a result of a general swing in education away from the teaching of Greek and Roman texts and towards literature written in English, Shakespeare became the object of intensive study in schools and universities. In the theatre, important turning points were the work in England of two theatre directors, William Poel (1852–1934) and his disciple Harley Granville-Barker (1877–1946), who showed that the application of knowledge, some of it newly acquired, of early staging conditions to performance of the plays could render the original texts viable in terms of the modern theatre. During the twentieth century appreciation of Shakespeare's work, encouraged by the availability of audio, film and video versions of the plays, spread around the world to such an extent that he can now be claimed as a global author.

The influence of Shakespeare's works permeates the English language. Phrases from his plays and poems – 'a tower of strength', 'green-eyed jealousy', 'a foregone conclusion' – are on the lips of people who may never have read him. They have inspired composers of songs, orchestral music and operas; painters and sculptors; poets, novelists and film-makers. Allusions to him appear in pop songs, in advertisements and in television shows. Some of his characters – Romeo and Juliet, Falstaff, Shylock and Hamlet – have acquired mythic status. He is valued for his humanity, his psychological insight, his wit and humour, his lyricism, his mastery of language, his ability to excite, surprise, move and, in the widest sense of the word, entertain audiences. He is the greatest of poets, but he is essentially a dramatic poet. Though his plays have much to offer to readers, they exist fully only in performance. In these volumes we offer individual introductions, notes on language and on specific points of the text, suggestions for further reading and information about how each work has been edited. In addition we include accounts of the ways in which successive generations of interpreters and audiences have responded to challenges and rewards offered by the plays. The Penguin Shakespeare series aspires to remove obstacles to understanding and to make pleasurable the reading of the work of the man who has done more than most to make us understand what it is to be human.

Stanley Wells

The Chronology of
Shakespeare's Works

A few of Shakespeare's writings can be fairly precisely dated. An allusion to the Earl of Essex in the chorus to Act V of *Henry V*, for instance, could only have been written in 1599. But for many of the plays we have only vague information, such as the date of publication, which may have occurred long after composition, the date of a performance, which may not have been the first, or a list in Francis Meres's book *Palladis Tamia*, published in 1598, which tells us only that the plays listed there must have been written by that year. The chronology of the early plays is particularly difficult to establish. Not everyone would agree that the first part of *Henry VI* was written after the third, for instance, or *Romeo and Juliet* before *A Midsummer Night's Dream*. The following table is based on the 'Canon and Chronology' section in *William Shakespeare: A Textual Companion*, by Stanley Wells and Gary Taylor, with John Jowett and William Montgomery (1987), where more detailed information and discussion may be found.

The Two Gentlemen of Verona	1590–91
The Taming of the Shrew	1590–91
Henry VI, Part II	1591
Henry VI, Part III	1591

Henry VI, Part I (perhaps with Thomas Nashe)	1592
Titus Andronicus (perhaps with George Peele)	1592
Richard III	1592–3
Venus and Adonis (poem)	1592–3
The Rape of Lucrece (poem)	1593–4
The Comedy of Errors	1594
Love's Labour's Lost	1594–5
Edward III (authorship uncertain, not later than 1595
not included in this series)	(printed in 1596)
Richard II	1595
Romeo and Juliet	1595
A Midsummer Night's Dream	1595
King John	1596
The Merchant of Venice	1596–7
Henry IV, Part I	1596–7
The Merry Wives of Windsor	1597–8
Henry IV, Part II	1597–8
Much Ado About Nothing	1598
Henry V	1598–9
Julius Caesar	1599
As You Like It	1599–1600
Hamlet	1600–1601
Twelfth Night	1600–1601
'The Phoenix and the Turtle' (poem)	by 1601
Troilus and Cressida	1602
The Sonnets (poems)	1593–1603 and later
Measure for Measure	1603
A Lover's Complaint (poem)	1603–4
Sir Thomas More (in part,	
not included in this series)	1603–4
Othello	1603–4
All's Well That Ends Well	1604–5
Timon of Athens (with Thomas Middleton)	1605
King Lear	1605–6

Macbeth (revised by Middleton)   1606
Antony and Cleopatra   1606
Pericles (with George Wilkins)   1607
Coriolanus   1608
The Winter's Tale   1609
Cymbeline   1610
The Tempest   1611
Henry VIII (by Shakespeare and John Fletcher;
    known in its own time as *All is True*)   1613
Cardenio (by Shakespeare and Fletcher; lost)   1613
The Two Noble Kinsmen (by Shakespeare
    and Fletcher)   1613–14

Introduction

All's Well That Ends Well, like several of Shakespeare's other comedies (*Twelfth Night*, *As You Like It*, *Much Ado About Nothing*), suggests by its title a simple, light-hearted, almost frivolous ease. Nothing could be less true of this intense and moving play, hung between fairy tale and an ironic rebuttal of easy resolutions. The set and lighting of Greg Doran's Stratford production at the Swan in 2003 expressed the characteristically subtle and ambiguous tones of this play: wintry trees were outlined against a metallic backdrop that changed from steely coldness to mellow warmth at different points in the play without ever wholly losing its echo of winter. Yet the problems of staging this bittersweet and difficult play are widely recognized. It is rarely performed; and, when it is, it risks a vitriolic critical response.

This is one of Shakespeare's earliest and worst efforts. It was misconceived, misbegotten and misnamed. Its ending is far from well. It finishes deplorably. What possible satisfaction can there be to anyone in the reunion of such an ignominious pair? A more unsympathetic hero and heroine it is impossible to find in the whole gallery of Shakespearean portraits.

So the *Sunday Times* pronounced on 4 December 1921,

in response to Robert Atkins's production of *All's Well That Ends Well*, which was only the second production of the play in almost seventy years. When John Barton directed *All's Well* in 1967, responses were polarized. Alan Brien of the *Daily Telegraph* wondered:

How can a producer today stage this skirmish in the sex war without favouring one side more than the other in a play whose hero almost every modern critic has hated and whose heroine few have ever positively liked?

Meanwhile the *Daily Express* critic's response was rapturous: 'It is a lovely and a loving play and I adored every moment of it.' This divergence of responses is as characteristic of scholars reading the play as it is of spectators viewing it, and since the late nineteenth century the play has commonly been discussed, alongside *Measure for Measure*, *Troilus and Cressida* and sometimes *Hamlet*, as a 'problem play', a term first coined by F. S. Boas in 1896, although the grouping (minus *Hamlet*) had already been proposed by Edward Dowden in 1877.

That grouping, moreover, by linking *All's Well* to plays from Shakespeare's middle period, moved the presumed date of the play away from the earliest part of Shakespeare's writing life (early 1590s) to the first years of the seventeenth century and thus shifted the critical approach in other ways too, since such a dating prevents a rejection of the play as a piece of juvenile ineptitude. The easy dismissal of it as an instance of early apprentice-work died hard, however, as the 1921 review demonstrates; and it is impossible to rule firmly on the date of the play, since there is no record of any allusion to it or performance of it in Shakespeare's lifetime. Indeed, no record of any performance before 1741 survives.

Dating the play is therefore entirely a matter of internal evidence, that is, evidence from within the text itself. Recent scholarship tends towards a dating of 1604–5, which puts the play as the latest of the so-called problem plays and places it firmly within Shakespeare's maturity (he would have been about forty at this time). The view that it represents a revision of an earlier play, *Love's Labour's Won*, is no longer widely held. J. L. Styan in his Commentary has called it a play without a past (*All's Well That Ends Well*, 1984), by which he means both that we know nothing about its early stage history and that it has had relatively little recent stage-life to speak of. Indeed, it has been so rarely performed, even in the twentieth century, that many of the critics who have written about the play across the centuries will never have seen it performed. Though the number of productions recorded over recent decades has seen significant increase, that number is still very small compared with productions of Shakespeare's better-known plays.

FAIRY TALE

All's Well That Ends Well, as its title suggests, has a strong element of the fairy tale about it. It is a rags-to-riches tale of an orphaned maiden who falls in love with a young nobleman, and whose miraculous cure of the ailing king enables her to choose the said count for her husband. Forced to marry her, the count rejects her by imposing upon her a seemingly impossible task:

> *When thou canst get the ring upon my finger, which never shall come off, and show me a child begotten of thy body that I am*

> *father to, then call me husband; but in such a 'then' I write a*
> *'never'.* (III.2.56–9)

The play goes on to combine folk-tale elements commonly
known as the 'clever wench' and the 'bed-trick'. By patient
endurance and clever wiles, the maiden, substituting
herself for another in the count's bed, succeeds in
conceiving his child. The ring she there gets from his
finger becomes the proof of her fulfilment of the task,
and the count must accept her as his wife. As the play
moves ever closer to this denouement, the increasingly
dominant presence of riddle, rhyme and proverb gives
emphasis to its fairy-tale shape throughout Act V. Helena,
her task accomplished but not yet made public, is confi-
dent of a happy ending: 'All's well that ends well yet, |
Though time seem so adverse and means unfit' (V.1.25–6).
Taken for dead by her husband and the court, Helena's
entry into the final scene is announced in a riddle by Diana,
the maiden whom she replaced in Bertram's bed:

> Dead though she be she feels her young one kick.
> So there's my riddle: one that's dead is quick.
> And now behold the meaning. (V.3.300–302)

The King's final words in character embody the proverbial consolation of the play's title: 'All yet seems well,
and if it end so meet, | The bitter past, more welcome is
the sweet' (330–31); and he repeats the same wisdom as
he turns from character into player in the Epilogue:

> The King's a beggar, now the play is done.
> All is well ended if this suit be won,
> That you express content; which we will pay
> With strife to please you, day exceeding day. (V.3.332–5)

Yet, within the fairy-tale drive towards happy ending, it is impossible not to hear the compromising prominence of 'if': '*if* it end so meet', '*if* this suit be won' (my italics here and throughout subsequent quotations). Helena's final appeal, 'Will you be mine now you are doubly won?', begs and deserves the answer 'yes'; but Bertram, who has lied throughout the scene, responds, outrageously, in conditional terms, and even then not directly to Helena but, characteristically, looking past her, in this case to the King:

> *If* she, my liege, can make me know this clearly
> I'll love her dearly, ever, ever dearly.

and Helena's answering affirmation of truth echoes that conditional syntax:

> *If* it appear not plain and prove untrue
> Deadly divorce step between me and you! (V.3.313–16)

All's well that ends well, then, only if more 'ifs' are fulfilled beyond the end of the play. And where is the fairy tale in that?

Fairy tales, of course, are structured by the imposition and fulfilment of seemingly impossible conditions, and the play returns again and again to the magic of 'if'. Occurrences are far too numerous to quote in full, but the word resounds from the very first scene, highlighting instances of possibility, impossibility and longing. In the first scene alone, both the Countess and Lafew mourn the passing of Helena's father in terms of impossible possibility. They praise his medical skill as seemingly great enough to oppose death: that skill, 'had it stretched so far, would have made nature immortal, and death

should have play for lack of work' (I.I.19–21); 'He was
skilful enough to have lived still, if knowledge could be
set up against mortality' (28–30). A few lines later, the
Countess responds to Lafew's warning to Helena against
excessive grief with another conditional:

LAFEW Moderate lamentation is the right of the dead, exces-
    sive grief the enemy to the living.
COUNTESS *If* the living be enemy to the grief, the excess makes
    it soon mortal. (53–6)

And Helena herself, left alone and pondering her inca-
pacity to remember her father despite her grief, expresses
through another conditional her feeling that without
Bertram's presence everyone and everything is dead:
'there is no living, none, | *If* Bertram be away' (83–4).

Helena's miraculous cure of the King, using her
father's medical arts, is repeatedly framed in terms of an
'if' that allows Helena's longing for a means to win
Bertram to echo the King's longing for recovery and both
their longings for her dead father, while at the same time
encapsulating both their fears: the King's fear that this
young, inexperienced girl cannot possibly cure him and
Helena's fear that she risks everything she has in
attempting to do so. Thus, the 'ifs' that express their fears
and longings also underline the necessary elements of
risk and daring that give their decisions and actions
symbolic weight. The final agreement in Act II, scene I
is expressed in terms of a stern condition agreed on both
sides:

KING

    Sweet practiser, thy physic I will try,
    That ministers thine own death *if* I die.

HELENA

    If I break time, or flinch in property

    Of what I spoke, unpitied let me die,

    And well deserved. (II.1.185–9)

The other side of this harsh condition, however, opens up a space for possible happiness:

HELENA   Not helping, death's my fee;

    But, *if* I help, what do you promise me?

KING

    Make thy demand. (189–91)

The last lines of the scene use 'if' to express a binding vow:

KING   *If* thou proceed

    As high as word, my deed shall match thy deed. (209–10)

The vocabulary of 'if' reappears, quite naturally and predictably, in Act II, scene 3, the scene where Helena makes her choice of a husband. When Bertram rejects Helena, the King's first conditionals dispute the grounds on which Bertram despises her and offer to make them good:

                 If she be

All that is virtuous, save what thou dislikest –

A poor physician's daughter – thou dislikest

Of virtue for the name.

. . .

If thou canst like this creature as a maid,

I can create the rest. Virtue and she

Is her own dower; honour and wealth from me.

    (II.3.120–23, 141–3)

Bertram's uncompromising refusal of the King's offer, 'I cannot love her nor will strive to do't', elicits a much more threatening conditional: 'Thou wrongest thyself *if* thou shouldst strive to choose' (II.3.144–5), which forces Bertram into acceptance. But his acceptance is merely nominal. The King can force him to submit to the form of marriage but not to its embodiment. He refuses not only to lie with Helena but even to remain with her or kiss her goodbye. His letter to the Countess informs his mother that he has '*wedded her, not bedded her, and sworn to make the "not" eternal*' (III.2.21–2), employing the conditional with unconditional intent: '*If there be breadth enough in the world I will hold a long distance*' (23–4); while his letter to Helena deliberately sets her a condition which he assumes she cannot meet: he will be her husband in deed if she can get the ring from his finger and show him the child he has begotten of her body (56–9).

Helena's love is expressed from the first in conditionals. These contrast the simple unconditionality of her love for Bertram with the fact that its fulfilment is conditional in ways beyond her control: for example, upon changes to her low social status and to Bertram's lack of affection for her. The Countess, insisting on her right to know whether Helena loves her son, faces her with two alternative answers, knowing already which is true: '*If* it be so, you have wound a goodly clew; | *If* it be not, forswear't' (I.3.177–8; the first line is proverbial, and a 'clew' is a ball of thread). Helena answers directly and with uncompromising clarity, to the point where she cuts off the verse rhythm with her bluntness (the last half-line of the following quotation is left uncompleted):

> Then I confess,
> Here on my knee, before high heaven and you,

That before you, and next unto high heaven,
I love your son. (186–9)

But she follows up that directness with an appeal for the
Countess's compassion through a passionate 'if' that seeks
to parallel her own love with the Countess's youthful
experience:

                                    . . . *if* yourself,
Whose aged honour cites a virtuous youth,
Did ever, in so true a flame of liking,
Wish chastely and love dearly, that your Dian
Was both herself and love – O then, give pity
To her whose state is such that cannot choose
But lend and give where she is sure to lose;
That seeks not to find that her search implies,
But riddle-like lives sweetly where she dies. (204–12)

Her plea directly recalls the Countess's prior admission,
earlier in the same scene, on first hearing from the Clown
of Helena's love for Bertram:

Even so it was with me when I was young.
    If ever we are nature's, these are ours; this thorn
Doth to our rose of youth rightly belong . . . (123–5)

Both speak a language that recognizes the inevitability
of bitterness inherent in any sweetness. Helena's experience of love as a death in life parallels the Countess's
knowledge, through the experience of love, that there is
no rose without a thorn in nature.

Helena's endurance and the working out of the plot
progress through a sequence of conditionals that express
both the hazards that must be negotiated and the single-

mindedness of Helena's determination to overcome them.
Her decision to plod the cold ground barefoot as a pilgrim
of St Jaques (III.4.4–6) is a bodily statement of both
penitence and resolution. (The resolution is, however,
crucially unclear. Helena seems to leave Rossillion so that
Bertram can freely return, yet as she arrives in Florence
and takes up residence in the house of the woman Bertram
courts, it is not certain how far we should understand
this as a matter of providence or of Helena's agency. I
discuss the question of providence versus agency further
below.) As the Countess and her Steward ponder how
they might have prevented her departure, both know that
in fact their 'if onlies' would have changed nothing
(20–25).

The series of 'ifs' with which the Widow, mother of
Diana (who is to become the bedmate for whom Helena
substitutes herself in Bertram's bed), offers Helena lodging
in Florence seems to mimic the careful sequence whereby
destiny works itself out through apparent randomness:

WIDOW

If you will tarry, holy pilgrim,
But till the troops come by,
I will conduct you where you shall be lodged;
The rather for I think I know your hostess
As ample as myself.

HELENA   Is it yourself?

WIDOW

If you shall please so, pilgrim. (III.5.38–43)

In the same way, when these two women enter a new
scene, mid-conversation on an 'if', we recognize the
conditional as again signalling to the audience a careful
and determined overcoming of obstacles:

HELENA
> *If* you misdoubt me that I am not she,
> I know not how I shall assure you further
> But I shall lose the grounds I work upon. (III.7.1–3)

We know that the 'if' contained in Helena's anticipation of possible success is an 'if' that exists solely to be resolved in the desired outcome of the bed-trick:

HELENA   Why then tonight
> Let us assay our plot, which, *if* it speed,
> Is wicked meaning in a lawful deed,
> And lawful meaning in a lawful act,
> Where both not sin, and yet a sinful fact.
> But let's about it. (43–8)

These two quotations are the first and last lines of the scene, and both their placing and the closing use of rhyme call attention to the certainty of the outcome. Conditions exist to be fulfilled in fairy tale.

'If' echoes more threateningly, but with an equally strong suggestion of a final favourable outcome, through the last scene, especially after the appearance of the ring. The King challenges Bertram, '*if* you know | That you are well acquainted with yourself' (V.3.105–6; in other words, without fail) to confess that he forced it from Helena. When Bertram denies foul play, the King, fearing that Bertram is responsible for Helena's death, threatens him:

>   *If* it should prove
> That thou art so inhuman – 'twill not prove so,
> And yet I know not; thou didst hate her deadly,
> And she is dead; which nothing but to close

Her eyes myself could win me to believe,
More than to see this ring. Take him away. (V.3.115–20)

Bertram responds with another conditional, intended to intensify the truth of his denial that the ring is hers:

>   *If* you shall prove
> This ring was ever hers, you shall as easy
> Prove that I husbanded her bed in Florence,
> Where yet she never was. (124–7)

Diana's appearance on the scene, claiming Bertram's vows to her, exacerbates the flow of threats, vows, conditions and riddles clustering around 'if' (169–70, 184–6, 189–95); and these multiply in ever quicker succession:

KING

If it were yours by none of all these ways
How could you give it him? (273–4)

DIANA

By Jove, *if* ever I knew man 'twas you. (285)

This culminates in the riddle that brings on Helena, alive ('one that's dead is quick', 301), and the final sequence of 'ifs' with which we began.

A PROBLEM PLAY

Though structured, then, on the classic fairy-tale foundation of impossible 'ifs' carried through to completion, the play refuses the easy affirmation with which fairy tales normally resolve that difficult sequence. It also refuses the boldly simple tones of fairy tale, exploring instead what it might really be like to live through the fairy tale: what the immovable yearnings, the impossible commands, the cruel humiliations and the tests of endurance would actually feel like within the experience of real human lives. Its title comes to sound like a warning, a bitter quotation of a facile optimism, as the play insists that we look at the bitterness underpinning every sweetness. Perhaps the most characteristic conditional of the play is this statement by an anonymous lord:

> The web of our life is of a mingled yarn, good and ill together. Our virtues would be proud *if* our faults whipped them not, and our crimes would despair *if* they were not cherished by our virtues. (IV.3.70–73)

The lord, like the title, seems to speak in conscious quotation marks, instructing the audience to pause and consider the general truth of the pronouncement, and this kind of consciously 'public' speaking is, unusually for Shakespeare, quite common in the play. Lafew's opening remark in Act II, scene 3 is another of these, equally clearly keyed towards undercutting the easy optimism of the fairy-tale structure:

> They say miracles are past, and we have our philosophical persons to make modern and familiar, things supernatural and causeless. Hence is it that we make trifles of terrors, ensconcing ourselves into seeming knowledge when we should submit ourselves to an unknown fear. (II.3.1–6)

Yet Lafew's statement has a double-edged effect, as he distances himself from the opinion he voices. Though we seem at first to hear him saying that miracles are past, the drift of his statement is actually to oppose the 'philosophical persons' who dismiss miracles thus, who rationalize supernatural things ('modern' means 'commonplace') and reduce terrors to trifles. His argument is precisely that we should divest ourselves of this kind of 'seeming knowledge' and submit ourselves to the recognition that the world is greater and more fearful than we can explain. Yet, despite the fact that such a recognition is parallel with the acceptance of the inexplicable demanded by fairy tale, Lafew's statement does not quite invite us to embrace that acceptance without question. The very difficulty of the language, and its invitation to consider the line it rejects, the rational dismissal of miracles, works against the submission to 'things supernatural and causeless' that it recommends.

This philosophical and sometimes bitter edge creates an unusual tone in a comedy and is one of the aspects of the play that contribute to its designation as a 'problem play'. The tone is there from the opening moment. All the court are dressed in mourning as they enter on the stage, and the first lines of the play are spoken from the deep sadness of both present and remembered grief:

COUNTESS In delivering my son from me, I bury a second husband.
BERTRAM And I in going, madam, weep o'er my father's death anew . . .

The conditionals already quoted above from the first scene are all focused around death, burial and the pain of remembrance; and Helena is introduced almost in passing, via the memory of her dead father: 'This young gentlewoman had a father – O that "had", how sad a passage 'tis!' (I.1.17–18). Both the filtering of Helena's youthful experience through the lens of the memory of one older and sadder than she is, and the breaking off to mourn the sadness of time passing – 'O that "had", how sad a passage 'tis!' – are utterly characteristic of this play. Helena, dressed in black and defined at first through her bereavement, is in one sense reminiscent of Hamlet; but where Hamlet finds himself in a court where everyone else is urging him to move on and forget the dead, Helena is surrounded by others continuing to mourn. Though the Countess and Lafew urge her, as Claudius and Gertrude urge Hamlet, to cease her tears 'lest it be rather thought you affect a sorrow than to have't' (50–51), they do not themselves achieve an easy passage from grief to forgetting.

HELENA

Helena's first soliloquy reveals a woman more complex than the sum of her grief. She is both like and unlike Hamlet, who denies insincerity when, in responding to Claudius's suggestion that his grief might seem affected, he insists 'I know not "seems"' (*Hamlet*, I.2.76). Helena, like Hamlet, is riddling and ambiguous, but, unlike him, claims affectation and sincerity together: 'I do affect a sorrow indeed, but I have it too' (I.1.52). (She means that the sorrow she affects or pretends to show for her father masks the more intense and present sorrow of her impossible love for Bertram.) Responding further to Lafew's parting injunction to her to 'hold the credit of your father' (keep up his good name), she offers an even more startlingly honest expression of how grief functions in ways that the bereaved normally scarcely dare admit:

> I think not on my father,
> And these great tears grace his remembrance more
> Than those I shed for him. What was he like?
> I have forgot him. (I.1.78–81)

and admits at the same time the pain that really torments her now:

>   My imagination
> Carries no favour in't but Bertram's.
> I am undone: there is no living, none,
> If Bertram be away. (81–4)

Helena uses this speech to reflect back on her silence, giving expression to what the Countess is later to call '[t]he mystery of your loneliness' (I.3.166).

Her second soliloquy, which closes the long first scene, is more thoughtful and more thought-provoking, as she meditates on the social impossibility of her love for Bertram reaching marriage:

> Our remedies oft in ourselves do lie,
> Which we ascribe to heaven. The fated sky
> Gives us free scope, only doth backward pull
> Our slow designs when we ourselves are dull. (I.1.212ff.)

The thought is an interesting one for a play with a fairy-tale shape, inviting us to ponder questions of free will, agency and divine providence. Even as the verse form, with its rhyming couplets, gives its content the feeling of closure, what is being said is actually opening up certain kinds of expected closure, and thereby disrupting our sense of what kind of story this is and how we should

view it. It is also complicating our sense of what kind of
figure Helena is. Is she sweet, silent, submissive, waiting
for impossible desires to be magically answered? Or is she
bold, determined, ready to take unusual and even unwom-
anly steps to fulfil her own desire? (One theatre critic,
Harold Hobson, called her 'a designing minx' and another,
J. C. Trewin, 'a calculating little opportunist' (Roger
Wood and Mary Clarke, *Shakespeare at the Old Vic*, 1955).)
Certainly the end of the scene contrasts with its beginning: where the opening moments of the play presented
Helena silent and socially marginal to the exchanges
between the noble family of Rossillion, the last line emphasizes the firmness that drives her from within: 'But my
intents are fixed, and will not leave me' (225).

The intervening moments between those two points,
moreover, have complicated Helena even further than
this contradiction would suggest, since, besides seeing
her socially humble and privately determined, we have
also seen her engaging in sexual banter with Parolles. As
Helena meditates, in her first soliloquy, on her desire for
Bertram and the seeming impossibility of fulfilling it
Parolles' entrance interrupts her with a question that is
brutally and ironically direct in the circumstances: 'Are
you meditating on virginity?' (I.I.109). Helena, up to this
moment a figure for chaste desire, takes Parolles on at
his own game and asks him, as a soldier, how virgins
should best defend themselves against an assault on their
virginity. It is as if 'Patience on a monument', Viola's
imagined figure of pining maidenly love in *Twelfth Night*
(II.4.113), has suddenly become Beatrice in *Much Ado
About Nothing*, with her frank and impudent wit. The talk
between Helena and Parolles is all double entendre and
sexual chop-logic: assailants will 'undermine' (penetrate)
and 'blow up' (bring to orgasm; make pregnant) virgins

(I.i.118); virgins are only born through the loss of virginity; virginity is 'too cold a companion' (130–31); but Helena 'will stand for't a little, though therefore I die a virgin' (132–3; with 'stand' and 'die' respectively recalling the sexual meanings of erection and orgasm). When Helena asks Parolles for advice on how a virgin might manage to lose her virginity 'to her own liking' (148–9), the degree to which she reminds the audience of her own personal situation is breathtaking; and when the conversation turns explicitly to Bertram it is with unexpected directness that Helena gives the sexual exchange one final turn that underlines the intensity of her desire. Wishing Bertram well, she meditates on her own utterance:

HELENA   'Tis pity –
PAROLLES
  What's pity?
HELENA
  That wishing well had not a body in't
  Which might be felt, that we, the poorer born,
  Whose baser stars do shut us up in wishes,
  Might with effects of them follow our friends,
  And show what we alone must think, which never
  Returns us thanks. (176–83)

That frankness about sexual desire, however, which nineteenth-century readers and critics found so problematic in this heroine, is also a frankness about love which gives Helena a moral authority to counteract her low social standing. When the Countess, already knowing of her love, demands an answer from Helena in person, Helena's confession, in its combination of assertiveness and submissiveness, strikes a unique note among Shakespeare's heroines:

> Then I confess,
> Here on my knee, before high heaven and you,
> That before you, and next unto high heaven,
> I love your son. (I.3.186–9)

That last half-line breaks off the verse rhythm with simple
finality before resuming in the next line, and even a
modern audience, much less highly attuned to the sound
of verse drama, registers the length and expressiveness
of that pause. The confession seems to raise Helena's
love above the social arena within which it is unseemly
into an idealized moral arena where true love is right
merely because it is true. Thus in a sense the same frankness that made Helena part of what has been seen as
problematic about this 'problem play' also accounts, in
this very different context, for an opposing critical
tendency to view her as quasi-divine, a noble soul who
loves beneath her, suffers for her love and, through her
suffering, redeems her unworthy lover.

This may be difficult to reconcile with the assertive,
independent spirit that was visible at the end of the first
scene, but that assertive, thinking quality itself becomes
increasingly difficult to hold on to as the play progresses.
The play drops soliloquy as a mode of expression for
Helena after Act III, scene 2 and turns to a more ritual-
ized and distanced concentration on the story almost
as fable, which represents Helena's attitude and mode
of speech in radically changed ways. A letter, in which
she depicts herself as undergoing ritual penance for
taking such an unseemly initiative in obtaining her
husband, is constructed in sonnet form and read aloud
by a steward:

I am Saint Jaques' pilgrim, thither gone.
  Ambitious love hath so in me offended
That barefoot plod I the cold ground upon,
  With sainted vow my faults to have amended. (III.4.4–7)

She justifies her subsequent actions not in realistic
thought-processes but in gnomic forms of speech that
sound like the pronouncements of an oracle:

Let us assay our plot, which, if it speed,
Is wicked meaning in a lawful deed,
And lawful meaning in a lawful act,
Where both not sin, and yet a sinful fact. (III.7.44–7)

And that disunity in the presentation of Helena is part
of the larger disunity of the play, which seems hung
between the two poles of romance and realism, or fairy
tale and feeling.

BERTRAM

The same problem surrounds the portrayal of Bertram.
Acceptance of him as a fit husband for Helena requires
that we don't analyse him too realistically; yet at the same
time the play seems to demand that we open our eyes
very realistically indeed to all that is unacceptable about
him. Probably the two most famous critical pronouncements on Bertram – Samuel Johnson's and George
Bernard Shaw's – both judge him from a realist perspective. Johnson's view, expressed in the Preface to his
edition of Shakespeare in 1765, is straightforwardly
condemnatory:

I cannot reconcile my heart to Bertram; a man noble without generosity, and young without truth; who marries Helena as a coward, and leaves her as a profligate: when she is dead by his unkindness, sneaks home to a second marriage, is accused by a woman whom he has wronged, defends himself by falsehood, and is dismissed to happiness.

Shaw's review of a production by the Irving Dramatic Club defends him as 'a perfectly ordinary young man, whose unimaginative prejudices and selfish conventionality make him out a very mean figure in the atmosphere created by the nobler nature of his wife' (*Saturday Review*, 2 February 1895).

It is impossible to believe that Shakespeare intends us to overlook the sheer brutality with which Bertram's rejection of Helena is depicted, a brutality which is neither necessary for the purposes of the plot nor present in the source (to which we will return). One kind of indirectness combines with another kind of directness to underline his cruelty. In rejecting her first before the King, he addresses himself entirely to the King, speaking of Helena only in the third person, almost as though she were not present at all, and certainly showing no delicacy towards her feelings:

> I know her well:
> She had her breeding at my father's charge.
> A poor physician's daughter my wife! Disdain
> Rather corrupt me ever! (II.3.112–15)

I cannot love her nor will strive to do't. (144)

Ordered to take her hand in marriage, he still refuses to
address a word to Helena but parrots the first part of the
order almost mockingly, while deliberately withholding
the second (as the unfinished rhythm emphasizes):

KING   Take her by the hand
  And tell her she is thine . . .
  . . .
BERTRAM   I take her hand. (II.3.172–5)

The most difficult scene for the audience to witness is
that in which Bertram's deliberate refusal to understand
Helena forces her to beg. On first seeing her coming, his
words to Parolles are brutal in the extreme: 'Here comes
my clog' (II.5.53). His direct words to Helena herself on
this occasion of their parting are equally cruel, ending
with his characteristic mode of speaking past her to
someone else:

BERTRAM   Well, what would you say?
HELENA
  I am not worthy of the wealth I owe,
  Nor dare I say 'tis mine – and yet it is;
  But, like a timorous thief, most fain would steal
  What law does vouch mine own.
BERTRAM   What would you have?
HELENA
  Something, and scarce so much; nothing indeed.
  I would not tell you what I would, my lord.
  Faith, yes:
  Strangers and foes do sunder and not kiss.
BERTRAM
  I pray you, stay not, but in haste to horse. (78–87)

The harshness of Bertram's words is emphasized the more by the hesitant rhythm and syntax of Helena's own speech. When the final scene shows him lying, content to besmirch anyone else's honour to maintain the appearance of his own, it is almost impossible to ignore the sense that the 'happy' ending overcomes him against his will.

A realist perspective, however, can elicit sympathy for, as well as hostility to, Bertram. He is, after all, a young man from whom all choice is taken away: chosen as a husband by a woman he has neither courted nor encouraged, overruled by the King, forced into a loveless marriage against his will and condemned on all sides for his unwillingness to cooperate. How might he behave in a way that would be both acceptable within the story and psychologically convincing? Is there any compatibility between the demands of realism and of romance? We will return to these questions.

It is perhaps not accidental that there are problems, as shown above, with both the principals, Helena and Bertram, since the play seems to parallel them from the start. Both have recently lost fathers and are hence wards of the court; and both are beholden to the same mother or 'mother' (Helena's father has 'bequeathed' her to the Countess's protection on his death (I.1.37), but the Countess also seems to have been involved in Helena's upbringing since childhood, as Bertram's sneering rejection of her underlines (II.3.112–15)). While Bertram is the Countess's true son in the biological sense, however, Helena becomes her 'true' daughter after Bertram discards her. From a position of fearing Helena's responses to the words 'mother' and 'daughter' (I.3.145–64) even as she guesses Helena's love for Bertram, the Countess comes to see Helena as her only child after Bertram has betrayed his honour in leaving her:

                                                He was my son,
                              But I do wash his name out of my blood
                              And thou art all my child. (III.2.66–8)

The discomfort we feel with both Bertram and Helena
and their behaviour arises partly out of the deliberate
wrenching of a more traditional story. Even without
knowing the source, readers and audiences may sense
that there is something forced and out of joint about
the story-line of the play, and comparison with the
play's source confirms this. Shakespeare was drawing
on the story of Giletta of Narbonne from Boccaccio's
Decameron, probably relayed through the English version
in the thirty-eighth novella in William Painter's *The
Palace of Pleasure*, first printed in 1566. In Painter's translation of Boccaccio the social distance between Beltramo
(Bertram) and Giletta (Helena) is much narrower, so that
Giletta's love for Beltramo is less inherently problematic
than in Shakespeare's version. No humiliating scene of
public choice and rejection exists in Painter, where, by
contrast, Giletta refuses many husbands offered to her
by her family without telling them why, and her choice
of Beltramo is relayed to him privately by the King. The
scene of their cruel parting is also Shakespeare's device.
In Painter we merely hear that Beltramo, having married
Giletta, departs for Tuscany rather than returning to his
own country, where Giletta is. It is clear in Painter that
Giletta, having become a pilgrim, arrives in the same
place as Beltramo by chance and only then devises the
bed-trick. Above all, when Giletta fulfils Beltramo's
condition and returns to him with two young sons in her
arms and prostrates herself at his feet, Beltramo's
response is one that fulfils the requirements of fairy tale.

The elements of repentance, embrace and 'happy ever after' are properly present in the prose tale:

[Beltramo] abjected his obstinate rigour, causing her to rise up, and embraced and kissed her, acknowledging her again for his lawful wife. And after he had apparelled her according to her estate . . . not only that day but many others he kept great cheer, and from that time forth he loved and honoured her as his dear spouse and wife. (From Painter, quoted in Appendix to G. K. Hunter's Arden edition (1959))

It can hardly be accidental that Shakespeare withholds these satisfactions and inserts scenes and details that problematize the 'all's well that ends well' of fairy tale.

Besides complicating the motives and public inter-actions of Bertram and Helena, Shakespeare adds char-acters and plot elements far beyond scope of the brief Painter novella. The Countess, Lafew, Parolles and Lavatch, the Clown, are all his additions. The Countess and Lafew, as we have seen, add a perspective of age, together with the sadness of both remembering and forgetting. Bernard Shaw thought the Countess 'the most beautiful old woman's part ever written' (*Saturday Review*, 2 February 1895). The passion of both Helena's desire and Bertram's disgust look different, framed by the perspective of passion spent. Ageing reminds us of the pangs with which some pleasures and pains are remembered while others are forgotten. The Countess remembers roses with their thorns; but if the roses are no longer as sweet, so the thorns are no longer as sharp. The bitter may become sweet; pain and loss may be transformed into precious gain. As the King says in the final scene of the play, 'Praising what is lost | Makes the remembrance dear' (V.3.19–20).

THE DESIRING BODY

Ageing is also one of many aspects of the play that direct our attention to the physical body. Helena's expression of longing in terms of the impatient body ('That wishing well had not a body in't | Which might be felt', I.1.178–9) is another of the ways in which she is paired with Bertram, whose body is equally impatient and demanding, but whose object of desire is not Helena but Diana. It is Helena, however, who understands that desire well enough to devise the bed-trick as the practical solution to her problem: 'Now his important [importunate, persistent] blood will naught deny | That she'll demand' (III.7.21–2). Helena understands Bertram because there are basic likenesses between them. In addition to the parallels already noted, and despite the difference in their social class and the seeming opposition between her 'virtue' and his lack of it, she shares with him a constrained position within this society that prevents her from simply following her desires and a strong will that determines to follow those desires regardless of the prohibitions upon them. Thus Helena's pursuit of Bertram is ultimately parallel with his flight from her. Both arise out of a passionate sense of self which rejects the idea that love or desire should be allowed to be determined by social and practical circumstances.

Helena's part in their shared understanding of physical passion, of the way the body shapes both desire and revulsion, is evident, as we have already seen, from the first scene, where she jokes edgily with Parolles about virginity. Indeed, one of the functions of Parolles is precisely to thrust the presence and importance of the physical body into the awareness of the more serious

characters and hence of the audience. That random question to Helena, 'Are you meditating on virginity?'
(I.I.109), constitutes almost his first words in the play,
and its very randomness calls attention to it as characteristic of Parolles rather than motivated by plot. Even
his greeting, the few words that precede the question, are
a potential slur on Helena's body: 'Save you, fair queen!'
(105; 'quean', pronounced like 'queen', being a term for
'whore'). For Helena, his mere presence, living in the
moment and for the body as he does, is a reminder of
the bodily price virtue may pay in postponing or sacrificing the fulfilment of desire. '[S]uperfluous folly', she
sees by Parolles's example, thrives, while 'virtue's steely
bones | Looks bleak i'th'cold wind' (102–4).

This is not a play – if this scene is performed – that
allows an audience to idealize Helena as a purely spiri-
tual creature, renouncing the physical body as gross and
inferior. On the contrary, Parolles's brutal jibes at the
'virtue' of chastity are there partly to provoke a further
demonstration of Helena's remarkable honesty:

PAROLLES . . . Virginity breeds mites, much like a cheese,
    consumes itself to the very paring, and so dies with feeding
    his own stomach . . . your virginity, your old virginity, is
    like one of our French withered pears: it looks ill, it eats
    drily; marry, 'tis a withered pear: it was formerly better;
    marry, yet 'tis a withered pear. Will you anything with it?
HELENA
    Not my virginity, yet . . . (140–62)

Parolles's advice that virginity is its own death, punning
ironically as it does on the secondary meaning of death as
orgasm, is a familiar theme in sixteenth- and seventeenth-
century literature. (Andrew Marvell's late-seventeenth-

century poem 'To His Coy Mistress' is perhaps the best-known treatment of it now.) A contemporary audience would have recognized it as a cliché and would probably have expected Helena to laugh it off. The searing vulnerability of her admission of longing in response to Parolles's grossness clarifies for the audience just how physical and unstoppable that longing is and just how much she fears the bleakness of 'virtue's steely bones' if virtue means renouncing her longing for Bertram. But the word 'yet' conveys a powerful sense of both yearning and possibility. As Barbara Everett showed at the end of her excellent Introduction to the previous Penguin edition of this play, 'yet' holds out a promise for the future sufficient to balance the strong sense of the past. Happiness is 'only to be reached by holding on to a *yetness* of things'.

The play's focus on physicality, on body, bones and blood, is both ironic and validatory. While Parolles's sardonic remarks about the withering of the physical body seem to mock desire, they are validated by the fact that Helena feels the power of physical longing so forcefully. The notably strong presence of older characters similarly mocks and validates the physical body simultaneously: the Countess, bereaved and widowed, remembers the force of youthful passion (I.3.123–30); Lafew, watching Helena choose a husband, longs to be one of the young men lined up for her choice (II.3.77–8); and Lavatch, the Clown, repeatedly expresses the simultaneous strength and folly of bodily desire. His desire to marry comes, he argues, out of two physical drives, the desire for 'issue o' my body' (children to carry on his bloodline) and sexual desire: 'My poor body, madam, requires it. I am driven on by the flesh' (I.3.25, 28–9). Throughout the scene in which the Countess reads Bertram's letter stating his rejection of Helena in bodily

terms (*'I have wedded her, not bedded her'*, III.2.21),
Lavatch interjects with a reductive parallel tale of his
own loss of desire:

> I have no mind to Isbel since I was at court. Our old lings
> and our Isbels o'th'country are nothing like your old ling
> and your Isbels o'th'court. The brains of my Cupid's
> knocked out, and I begin to love as an old man loves money,
> with no stomach. (III.2.12–16; with a bawdy play on 'ling',
> which is a long, thin fish)

Lavatch's linking of loss of desire with the ageing process
parallels in reverse the youthful, hot-blooded refusal to
be coerced without desire that underpins Bertram's action.
He is, in the Countess's words, a 'rash and unbridled boy'
(27), as physical as the Clown in his failure of sexual
desire, but for very different reasons.

Lavatch has a further mocking perspective on sex,
which positions it as the loss of manhood rather than its
expression. Commenting on Bertram's flight from the
embraces of Helena to war, he offers the Countess this
mock-comfort:

CLOWN Nay, there is some comfort in the news, some comfort:
    your son will not be killed so soon as I thought he would.
COUNTESS Why should he be killed?
CLOWN So say I, madam, if he run away, as I hear he does.
    The danger is in standing to't; that's the loss of men, though
    it be the getting of children. (35–41)

'Standing to't' (compare Helena's remarks in conversation with Parolles, quoted above) plays on a sexual and
a military meaning, setting one kind of erectness against
another, so that standing straight, as an honourable soldier

must do, is paralleled with the sexual act. Standing firm to face the enemy, Lavatch jokes, is 'the loss of men' (death); but maintaining an erection, resulting in the begetting of children, is 'the loss of men' in other ways too, since not only do men who impregnate women saddle themselves with both women and children and close down their opportunities as single men but the emission of semen was seen as a loss of male essence and orgasm as a kind of death. Both kinds of 'standing to't', then, are seen as the death of manhood, though one is literal death with some kind of honour, while the other is metaphorical death with a potential loss of honour. Parolles has already voiced very similar thoughts about the loss of honour in urging Bertram to leave Helena for the wars:

> To th'wars, my boy, to th'wars!
> He wears his honour in a box unseen
> That hugs his kicky-wicky here at home,
> Spending his manly marrow in her arms . . . (II.3.276–9)

Parolles here mocks the sexual act in the same way as Lavatch, as a spilling of 'manly marrow' in an emasculating embrace that keeps a man from visibly proving his honour in acts of war. ('Box', like 'case' elsewhere in the play, alludes to the female genitals, while 'kicky-wicky', a term not recorded elsewhere, is clearly a derisive term for 'lover'.) Yet his reference on another occasion to sexual union as 'The great prerogative and rite of love' (II.4.39), even though the term sits ironically within the context of Parolles using it to tell Helena that Bertram is postponing its fulfilment, nevertheless validates the bodily act as serious and worthy of respect.

Indeed, the bringing together of respect and scorn for the act that is potentially either the mere satisfaction of

lust or the seal of loving marriage is at the core of what
makes the play a problem, since the bed-trick at the heart
of the plot seeks to turn the one into the other. In seemingly fulfilling his desire for Diana, Bertram in fact proves
to be unwittingly fulfilling the long-postponed 'rite of
love' with Helena; and we are asked to accept that resolution as satisfactory despite having been shown all the
flaws in its construction. An act of paradoxical acceptance is required: we are invited to take the act of love as
a fulfilment of the sacrament of marriage, making man
and woman one flesh, while at the same time remem-
bering that the fulfilment of that sacrament on Bertram's
part arose, coincidentally, out of an intention to pursue
the sexual act as pure bodily pleasure in a straightforward
betrayal of his marriage vows. The play's complete
knowingness about this paradox is characteristically
uttered by the Clown, who plays on the mystery of the
marriage sacrament as a joking excuse for adultery:

> He that comforts my wife is the cherisher of my flesh and
> blood; he that cherishes my flesh and blood loves my flesh
> and blood; he that loves my flesh and blood is my friend;
> *ergo*, he that kisses my wife is my friend. If men could be
> contented to be what they are, there were no fear in marriage
> . . . (I.3.46–51)

It is both a cynical and a witty advance parody of the
trick whereby Helena wrenches an act of adultery into
one of faithful marriage:

> . . . wicked meaning in a lawful deed,
> And lawful meaning in a lawful act,
> Where both not sin, and yet a sinful fact. (III.7.45–7)

In a similar way, the Clown's desire to discard Isbel ('I have no mind to Isbel since I was at court', III.2.12), whom he so recently either married or intended to marry, parodies Bertram's intention to discard his own wife. Indeed, Lavatch makes his announcement with utter casualness at the very moment when the Countess is opening the letter from Bertram that announces his intention with such painful seriousness.

HONOUR AND BLOOD

The relations between honour and desire, between law and passion, are explored throughout the play at numerous levels and naturally are closely tied to the focus on body and blood. Blood is especially useful as a potential metaphor for noble birth and humanity as well as passionate anger and desire, and the play returns frequently to the irony whereby one kind of concern with 'blood' vies with another. The Countess, when reflecting on how thorns cling naturally to the 'rose of youth', offers a cryptic formulation that resists easy interpretation: 'Our blood to us, this to our blood is born. | It is the show and seal of nature's truth' (I.3.126–7). She may mean that passion is part of human nature and that suffering is part of passion; or that we are born into a certain social position, yet inherit the natural passion of humanity regardless of place. The King's remarks in responding to Bertram's sense of outrage at being chosen as husband by a mere physician's daughter are clearer in their meaning:

'Tis only title thou disdainest in her, the which
I can build up. Strange is it that our bloods,
Of colour, weight, and heat, poured all together,

> Would quite confound distinction, yet stands off
> In differences so mighty. (II.3.116–20)

Blood as physical substance, the King argues, is the same
in every human being. Yet Bertram, in making a fuss
about Helena's ignoble birth, seems to insist on an
inherent difference between their bloods which is in fact
not given but a matter of arbitrary appearance that he,
the King, can transform. Lafew, seeing the apparent scorn
of Helena by all the court's young men of noble birth,
so insistent on the superiority of their 'blood', condemns
them as bloodless 'boys of ice' (92).

Honour for women in this play, however, is less a
matter of their own noble blood than of refusing the
pressure of young men's 'important blood', or urgent
desire. Diana, the object of Bertram's lust, is characterized by a striking concern for her honour, and part of
her function is to expose Bertram as a liar in seeking to
use false promises of marriage to persuade her to yield
to his desire:

>   He had sworn to marry me
> When his wife's dead; therefore I'll lie with him
> When I am buried. (IV.2.71–3)

Her own determination to stay a virgin both enables and
justifies the bed-trick:

> Marry that will, I live and die a maid.
> Only, in this disguise, I think't no sin
> To cozen [cheat] him that would unjustly win. (74–6)

While Bertram imagines that he 'fleshes his will in the
spoil of her honour' (IV.3.15), as his fellow soldiers

put it, he is in fact lying with a woman for whom he feels no desire, and whom he has vowed never to bed. Diana's concept of honour and determination to remain a maid provide a notable contrast with Helena, who never has any intention of remaining either unmarried or a virgin. Indeed, her exchange on the subject with Parolles shows how fearful a prospect she finds the idea of sacrificing the flesh of desire to the bones of a cold virtue. She conceives of virtue differently, not in opposition to the desiring body but in harmony with it. In this she is deeply unlike Isabella in *Measure for Measure*, the other female protagonist Shakespeare shows involved in a bed-trick, since Isabella's concern, as a novice, is to keep her chastity, while Helena's is to conceive a child. Thus where Isabella's trick is to substitute another woman for herself in Angelo's bed in order to preserve her own virginity, Helena's is to substitute herself for another woman in Bertram's in order to lose it. Her triumph is to lose her virginity chastely, to the man she loves, within the honourable context of marriage. When, in describing herself in the third person to Diana and her mother, she singles out 'reservèd honesty' (strict honour) as 'all her deserving' (III.5.61, 60), she is simultaneously describing a chastity that she wishes to end and a different kind of honour that attaches, within her own sense of values, to her legitimate search to unite herself with her rightful husband.

Helena and Diana are not the only two characters to bring differing conceptions of honour into opposition within the play. Bertram and the King clash more violently. Whereas Diana's and Helena's personal codes of honour complement one another in their opposition and come together to achieve a shared outcome, Bertram's insistence that the King's intent to marry him to Helena demeans his honour offers a direct affront to the King's sense that his own honour is at stake in having his authority thus scorned (II.3.148). And Parolles adds a further perspective to these proud definitions by simply distancing himself entirely from such a concept. When Helena first sees Parolles approaching in Act I, scene 1, she compares the durability of creatures such as he, who freely bluff and cheat their way through life, prioritizing the demands of the moment, and characters like herself, self-denying and virtuous, living on seemingly vain hopes of future reward. His kind of folly, as she says, flourishes by simply and boldly insisting on its place in the world, while her own 'steely' virtue suffers unrewarded (I.1.102–3). As Parolles himself says knowingly, after he has been exposed as a liar and a traitor: 'Simply the thing I am | Shall make me live' (IV.3.323–4). He will survive because his heart is straightforwardly not great enough to register great pain. Just as Lavatch's brief witticism on husband and wife as one flesh simultaneously parodies and highlights the poignancy of the central narrative concern with marital union so, in a more extended way, the sub-plot that plays out the capture and exposure of Parolles parodies and highlights the central concern with honour. Helena's ideal of marriage survives its parody to retain a moral purity that transcends the Clown's wit; but Bertram's ideal of honour collapses as he himself is later revealed, in a scene that parallels the unmasking of Parolles, as a liar and a traitor. Moreover Parolles, repeatedly referred to in the play via his clothes and accessories ('The soul of this man is his clothes' (II.5.43–4); 'That jackanapes with scarfs' (III.5.84)), is a caricature of the superficiality and shallowness that characterize Bertram, for all his high-sounding claims to honour. It is not accidental that we never learn what the war that occupies him is about or who wins it. The absence of such knowledge serves to underline our sense that it exists as a mere vehicle for Bertram's fraudulent 'honour'. He is not proving himself a man by fighting for a worthy cause but rather escaping from manhood by losing himself in unquestioning activity far from the place of his personal responsibilities.

REALISM AND ROMANCE

It would be a mistake, however, to take refuge in such a purely realist explanation of Bertram's behaviour. The starting point for this introduction was the fairy-tale shape of *All's Well*. The development of that argument turned on recognizing the play's concern to show what such a fairy tale might really look and feel like from inside, the absurd and outrageous demands, refusals and conditions of the form. The argument that Bertram is immaturely refusing to face up to his situation fits within the realist perspective, but ignores the overall thrust of the play's shape, which is always in tension with that realism. The perspectives of realism and romance are truly not consistent with each other. If Helena looks like an ideally noble character by the end, that is primarily because of her place within the tale. We have only to look at the incompatibility between some of her utterances, statements by other characters and the lines of the plot to see that the play is underpinned by a providential shaping that is in potential conflict with psychological realism and coherence.

Helena's early soliloquies give us a strong sense of a mind thinking and feeling intensely and an individual claiming agency for her own fate:

> Our remedies oft in ourselves do lie,
> Which we ascribe to heaven.
>
> . . .
>
> But my intents are fixed, and will not leave me.
>   (I.1.212–13, 225)

Yet her motives for going to Florence, as we have seen, are apparently to allow Bertram to return home to Rossillion without having to find her there and to make amends for her fault in forcing Bertram into marriage with her against his will, not to follow Bertram in order to fulfil his condition. The chance whereby she just happens to take up lodging with the woman whose daughter Bertram is pursuing thus looks like the working out of a higher destiny rather than an expression of Helena's own will or agency. Soon after Helena's statement of resolve at the end of the first scene, the Countess is speaking of Helena in a way that suggests the priority of the story itself over the realism of the characters, a perspective that also forces us to see the characters, including Helena, as chess-pieces moved to stand still or take action by the hand of Providence: 'Her father bequeathed her to me, and she herself, without other advantage, may lawfully make title to as much love as she finds. There is more owing her than is paid, and more shall be paid her than she'll demand' (I.3.97–101). In this way, patience and humility are seen to be necessary functions of the tale rather than psychological attributes; and from this perspective there is no need to worry about the inconsistency between the patient, long-suffering Helena and the actively resolute Helena. Helena's own form of expression, later in this same scene – asking the Countess's compassion after confessing her love – seems to make her into a vehicle instrumental in uttering truths greater than herself rather than an individual articulating her inner state:

> O then, give pity
> To her whose state is such that cannot choose
> But lend and give where she is sure to lose;
> That seeks not to find that her search implies,
> But riddle-like lives sweetly where she dies. (I.3.208–12)

And by the beginning of the next act, in speaking to the King, that gnomic form of speech that sounds like higher wisdom ('But most it is presumption in us when | The help of heaven we count the act of men', II.1.151–2) is in blatant contradiction to the voice of the active young woman determined to shape her own fate in the first scene.

The 'all's well that ends well' motif is problematized both by the Clown's examination of the term 'well' (I.3.16–19 and II.4.2–5) and by the double-edged repetitive play on the proverb in the last scene. Despite this problematization, however, the characters' potential for interiority is still suspended in highly artificial verse forms and plot-shapes and their agency restricted within a providential structure that seems to impose itself from beyond them. If we accept that the play 'ends well', we accept it as the given shape of a particular kind of story. The play teaches us to look hard at the gap between art and life by exposing the formal structure of the play for what it is: an artificial closure imposed upon a difficult world of recalcitrant people. But that structure is one which, even as it gives us reasons to reject the idea of miracles, insists upon their possibility.

Janette Dillon

The Play in Performance

Two books have been indispensable to the writing of this section, furnishing most of the basic information and quotations from the play's stage history: Joseph Price's *The Unfortunate Comedy: A Study of 'All's Well That Ends Well' and Its Critics* (1968) and J. L. Styan's *All's Well That Ends Well* in the Macmillan Shakespeare in Performance Series (1984). Where sources of quotations are unacknowledged, they are taken from one of these two sources.

As noted in the Introduction, *All's Well That Ends Well* has a relatively thin theatrical history. We know of no performances for the first century and a half of its life; and while that tells us nothing about how much or how little it was performed up to the closing of the theatres in 1642, since records for that period are so poor, it does suggest that from the reopening of the theatres in 1660 up to the date of its first recorded performance in 1741 it was very little performed, if at all. Henry Giffard's 1741 production at Goodman's Fields, moreover, was advertised as 'written by Shakespeare and not acted since his time', which lends weight to that supposition. Between 1741 and Frank Benson's revival of Shakespeare's text at Stratford-upon-Avon in 1916 it was acted only in much-altered versions.

Something of the present-day superstition that now attaches to *Macbeth* seems to have dogged *All's Well* in the eighteenth century, when it was labelled 'the unfortunate comedy', as Thomas Davies recorded in 1783, 'from the disagreeable accidents which fell out several times during the acting of it'. Giffard's production was ousted a few weeks into the run by David Garrick's success as Richard III and the resulting dominance of tragedy in the Goodman's Fields repertoire. It was cancelled after only one night at Drury Lane the following year because Peg Woffington, playing Helena, fell ill. The production was rescheduled, but William Milward, playing the King, then fell ill and died. When it finally reached the stage a month or so later, Peg Woffington fainted during the first act; and a dispute between actors Theophilus Cibber and Charles Macklin over the casting of Parolles was the source of further difficulty.

Parolles was the star part for eighteenth-century actors and audiences. Nicholas Rowe, writing in 1709, is the first on record to comment on the appeal of the role. He called it 'as good as any thing of that kind in Plautus or Terence', thus flagging up the classical precedents for the role of the braggart-soldier. Samuel Johnson compared Parolles with Falstaff in his 1765 edition of Shakespeare's plays, singing his praise as having 'more wit than virtue'. The first recorded response to the play in performance is in a letter written by William Shenstone about the Drury Lane production of 1742, in which Theophilus Cibber played Parolles (Cibber took over the role from Joseph Peterson, whose own success in the part must have contributed to the quarrel between Cibber and Macklin over who should take it on after that):

Me nothing has so much transported as young Cibber's exhibition of Parolles, in Shakespear's '*All's well that ends well*'. The character is admirably written by the author . . . I think Cibber elicited from me as sincere a laugh as I can ever recollect. Nothing, sure, can be comparable to this representation of Parolles in his bully-character; except the figure he makes as a shabby gentleman. In his first dress he is tawdry, as you may imagine; in the last, he wears a rusty black coat, a black stock [neck-cloth], a black wig with a Ramillie [a long plait at the back], a pair of black gloves; and a face! – which causes five minutes' laughter.

While Shenstone describes the part as 'admirably written', one can't help noticing here the classic visual appeal of the clown, who 'wears' the part as a vehicle for his personal charisma, making people laugh just by the way he is rather than through the lines he speaks.

Though we don't know which text was used for this production, it is likely that it was edited to highlight the role of Parolles. Certainly Garrick's text for the play's revival in 1756 did this, playing down the part of Helena in order to maximize the central comic role, and transferring the epilogue to Parolles. It was the comedian Harry Woodward who took top billing in the role in Garrick's production. Charles I's glossing of the title as 'Monsieur Parolles' in his copy of the second Folio, published in 1632, may well indicate that this part was the major attraction from the play's earliest performances. It is notable that even as late as Frank Benson's production in 1916, Benson himself took the part of Parolles, casting his wife as Helena. William Poel, who tried to cast a woman as Parolles (Clare Greet, known for her performance of female comic stereotypes), ended up playing the part himself in his 1920 production; and the young Laurence Olivier took the role in a production at the Birmingham Repertory Theatre in 1927, playing it, in J. C. Trewin's opinion, as 'an amiable, too smart young man'.

No part, however, has polarized responses more than that of Helena. Though Garrick cut her part primarily in order to enhance that of Parolles, her sexual explicitness in joking with Parolles was already becoming unacceptably frank for eighteenth-century audiences, and her trickery of Bertram was coming to be seen as unfeminine. Francis Gentleman, writing of the Garrick script in his introduction to the Bell Acting Edition, published in 1774, thought it compared well with the original in respect of the scene with Parolles. This scene, he wrote, 'as it stands originally, is not only indelicate, but trifling: above half of it is omitted, and indeed the whole might very well be spared'. Charlotte Lennox, an eighteenth-century novelist and translator, who published a work on Shakespeare's sources in 1753, described Helena as 'cruel, artful, and insolent'. By the nineteenth century, although the emphasis of the play in performance had shifted from Parolles to Helena, this was a purified and idealized Helena, whose wit and initiative had been sacrificed to the portrayal of patient sweetness. John Philip Kemble's revision, performed through the first half of the nineteenth century, excised her seemingly inappropriate assertiveness in pursuing Bertram as a husband and her unmaidenly confidence in dealing with an anal fistula, as well as her banter about virginity with Parolles. Even during the nineteenth century, however, there was no agreement about her. Amongst Romantic critics, for example, William Hazlitt described her as having 'great sweetness and delicacy'; Samuel Taylor Coleridge, despite judging her to be 'Shakespeare's loveliest character', elsewhere confessed to finding her character 'not very delicate'; while Mrs Anna Jameson (author of a book on Shakespeare's heroines) magisterially pronounced that 'there never was, perhaps, a more beautiful picture of a woman's love . . . Her love is like a religion, pure, holy, and deep.'

Changing ideas about women towards the end of the nineteenth century, however, and the shock of Ibsen's arrival on the English stage, allowed the sexual frankness and assertiveness of Helena's character to resurface as a positive feature. Suddenly she seemed to be a modern woman, ahead of her time. For William Poel, producing the play in 1920, Helena's initiative seemed to speak of the emancipation of women and the overcoming of class barriers; and Robert Atkins's production at the Old Vic the following year restored dialogue previously seen as too explicit. Bernard Shaw thought the part still ahead of its time in 1928: 'In Shakespeare there are parts – like that of Helena in *All's Well* for instance – which are still too genuine and beautiful and modern for the public.'

This may partly explain why no actress seems to have created a truly satisfactory rendition of Helena until Tyrone Guthrie's production at Stratford, Ontario, in 1953. There were eight major productions in the first forty years of the twentieth century, but none before then that totally convinced. Ivor Brown, reviewing for *Punch*, for example, found Catherine Lacey's performance in Atkins's third production of the play in 1940 overwhelmingly lovable, but not particularly credible: 'You need not believe in her, but love her you must – and love her you will.' Critics agreed, however, that Irene Worth's 'disconcerting simplicity', to use Joseph Price's term, brought fulfilment to the role at Stratford, Ontario. Claire Bloom, who played the part in the same year in Michael

Benthall's production at the Old Vic, also convinced, according to Roger Wood and Mary Clarke in their review of the 1953–4 season, by 'playing Helena quite straight-forwardly as if she believed implicitly in the character's behaviour'. She offered a performance that openly acknowledged the difference between the two halves of the play, 'an April creature of quick tears and laughter in the early scenes and strangely moving in her very still-ness and solemnity at the end' (Wood and Clarke, *Shakespeare at the Old Vic*, 1955). Guthrie directed both Irene Worth and Zoe Caldwell (in his later 1959 version of the play at Stratford-upon-Avon) towards an austerity and seriousness that suggested the Shavian 'new woman', toning down romantic sweetness in order to make way for a briskness of approach that could make sense of Helena's medical practicality towards the King's fistula.

Later actresses continued to emphasize both her prac-ticality and her anguish, and social class became a domi-nant perspective. Estelle Kohler and Lynn Farleigh, in John Barton's productions of 1967 and 1968, were depicted as middle-class fish out of water, with Kohler playing up a rather brazen persona, knowingly and oppor-tunistically exploiting a girlish sexuality (Milton Shulman described her as 'an efficient man-trap'). Angela Down, playing the part for Elijah Moshinsky's BBC TV version in 1980, emphasized Helena's continuing pain and unremitting seriousness even further; while Trevor Nunn's production of 1981–2 sought to restore some romantic element, at the same time retaining a strongly visible class perspective in an Edwardian setting that showed Helena wearing the house keys at her waist as against Bertram at leisure in the officers' club. Sophie Thompson, in Peter Hall's 1993 production, was described by the critic for the *London Evening Standard* as having 'the air of a retiring schoolgirl who summons up undreamt-of reserves of gumption to achieve her goal'; and most recently Claudie Blakley, in Greg Doran's 2003 production at the Swan in Stratford-upon-Avon, brought ardency and determination together in a way that clarified her choice to move from lover to wife through pilgrimage.

While directors tend to find Helena the most problematic character to stage, Bertram also presents challenges. One way in which directors have excused him is to stress his youth and immaturity (a line also endorsed by several academic critics, notably E. M. W. Tillyard, who noted the growth of the hero as a motif common to all the problem plays). Good looks also help the performer of this part to overcome potential audience distaste for his behaviour. Mike Gwilym and Philip Franks took the role at Stratford-upon-Avon and the London Barbican respectively in Trevor Nunn's RSC production in 1981–2; Tyrone Guthrie cast the youthful Edward De Souza in his 1959 production; John Neville, in Michael Benthall's production for the Old Vic in the same year, 'had no hope of making Bertram heroic, but played him with considerable spirit aided by a handsome voice and presence' (Wood and Clarke); and Maurice Colbourne's Bertram in W. Bridges-Adams's production at Stratford-upon-Avon in 1922 was, according to one member of the audience, 'like an armoured knight in a Burne-Jones window: a figure too beautiful to be taken seriously'. John Houseman's direction of John Ragin's Bertram at Stratford, Connecticut, in 1959 made the part credible, in Joseph Price's view, by playing up a realistically youthful alternation between impulsiveness and anxiety.

Price lists the most crucial questions raised by the play for directors since the 1950s:

Could the romantic and realistic portions ever blend in the theatre to satisfy any one of the numerous critical interpretations of the play? Could the full text produce a coherent comedy, a sentimental romance, a modern problem play, a dark and bitter satire, a philosophical commentary? Regardless of approach, could Bertram ever be played as an attractive mate for Helena? Could Helena herself ever yield to a consistent interpretation when the 'ribaldries' of her repartee with Parolles on virginity are enclosed by two soliloquies of touching beauty? Should the surprising deceits of Helena be applauded, ignored as mere convention, or decried? Should the unpleasant deceits of Bertram be treated comically or tragically? Should the humorous deceits of Parolles suffer a tragic denouement or a flippant reconciliation with life? How should the minor characters be played – Lafeu as the meddling buffoon or the King's confidant, Lavache as the playful clown or the bitter fool, the King as the impulsive tyrant or the fatherly ruler, Diana as an impudent schemer or virtuous maiden, the Widow as the greedy opportunist or the maternal sympathizer?

The questions listed by Price focus primarily on issues of character and coherence. There are, however, two further areas of difficulty which can create immense practical challenges in production: the obscurity of the text and the unseemly haste of the last scene. G. K. Hunter, in his introduction to the Arden edition (1959), describes the text as 'laboured and complex, but not rich', going on to assert in no uncertain terms that '[t]he amount of mental energy required is out of all proportion to any dramatic illumination of the context'. Consider, for example, these remarks by the Countess in the opening moments of the play:

I have those hopes of her good, that her education promises her dispositions she inherits – which makes fair gifts fairer; for where an unclean mind carries virtuous qualities, there commendations go with pity: they are virtues and traitors too. (I.1.38–42)

or this exchange a few lines later:

LAFEW Moderate lamentation is the right of the dead, excessive grief the enemy to the living.
COUNTESS If the living be enemy to the grief, the excess makes it soon mortal. (53–6)

Delivery of lines like these needs to be exceptionally clear and confident if audiences are to make sense of them.

As the second of these quotations illustrates, there is also, besides a general difficulty of expression, the problem of the play's tendency to give characters universalizing, proverbial-sounding lines (see Introduction, 'Helena'), which are almost impossible to speak within a naturalistic performance style, still dominant through much of the twentieth century and dedicated to a concentration on making characters seem real and believable. Nicholas Hytner, preparing to rehearse his production of *Henry V* in 2002, speaks for several recent generations in expressing the view that: 'In my experience, you can only act Shakespeare by taking his people literally; by assuming that Hamlet is real. And then audiences, certainly in this country, will believe you' (*Times Literary Supplement*, 1 November 2002). Though views like this have underpinned so much twentieth-century performance, they can create more problems than they solve when applied to plays that are not written with the same preconceptions about characters. One of the great strengths of Doran's production at the Swan was its trust in the play's didactic moments. Watching this performance illuminated the prominence the play gives to older characters: not only has their experience important things to teach us but the experience of listening to such teaching, far from being boring, as one might predict for a contemporary audience, can be both moving and inspiring. *All's Well That Ends Well*, with its changeable heroine and fairy-tale plot written for a different age, its tension between individuality and destiny, resists a consistent literalism and refuses to allow its characters to be taken for real.

The play's resistance to realism is also at the heart of the problem with the ending. It seems to impose a resolution with unhappy and unbelievable speed, showing Bertram at his least likeable or trustworthy even as the ring is produced, still making more conditions even as the original conditions are already shown to be fulfilled: 'If she, my liege, can make me know this clearly | I'll love her dearly, ever, ever dearly' (V.3.313–14). But performance is occasionally capable of transforming a willing audience, of persuading them against their better judgement to believe in magical resolutions, especially if they can be encouraged to let go of literal and realistic responses and to trust in the intensity of the moment. Muriel St Clare Byrne describes the force of that intensity for her as she watched Zoe Caldwell play Helena in Tyrone Guthrie's 1959 Stratford-upon-Avon production and experienced the overwhelming of her rational view that Bertram's outrageous words were simply unspeakable and unacceptable:

I saw nothing but Helena and what she did, heard nothing but what she had said, accepted the gesture of contrition and perhaps of the beginnings of love with which he knelt and clung to her. It was her moment: her words and the stage picture had said all there was to say. And from Dame Edith [Evans, playing the Countess] down, every single member of the cast *acted* that moment: you did not watch them, you felt them feeling its impact. There was no need for Bertram to speak, and if his words had been adequate they would have been out of character. (Actually, of course, the 'impossible' couplet was spoken simply and firmly. The literary eye is often deceived until the ears gain theatrical experience.)

Though performances can sometimes overcome audiences' doubts and preconceptions in this way, the play has remained one that most directors prefer to pass by. Greg Doran, writing in the programme for the 2003 Swan production, describes his personal journey to Wilton House, where we know Shakespeare's company performed in 1603, probably before the performance but perhaps during the writing of *All's Well*, in order to look for 'clues to this, Shakespeare's most melancholy and in some ways problematic comedy'. For him, the solution lies partly in seeing both Helena and Parolles as projections of Shakespeare's own life, as it seems to emerge in the *Sonnets*, loving one high above his station and using words both to express and to disguise his passions. For most directors and reviewers, however, the practical questions centre around three linked areas of focus: the difficulties inherent in Bertram and Helena both individually and as a pair; the outrageous plot; and the question of whether to seek to resolve these by playing up the miraculous and romantic elements, playing up the hard, realistic edge, or looking for a way to allow both to co-exist. Its combination of fairy tale and real life, as the *London Evening Standard* reviewer wrote on 12 December 1993, can seem merely jarring:

All's Well is a Gordian knot of discordant themes and registers. Generically a comedy, it is neither funny nor uplifting; its plot has a folkloric simplicity warped by imbuing the characters with credible inner lives.

In describing it as 'not a play people leap towards with glad cries', then, Richard Edmonds of the *Birmingham Post* (12 December 2003) speaks for a wide constituency of scholars and reviewers alike. Even G. K. Hunter, introducing the Arden edition, wrote that it was 'not a play that is often read or performed, and on the rare occasions when it is seen or heard it does not seem to give much general pleasure'. It is scarcely surprising, given the dominance of such negative views, that the play is so rarely performed. Directors who choose to stage it risk their reputations in taking on this difficult and characteristically unloved play; and for this very reason the play may be seen as something of a test case. Roger Wood and Mary Clarke, writing about the play's run at the Old Vic in 1953, note that it was deliberately chosen by the Old Vic in order to test the extent to which audiences would support 'the lesser known and indeed inferior plays'. The signs were, they concluded from that production, that, despite its excellent reviews and good-sized audiences over thirty-five performances, 'the public for the rarer plays is, as yet, a limited and specialized one'.

And yet this need not be so. Judi Dench, who played the Countess in Doran's 2003 production, evidently experienced the relative unfamiliarity of the play as liberating: 'I had never seen the play and had never heard it read . . . It's a new story to me and to most people who come to the theatre to see it. They don't know the ending' (quoted by Marion McMullen, *Coventry Evening Tele-*

graph, 12 December 2003). Certainly this production moved audiences, both those who did not previously know the play and those who knew it but had no particular liking for it. Reviews show clearly the way performance can transform critical opinion:

All's Well That Ends Well is one of the least loved of Shakespeare's plays, but watching Gregory Doran's superb production . . . one wonders why . . . [T]his neglected play is revealed to be something very special indeed, a twisted, wintry work that holds out the tentative promise of spring. (Charles Spencer, *Daily Telegraph*, 12 December 2003)

If there was ever such a thing as a feel-bad comedy, then *All's Well* is surely it . . . [but] this was one of the most visually satisfying, and consummately acted, shows that I have seen in Stratford for some years. (Greg Walker, *Cahiers Élisabéthains*, forthcoming)

It is Dench who is drawing the crowds, but the triumph lies in the restoration of an unforgivably neglected play. (Michael Billington, *Guardian*, 12 December 2003)

Attending this production as an admirer of the play, I nevertheless found that performance transformed my perception of it. Where, in reading the play, the problem of pairing Helena and Bertram had seemed paramount, I found as I watched this production that the emphasis shifted from that relationship to the relationship between Helena and the Countess. The love between these two women, and the suffering that each is caused by the loss, or fear of loss, of the other, seemed to be the real centre of engagement; and the problem of Bertram's ungracious acceptance of Helena in the final scene seemed less significant because it was so quickly overwhelmed by the powerful tableau of the reconciliatory embrace between the women. Most readers, reading the play even now, will not have seen a production of this play. It is thus all the more important to hold in the imagination the capacity of performance to transform the text in ways that are almost, as the ending of the play itself is, beyond belief.

Janette Dillon

Further Reading

The sources, date and textual status of *All's Well* are ably and comprehensively examined by three major editions of the play: G. K. Hunter's Arden (1959), Russell Fraser's New Cambridge (1985) and Susan Snyder's admirable Oxford (1993). Howard C. Cole in *The 'All's Well' Story From Boccaccio to Shakespeare* (1981) gives an exhaustive account of the fascination of the play's story for European writers before Shakespeare: 'its tradition had been shaped by the wit and irony of Boccaccio, the cynicism of Accolti, and the nervous expurgations and glosses of Borghini, Salviati, Painter.' *All's Well*'s relationship to its sister play, *Measure for Measure* – a popular topic – is emphatically addressed by Russell Fraser in his New Cambridge edition: 'I take *All's Well* to present a sceptical recension of the same material which Shakespeare has been deploying in *Measure for Measure*, or a second look at the material, refined to the point of abstraction, making it the more radical case. I follow Collier and Malone and date the play about 1605.' This date is rejected by David Haley in his *Shakespeare's Courtly Mirror: Reflexivity and Prudence in 'All's Well That Ends Well'* (1993), who argues, somewhat tenuously, that the play's providential theme connects it with issues of historical providence in *Richard II*, *Henry IV* and *Henry V*. He therefore dates the play in early 1600, looking back to *Henry V* in the spring of 1599 and *Every Man Out of His Humour* in the autumn.

Susan Snyder in her Oxford edition has fresh and interesting things to say about the play's controversial main character, Helena, not least that she should be called Helen, the spelling most frequently used in the 1623 Folio. She can best be understood, Snyder maintains, in the context of a hybrid plot and an experimental genre. Indeed, our approach to the play should take its 'dislocations and deferrals as the point of entry'. The history of the play's reception in study and theatre – a history itself of dislocations and deferrals – is given in Joseph Price's *The Unfortunate Comedy* (1968), and the deferred theatrical tradition is further examined in J. L. Styan's book (1984) on the play in performance (see The Play in Performance above), which notes that, because of the indelicacy of its plot, the play doesn't have much of a theatrical history: it comes to us 'largely unencumbered by the debris of stage tradition'. Styan's study is usefully divided into two parts: a full general discussion and a scene-by-scene discussion of performance issues in the play.

A dislocated and dislocating *All's Well* helps to explain the play's lack of popularity before, and relative surge of popularity during, the twentieth century. Russell Fraser expresses the view that: '*All's Well* is a great play whose time has come round.' Though this perhaps overstates the current enthusiasm for the play, there is certainly more evidence of interest in staging it over recent years than at any time in its history. The play's rehabilitation began in 1931 with W. W. Lawrence's *Shakespeare's Problem Comedies* and continued with minor dislocations to the present day. (One such dislocation was E. M. W. Tillyard's own *Shakespeare's Problem Comedies* (1950), which designated the play a failure because of the difficulty of reconciling the romantic plot with a realistic treatment of the plot's characters.) Major advocates of the play's distinction include: R. G. Hunter's *Shakespeare and the Comedy of Forgiveness* (1965); Northrop Frye's *The Myth of Deliverance: Reflections on Shakespeare's Problem Comedies* (1983); A. P. Rossiter's lively and idiosyncratic *Angel with Horns* (1961); Joseph Westlund's *Shakespeare's Reparative Comedies: A Psychoanalytic View of the Middle Plays* (1984), in which we see *All's Well* in the illuminating company of *The Merchant of Venice*, *Much Ado*, *As You Like It*, *Twelfth Night* and *Measure for Measure*; and P. C. McGuire's *Shakespeare: The Jacobean Plays* (1994).

Nicholas Marsh has recently provided a useful analysis of the play alongside *Measure for Measure* and *Troilus and Cressida* in *Shakespeare: Three Problem Plays* (2003), where he shows how much is to be learned by ordering and inspecting certain kinds of information in tabular form (chapter 6). Volume IV of the *Blackwell Companion to Shakespeare's Works* (2003) includes Barbara Howard Traister's '"Doctor She": Healing and Sex in *All's Well That Ends Well*', a reading which argues that Helena herself is in need of healing, and an essay on marriage and the bed-tricks (Theodora Jankowski's 'Hymeneal Blood, Interchangeable Women, and the Early Modern Marriage Economy in *Measure for Measure* and *All's Well That Ends Well*').

The psychoanalytically-minded have been much drawn to *All's Well*. Richard Wheeler's enthralling *Shakespeare's Development and the Problem Comedies* (1981) argues that in *All's Well* Bertram is a 'typical comic hero who finds himself at the center of deep psychologic conflict from which his predecessors have been carefully protected'. And what we have from Helena is no high-spirited playfulness but 'anguished adoration'. Wheeler asks us – as many others do (notably Susan Snyder) – to see the play in the context of Shakespeare's sonnets, where Helena and the Poet's submissive posture 'is experienced in the tragedies as excruciating shame, helplessness, and rage'. Like Wheeler, David Haley in *Shakespeare's Courtly Mirror* tends to see the play as focusing on Bertram rather than on Helena (contrast, say, Carol T. Neely's book *Broken Nuptials in Shakespeare's Plays* (1985), which studies the play in the context of the broken nuptials in *Much Ado*, *Antony and Cleopatra*, *Othello* and *The Winter's Tale*). Bertram is 'a specimen of the unformed nobleman', the observed of all observers, bursting with aristocratic potential. His rejection of Helena is, so Haley would have us believe, 'a creative act', where 'the sullen disdain that his resistance puts on masks the heroic resolution of an aristocrat'. Haley, however, is no psychologizer and sees the play as enacting 'a dialectic between prudence and Providence' where prudence = politics: 'The court in *All's Well* is a mirror of heroic prudence. The courtier's praxis issues from his deliberations, which is identical with courtly reflexivity.' It's a humanistic not a divine providence and takes human forms: 'the courtier's heroic prudence, the alchemical work of renewal, Helena's purposeful love'.

Several shorter pieces illuminate understanding of the play by way of a narrower focus. A variety of insights are drawn, for example, from close attention to the play's opening scene and to its language. In an essay in a collection about Shakespeare's beginnings J. L. Styan notes two ways in which the opening of *All's Well* is unusual: it opens with prose rather than verse, and its prose is obscure and difficult to understand, signalling the presence of a suppression and enigma that are to be important throughout ('The Opening of *All's Well That Ends Well*: A Performance Approach' in *Entering the Maze: Shakespeare's Art of Beginning*, ed. Robert F. Willson, Jr. (1995)). The play, Styan notes, 'will have to do with leaving home and coming back, with giving birth and with dying'; and this is a perception also informing essays by David Bevington ('All's Well That Plays Well' in *Subjects on the World's Stage: Essays on British Literature of the Middle Ages and Renaissance*, ed. David C. Allen and Robert A. White (1995)) and Patricia Parker ('*All's Well That Ends Well*: Increase and Multiply' in *Creative Imitation: New Essays on Renaissance Literature in Honor of Thomas M. Greene*, ed. David Quint et al. (1992)). Bevington argues that Act I, scene 1 sets in motion 'the play as a whole, for its two halves juxtapose sadness and laughter, death and sexual vitality, Lent and carnival, good-bye and hello'. The dual character of Helena is key, he suggests, to the unity of both this scene and the whole play. For Parker, paradoxes about the opening scene (with its 'oppressive sense of ending') and the play's language are key to its meaning. Though the play places so much emphasis on closure or ending it appears, as she shows, 'to gain its own life or "increase" . . . from the opening up of space and the putting off of endings'. The play returns again and again to linguistic figures of increase or dilation, and Parolles, with his unstoppable stream of words (including his instruction in how to 'take a more dilated farewell' (II.1.56–7)), is himself a representative figure for this increase, which also finds a parallel in Helena's physical fertility. Parolles's language is also centrally symbolic to François Laroque's perception of a 'semantic crisis' at the heart of the play ('Words and

Things in *All's Well That Ends Well*' in *French Essays on Shakespeare and His Contemporaries*, ed. Jean-Marie Maguin (1995)). He sees words in conflict with things in the play, as Parolles is in conflict with Lafew, and finds that the desire for amplification reduces language to meaninglessness.

A good all-round yet sophisticated introduction to *All's Well* is Sheldon Zitner's New Harvester Introduction (1989). He deals with the play illuminatingly by topic: power and status, gender and sexuality, young and old, making it theatre. Like David Haley, Zitner argues for the seriousness of Shakespeare's treatment of providence but draws different conclusions: 'In *All's Well* the supernatural has the effect of softening and deflecting Helena's activism from calculating bustle to a more elevated risk-taking.' And, like many other critics, he acknowledges the importance of the sonnets: 'The "I" of the sonnets is himself a kind of Helena, a provincial gaining entrée to court circles by virtue of a rare skill, forming passionate attachments "beyond his sphere".' In countering the usual view of the problem comedies, and this one in particular, as much obsessed with death, Zitner ends his book on a refreshingly positive note: 'If anything, we should say that Shakespeare's comedies are "life-haunted".'

Michael Taylor, 1998
Revised by Janette Dillon, 2005

ALL'S WELL THAT ENDS WELL

The Characters in the Play

BERTRAM, Count of Rossillion, a ward of the King of France
The COUNTESS of Rossillion, Bertram's mother
HELENA, a young girl brought up by the Countess
PAROLLES, Bertram's friend
Rynaldo, STEWARD in the Countess's household
Lavatch, CLOWN in the Countess's household
A PAGE in the Countess's household

The KING of France
LAFEW, an old Lord
The brothers Dumaine, two French LORDS: later Captains serving the Duke of Florence
Other LORDS
Two French SOLDIERS
A GENTLEMAN, Astringer to the Court of France
MESSENGER
ATTENDANT

The DUKE of Florence
WIDOW Capilet of Florence
DIANA, the Widow's daughter
MARIANA, a friend of the Widow

Lords, attendants, soldiers, citizens

Enter young Bertram, Count of Rossillion, his mother
the Countess, Helena, and Lord Lafew; all in black

COUNTESS In delivering my son from me, I bury a second
husband.

BERTRAM And I in going, madam, weep o'er my father's
death anew; but I must attend his majesty's command,
to whom I am now in ward, evermore in subjection.

LAFEW You shall find of the King a husband, madam; you,
sir, a father. He that so generally is at all times good
must of necessity hold his virtue to you, whose worthiness would stir it up where it wanted, rather than lack it
where there is such abundance.

COUNTESS What hope is there of his majesty's amend-
ment?

LAFEW He hath abandoned his physicians, madam, under
whose practices he hath persecuted time with hope, and
finds no other advantage in the process but only the
losing of hope by time.

COUNTESS This young gentlewoman had a father – O
that 'had', how sad a passage 'tis! – whose skill was
almost as great as his honesty; had it stretched so far,
would have made nature immortal, and death should
have play for lack of work. Would for the King's sake he
were living! I think it would be the death of the King's
disease.

10

20

LAFEW How called you the man you speak of, madam?

COUNTESS He was famous, sir, in his profession, and it
was his great right to be so: Gerard de Narbon.

LAFEW He was excellent indeed, madam. The King very
lately spoke of him admiringly, and mourningly. He
was skilful enough to have lived still, if knowledge could
30   be set up against mortality.

BERTRAM What is it, my good lord, the King languishes
of?

LAFEW A fistula, my lord.

BERTRAM I heard not of it before.

LAFEW I would it were not notorious. Was this gentlewoman the daughter of Gerard de Narbon?

COUNTESS His sole child, my lord, and bequeathed to my
overlooking. I have those hopes of her good, that her
education promises her dispositions she inherits – which
40   makes fair gifts fairer; for where an unclean mind
carries virtuous qualities, there commendations go with
pity: they are virtues and traitors too. In her they are the
better for their simpleness. She derives her honesty and
achieves her goodness.

LAFEW Your commendations, madam, get from her tears.

COUNTESS 'Tis the best brine a maiden can season her
praise in. The remembrance of her father never
approaches her heart but the tyranny of her sorrows
takes all livelihood from her cheek. No more of this,
50   Helena; go to, no more, lest it be rather thought you
affect a sorrow than to have't.

HELENA I do affect a sorrow indeed, but I have it too.

LAFEW Moderate lamentation is the right of the dead,
excessive grief the enemy to the living.

COUNTESS If the living be enemy to the grief, the excess
makes it soon mortal.

BERTRAM Madam, I desire your holy wishes.

LAFEW How understand we that?

COUNTESS

> Be thou blessed, Bertram, and succeed thy father
> In manners as in shape! Thy blood and virtue   60
> Contend for empire in thee, and thy goodness
> Share with thy birthright! Love all, trust a few,
> Do wrong to none. Be able for thine enemy
> Rather in power than use, and keep thy friend
> Under thy own life's key. Be checked for silence,
> But never taxed for speech. What heaven more will,
> That thee may furnish and my prayers pluck down,
> Fall on thy head! Farewell. – My lord,
> 'Tis an unseasoned courtier: good my lord,
> Advise him.

LAFEW   He cannot want the best   70
> That shall attend his love.

COUNTESS Heaven bless him! Farewell, Bertram.   *Exit*

BERTRAM The best wishes that can be forged in your thoughts be servants to you! (*To Helena*) Be comfortable to my mother, your mistress, and make much of her.

LAFEW Farewell, pretty lady. You must hold the credit of your father.   *Exeunt Bertram and Lafew*

HELENA

> O, were that all! I think not on my father,
> And these great tears grace his remembrance more
> Than those I shed for him. What was he like?   80
> I have forgot him. My imagination
> Carries no favour in't but Bertram's.
> I am undone: there is no living, none,
> If Bertram be away. 'Twere all one
> That I should love a bright particular star
> And think to wed it, he is so above me.
> In his bright radiance and collateral light
> Must I be comforted, not in his sphere.

Th'ambition in my love thus plagues itself:
90 The hind that would be mated by the lion
Must die for love. 'Twas pretty, though a plague,
To see him every hour, to sit and draw
His archèd brows, his hawking eye, his curls,
In our heart's table – heart too capable
Of every line and trick of his sweet favour.
But now he's gone, and my idolatrous fancy
Must sanctify his relics. Who comes here?

Enter Parolles

One that goes with him. I love him for his sake,
And yet I know him a notorious liar,
100 Think him a great way fool, solely a coward,
Yet these fixed evils sit so fit in him
That they take place when virtue's steely bones
Looks bleak i'th'cold wind. Withal, full oft we see
Cold wisdom waiting on superfluous folly.

PAROLLES Save you, fair queen!

HELENA And you, monarch!

PAROLLES No.

HELENA And no.

PAROLLES Are you meditating on virginity?

110 HELENA Ay. You have some stain of soldier in you: let me
ask you a question. Man is enemy to virginity; how may
we barricado it against him?

PAROLLES Keep him out.

HELENA But he assails, and our virginity, though valiant,
in the defence yet is weak. Unfold to us some warlike
resistance.

PAROLLES There is none. Man setting down before you
will undermine you and blow you up.

HELENA Bless our poor virginity from underminers and
120 blowers-up! Is there no military policy how virgins
might blow up men?

PAROLLES Virginity being blown down, man will quick-
lier be blown up; marry, in blowing him down again,
with the breach yourselves made you lose your city. It
is not politic in the commonwealth of nature to preserve virginity. Loss of virginity is rational increase, and
there was never virgin got till virginity was first lost.
That you were made of is mettle to make virgins. Virginity, by being once lost, may be ten times found; by
being ever kept it is ever lost. 'Tis too cold a com-   130
panion. Away with't!

HELENA I will stand for't a little, though therefore I die
a virgin.

PAROLLES There's little can be said in't; 'tis against the
rule of nature. To speak on the part of virginity is to
accuse your mothers, which is most infallible dis-
obedience. He that hangs himself is a virgin; virginity
murders itself, and should be buried in highways out of
all sanctified limit, as a desperate offendress against
nature. Virginity breeds mites, much like a cheese, con-   140
sumes itself to the very paring, and so dies with feeding
his own stomach. Besides, virginity is peevish, proud,
idle, made of self-love which is the most inhibited sin in
the canon. Keep it not; you cannot choose but lose by't.
Out with't! Within ten year it will make itself two, which
is a goodly increase, and the principal itself not much
the worse. Away with't!

HELENA How might one do, sir, to lose it to her own
liking?

PAROLLES Let me see. Marry, ill, to like him that ne'er it   150
likes. 'Tis a commodity will lose the gloss with lying;
the longer kept, the less worth. Off with't while 'tis
vendible; answer the time of request. Virginity, like an
old courtier, wears her cap out of fashion, richly suited
but unsuitable, just like the brooch and the toothpick,

which wear not now. Your date is better in your pie and
your porridge than in your cheek; and your virginity,
your old virginity, is like one of our French withered
pears: it looks ill, it eats drily; marry, 'tis a withered
160   pear; it was formerly better; marry, yet 'tis a withered
pear. Will you anything with it?

HELENA

Not my virginity, yet . . .
There shall your master have a thousand loves,
A mother, and a mistress, and a friend,
A phoenix, captain, and an enemy,
A guide, a goddess, and a sovereign,
A counsellor, a traitress, and a dear;
His humble ambition, proud humility,
His jarring concord, and his discord dulcet,
170   His faith, his sweet disaster; with a world
Of pretty, fond, adoptious christendoms
That blinking Cupid gossips. Now shall he –
I know not what he shall. God send him well!
The court's a learning-place, and he is one –

PAROLLES

What one, i'faith?

HELENA

That I wish well. 'Tis pity –

PAROLLES

What's pity?

HELENA

That wishing well had not a body in't
Which might be felt, that we, the poorer born,
180   Whose baser stars do shut us up in wishes,
Might with effects of them follow our friends,
And show what we alone must think, which never
Returns us thanks.

Enter Page

PAGE Monsieur Parolles, my lord calls for you.   *Exit*

PAROLLES Little Helen, farewell. If I can remember thee
    I will think of thee at court.

HELENA Monsieur Parolles, you were born under a
    charitable star.

PAROLLES Under Mars, I.

HELENA I especially think under Mars.   190

PAROLLES Why under Mars?

HELENA The wars hath so kept you under that you must
    needs be born under Mars.

PAROLLES When he was predominant.

HELENA When he was retrograde, I think rather.

PAROLLES Why think you so?

HELENA You go so much backward when you fight.

PAROLLES That's for advantage.

HELENA So is running away, when fear proposes the
    safety. But the composition that your valour and fear   200
    makes in you is a virtue of a good wing, and I like the
    wear well.

PAROLLES I am so full of businesses I cannot answer thee
    acutely. I will return perfect courtier, in the which my
    instruction shall serve to naturalize thee, so thou wilt be
    capable of a courtier's counsel, and understand what
    advice shall thrust upon thee; else thou diest in thine
    unthankfulness, and thine ignorance makes thee away.
    Farewell. When thou hast leisure, say thy prayers; when
    thou hast none, remember thy friends. Get thee a good   210
    husband, and use him as he uses thee. So, farewell. *Exit*

HELENA
    Our remedies oft in ourselves do lie,
    Which we ascribe to heaven. The fated sky
    Gives us free scope, only doth backward pull
    Our slow designs when we ourselves are dull.
    What power is it which mounts my love so high,

That makes me see, and cannot feed mine eye?
The mightiest space in fortune nature brings
To join like likes, and kiss like native things.
220 Impossible be strange attempts to those
That weigh their pains in sense, and do suppose
What hath been cannot be. Who ever strove
To show her merit that did miss her love?
The King's disease – my project may deceive me,
But my intents are fixed, and will not leave me.   *Exit*

I.2   *Flourish of cornets. Enter the King of France with*
         letters, and divers Attendants

KING
The Florentines and Senoys are by th'ears,
Have fought with equal fortune, and continue
A braving war.

FIRST LORD   So 'tis reported, sir.

KING
Nay, 'tis most credible. We here receive it
A certainty, vouched from our cousin Austria,
With caution that the Florentine will move us
For speedy aid; wherein our dearest friend
Prejudicates the business, and would seem
To have us make denial.

FIRST LORD   His love and wisdom,
10 Approved so to your majesty, may plead
For amplest credence.

KING   He hath armed our answer,
And Florence is denied before he comes;
Yet, for our gentlemen that mean to see
The Tuscan service, freely have they leave
To stand on either part.

SECOND LORD   It well may serve

A nursery to our gentry, who are sick
For breathing and exploit.

KING   What's he comes here?

Enter Bertram, Lafew, and Parolles

FIRST LORD

It is the Count Rossillion, my good lord,
Young Bertram.

KING   Youth, thou bearest thy father's face;
Frank nature, rather curious than in haste,   20
Hath well composed thee. Thy father's moral parts
Mayst thou inherit too! Welcome to Paris.

BERTRAM

My thanks and duty are your majesty's.

KING

I would I had that corporal soundness now,
As when thy father and myself in friendship
First tried our soldiership. He did look far
Into the service of the time, and was
Discipled of the bravest. He lasted long,
But on us both did haggish age steal on,
And wore us out of act. It much repairs me   30
To talk of your good father. In his youth
He had the wit which I can well observe
Today in our young lords, but they may jest
Till their own scorn return to them unnoted
Ere they can hide their levity in honour.
So like a courtier, contempt nor bitterness
Were in his pride or sharpness; if they were,
His equal had awaked them, and his honour,
Clock to itself, knew the true minute when
Exception bid him speak, and at this time   40
His tongue obeyed his hand. Who were below him
He used as creatures of another place,
And bowed his eminent top to their low ranks,

Making them proud of his humility,
In their poor praise he humbled. Such a man
Might be a copy to these younger times;
Which, followed well, would demonstrate them now
But goers backward.

BERTRAM   His good remembrance, sir,
Lies richer in your thoughts than on his tomb;
50   So in approof lives not his epitaph
As in your royal speech.

KING

Would I were with him! He would always say –
Methinks I hear him now; his plausive words
He scattered not in ears, but grafted them
To grow there and to bear – 'Let me not live',
This his good melancholy oft began
On the catastrophe and heel of pastime,
When it was out, 'Let me not live,' quoth he,
'After my flame lacks oil, to be the snuff
60   Of younger spirits, whose apprehensive senses
All but new things disdain; whose judgements are
Mere fathers of their garments; whose constancies
Expire before their fashions.' This he wished.
I, after him, do after him wish too,
Since I nor wax nor honey can bring home,
I quickly were dissolvèd from my hive
To give some labourers room.

SECOND LORD   You're loved, sir;
They that least lend it you shall lack you first.

KING

I fill a place, I know't. How long is't, Count,
70   Since the physician at your father's died?
He was much famed.

BERTRAM   Some six months since, my lord.

KING

    If he were living I would try him yet.

    Lend me an arm. – The rest have worn me out

    With several applications; nature and sickness

    Debate it at their leisure. Welcome, Count,

    My son's no dearer.

BERTRAM   Thank your majesty.

                              Exeunt. Flourish

    Enter the Countess, Rynaldo her Steward, and   1.3

    Lavatch her Clown

COUNTESS I will now hear. What say you of this gentle-

    woman?

STEWARD Madam, the care I have had to even your

    content I wish might be found in the calendar of my

    past endeavours, for then we wound our modesty, and

    make foul the clearness of our deservings, when of our-

    selves we publish them.

COUNTESS What does this knave here? Get you gone,

    sirrah. The complaints I have heard of you I do not all

    believe; 'tis my slowness that I do not, for I know you   10

    lack not folly to commit them, and have ability enough

    to make such knaveries yours.

CLOWN 'Tis not unknown to you, madam, I am a poor

    fellow.

COUNTESS Well, sir.

CLOWN No, madam, 'tis not so well that I am poor,

    though many of the rich are damned; but if I may have

    your ladyship's good will to go to the world, Isbel the

    woman and I will do as we may.

COUNTESS Wilt thou needs be a beggar?   20

CLOWN I do beg your good will in this case.

COUNTESS In what case?

CLOWN In Isbel's case and mine own. Service is no
heritage, and I think I shall never have the blessing of
God till I have issue o'my body; for they say barnes are
blessings.

COUNTESS Tell me thy reason why thou wilt marry.

CLOWN My poor body, madam, requires it. I am driven
on by the flesh, and he must needs go that the devil
30   drives.

COUNTESS Is this all your worship's reason?

CLOWN Faith, madam, I have other holy reasons, such as
they are.

COUNTESS May the world know them?

CLOWN I have been, madam, a wicked creature, as you
and all flesh and blood are, and indeed I do marry that I
may repent.

COUNTESS Thy marriage, sooner than thy wickedness.

CLOWN I am out o'friends, madam, and I hope to have
40   friends for my wife's sake.

COUNTESS Such friends are thine enemies, knave.

CLOWN Y'are shallow, madam; e'en great friends, for the
knaves come to do that for me which I am aweary of.
He that ears my land spares my team, and gives me
leave to in the crop. If I be his cuckold, he's my drudge.
He that comforts my wife is the cherisher of my flesh
and blood; he that cherishes my flesh and blood loves
my flesh and blood; he that loves my flesh and blood is
my friend; *ergo*, he that kisses my wife is my friend. If
50   men could be contented to be what they are, there were
no fear in marriage; for young Charbon the puritan and
old Poysam the papist, howsome'er their hearts are
severed in religion, their heads are both one: they may
jowl horns together like any deer i'th'herd.

COUNTESS Wilt thou ever be a foul-mouthed and
calumnious knave?

CLOWN A prophet I, madam, and I speak the truth the
next way:

> For I the ballad will repeat
> > Which men full true shall find: 60
> Your marriage comes by destiny,
> > Your cuckoo sings by kind.

COUNTESS Get you gone, sir. I'll talk with you more anon.

STEWARD May it please you, madam, that he bid Helen
come to you: of her I am to speak.

COUNTESS Sirrah, tell my gentlewoman I would speak
with her – Helen, I mean.

CLOWN

> Was this fair face the cause, quoth she,
> > Why the Grecians sackèd Troy?
> Fond done, done fond,   70
> > Was this King Priam's joy?
> With that she sighèd as she stood,
> With that she sighèd as she stood,
> > And gave this sentence then:
> Among nine bad if one be good,
> Among nine bad if one be good,
> > There's yet one good in ten.

COUNTESS What, one good in ten? You corrupt the song,
sirrah.

CLOWN One good woman in ten, madam, which is a   80
purifying o'th'song. Would God would serve the world
so all the year! We'd find no fault with the tithe-woman
if I were the parson. One in ten, quoth 'a! An we might
have a good woman born but one every blazing star or
at an earthquake, 'twould mend the lottery well; a man
may draw his heart out ere 'a pluck one.

COUNTESS You'll be gone, sir knave, and do as I command you!

CLOWN That man should be at woman's command, and

90   yet no hurt done! Though honesty be no puritan, yet it
     will do no hurt. It will wear the surplice of humility over
     the black gown of a big heart. I am going, forsooth. The
     business is for Helen to come hither.   *Exit*

COUNTESS Well, now.

STEWARD I know, madam, you love your gentlewoman
     entirely.

COUNTESS Faith, I do. Her father bequeathed her to me,
     and she herself, without other advantage, may lawfully
     make title to as much love as she finds. There is more
100 owing her than is paid, and more shall be paid her than
     she'll demand.

STEWARD Madam, I was very late more near her than I
     think she wished me. Alone she was, and did communi-
     cate to herself her own words to her own ears; she
     thought, I dare vow for her, they touched not any
     stranger sense. Her matter was, she loved your son.
     Fortune, she said, was no goddess, that had put such
     difference betwixt their two estates; Love no god, that
     would not extend his might only where qualities were
110 level; Dian no queen of virgins, that would suffer her
     poor knight surprised without rescue in the first assault
     or ransom afterward. This she delivered in the most
     bitter touch of sorrow that e'er I heard virgin exclaim
     in, which I held my duty speedily to acquaint you
     withal, sithence, in the loss that may happen, it con-
     cerns you something to know it.

COUNTESS You have discharged this honestly; keep it to
     yourself. Many likelihoods informed me of this before,
     which hung so tottering in the balance that I could
120 neither believe nor misdoubt. Pray you leave me. Stall
     this in your bosom, and I thank you for your honest
     care. I will speak with you further anon.   *Exit Steward*
           Enter Helena

COUNTESS

Even so it was with me when I was young.
    If ever we are nature's, these are ours; this thorn
Doth to our rose of youth rightly belong;
    Our blood to us, this to our blood is born.
It is the show and seal of nature's truth,
Where love's strong passion is impressed in youth.
By our remembrances of days foregone,
Such were our faults, or then we thought them none.   130
Her eye is sick on't; I observe her now.

HELENA

What is your pleasure, madam?

COUNTESS   You know, Helen,
I am a mother to you.

HELENA

Mine honourable mistress.

COUNTESS   Nay, a mother:
Why not a mother? When I said 'a mother',
Methought you saw a serpent. What's in 'mother'
That you start at it? I say I am your mother,
And put you in the catalogue of those
That were enwombèd mine. 'Tis often seen
Adoption strives with nature, and choice breeds   140
A native slip to us from foreign seeds.
You ne'er oppressed me with a mother's groan,
Yet I express to you a mother's care.
God's mercy, maiden! Does it curd thy blood
To say I am thy mother? What's the matter,
That this distempered messenger of wet,
The many-coloured Iris, rounds thine eye?
Why, that you are my daughter?

HELENA   That I am not.

COUNTESS

I say I am your mother.

HELENA   Pardon, madam.
150   The Count Rossillion cannot be my brother.
       I am from humble, he from honoured name;
       No note upon my parents, his all noble.
       My master, my dear lord he is, and I
       His servant live, and will his vassal die.
       He must not be my brother.

COUNTESS   Nor I your mother?

HELENA
       You are my mother, madam; would you were –
       So that my lord your son were not my brother –
       Indeed my mother! Or were you both our mothers
       I care no more for than I do for heaven,
160   So I were not his sister. Can't no other
       But, I your daughter, he must be my brother?

COUNTESS
       Yes, Helen, you might be my daughter-in-law.
       God shield you mean it not! 'Daughter' and 'mother'
       So strive upon your pulse. What, pale again?
       My fear hath catched your fondness. Now I see
       The mystery of your loneliness, and find
       Your salt tears' head. Now to all sense 'tis gross:
       You love my son. Invention is ashamed
       Against the proclamation of thy passion
170   To say thou dost not. Therefore tell me true;
       But tell me then, 'tis so; for, look, thy cheeks
       Confess it t'one to th'other, and thine eyes
       See it so grossly shown in thy behaviours
       That in their kind they speak it; only sin
       And hellish obstinacy tie thy tongue,
       That truth should be suspected. Speak, is't so?
       If it be so, you have wound a goodly clew;
       If it be not, forswear't; howe'er, I charge thee,
       As heaven shall work in me for thine avail,

To tell me truly.

HELENA   Good madam, pardon me.   180

COUNTESS

Do you love my son?

HELENA   Your pardon, noble mistress.

COUNTESS

Love you my son?

HELENA   Do not you love him, madam?

COUNTESS

Go not about; my love hath in't a bond
Whereof the world takes note. Come, come, disclose
The state of your affection, for your passions
Have to the full appeached.

HELENA   Then I confess,
Here on my knee, before high heaven and you,
That before you, and next unto high heaven,
I love your son.
My friends were poor, but honest; so's my love.   190
Be not offended, for it hurts not him
That he is loved of me. I follow him not
By any token of presumptuous suit,
Nor would I have him till I do deserve him,
Yet never know how that desert should be.
I know I love in vain, strive against hope,
Yet in this captious and intenable sieve
I still pour in the waters of my love
And lack not to lose still. Thus, Indian-like,
Religious in mine error, I adore   200
The sun that looks upon his worshipper
But knows of him no more. My dearest madam,
Let not your hate encounter with my love,
For loving where you do; but if yourself,
Whose aged honour cites a virtuous youth,
Did ever, in so true a flame of liking,

Wish chastely and love dearly, that your Dian
Was both herself and love – O then, give pity
To her whose state is such that cannot choose
210   But lend and give where she is sure to lose;
That seeks not to find that her search implies,
But riddle-like lives sweetly where she dies.

COUNTESS

Had you not lately an intent – speak truly –
To go to Paris?

HELENA   Madam, I had.

COUNTESS   Wherefore? tell true.

HELENA

I will tell truth, by grace itself I swear.
You know my father left me some prescriptions
Of rare and proved effects, such as his reading
And manifest experience had collected
For general sovereignty; and that he willed me
220   In heedfullest reservation to bestow them,
As notes whose faculties inclusive were
More than they were in note. Amongst the rest
There is a remedy, approved, set down,
To cure the desperate languishings whereof
The King is rendered lost.

COUNTESS   This was your motive
For Paris, was it? Speak.

HELENA

My lord your son made me to think of this,
Else Paris and the medicine and the King
Had from the conversation of my thoughts
230   Haply been absent then.

COUNTESS   But think you, Helen,
If you should tender your supposèd aid,
He would receive it? He and his physicians
Are of a mind: he, that they cannot help him;

They, that they cannot help. How shall they credit
A poor unlearnèd virgin, when the schools,
Embowelled of their doctrine, have left off
The danger to itself?

HELENA   There's something in't
More than my father's skill, which was the greatest
Of his profession, that his good receipt
Shall for my legacy be sanctified   240
By th'luckiest stars in heaven; and would your honour
But give me leave to try success, I'd venture
The well-lost life of mine on his grace's cure
By such a day, an hour.

COUNTESS   Dost thou believe't?

HELENA
Ay, madam, knowingly.

COUNTESS
Why, Helen, thou shalt have my leave and love,
Means and attendants, and my loving greetings
To those of mine in court. I'll stay at home
And pray God's blessing into thy attempt.
Be gone tomorrow, and be sure of this,   250
What I can help thee to, thou shalt not miss.   *Exeunt*

*

Enter the King with divers young Lords taking leave   **II.I**
for the Florentine war; Bertram and Parolles;
Attendants. Flourish of cornets

KING
Farewell, young lords; these warlike principles
Do not throw from you; and you, my lords, farewell.
Share the advice betwixt you; if both gain all,
The gift doth stretch itself as 'tis received,

And is enough for both.

FIRST LORD   'Tis our hope, sir,
After well-entered soldiers, to return
And find your grace in health.

KING
No, no, it cannot be; and yet my heart
Will not confess he owes the malady
That doth my life besiege. Farewell, young lords.
Whether I live or die, be you the sons
Of worthy Frenchmen. Let higher Italy –
Those bated that inherit but the fall
Of the last monarchy – see that you come
Not to woo honour, but to wed it. When
The bravest questant shrinks, find what you seek,
That fame may cry you loud. I say farewell.

FIRST LORD
Health at your bidding serve your majesty!

KING
Those girls of Italy, take heed of them:
They say our French lack language to deny
If they demand. Beware of being captives
Before you serve.

BOTH LORDS   Our hearts receive your warnings.

KING
Farewell. (*To some Attendants*) Come hither to me.
     He withdraws

FIRST LORD
O my sweet lord, that you will stay behind us!

PAROLLES
'Tis not his fault, the spark.

SECOND LORD   O, 'tis brave wars!

PAROLLES
Most admirable! I have seen those wars.

BERTRAM

    I am commanded here, and kept a coil with

    'Too young', and 'The next year', and ''Tis too early'.

PAROLLES

    An thy mind stand to't, boy, steal away bravely.

BERTRAM

    I shall stay here the forehorse to a smock,   30

    Creaking my shoes on the plain masonry,

    Till honour be bought up, and no sword worn

    But one to dance with. By heaven, I'll steal away!

FIRST LORD

    There's honour in the theft.

PAROLLES   Commit it, Count.

SECOND LORD I am your accessary; and so farewell.

BERTRAM I grow to you, and our parting is a tortured
    body.

FIRST LORD Farewell, captain.

SECOND LORD Sweet Monsieur Parolles!

PAROLLES Noble heroes, my sword and yours are kin.   40
    Good sparks and lustrous, a word, good metals. You
    shall find in the regiment of the Spinii one Captain
    Spurio, with his cicatrice, an emblem of war, here on his
    sinister cheek; it was this very sword entrenched it. Say
    to him I live, and observe his reports for me.

FIRST LORD We shall, noble captain.   *Exeunt the Lords*

PAROLLES Mars dote on you for his novices! (*To Bertram*)
    What will ye do?

BERTRAM Stay: the King.

PAROLLES Use a more spacious ceremony to the noble   50
    lords; you have restrained yourself within the list of too
    cold an adieu. Be more expressive to them, for they
    wear themselves in the cap of the time; there do muster
    true gait, eat, speak, and move, under the influence of
    the most received star; and though the devil lead the

measure, such are to be followed. After them, and take a
more dilated farewell.

BERTRAM And I will do so.

PAROLLES Worthy fellows, and like to prove most sinewy
60   sword-men.   *Exeunt Bertram and Parolles*
        Enter Lafew. The King comes forward

LAFEW (*kneeling*)
    Pardon, my lord, for me and for my tidings.

KING
    I'll sue thee to stand up.

LAFEW
    Then here's a man stands that has brought his pardon.
    I would you had kneeled, my lord, to ask me mercy,
    And that at my bidding you could so stand up.

KING
    I would I had, so I had broke thy pate
    And asked thee mercy for't.

LAFEW   Good faith, across!
    But, my good lord, 'tis thus: will you be cured
    Of your infirmity?

KING   No.

LAFEW   O, will you eat
    No grapes, my royal fox? Yes, but you will
70   My noble grapes, and if my royal fox
    Could reach them. I have seen a medicine
    That's able to breathe life into a stone,
    Quicken a rock, and make you dance canary
    With sprightly fire and motion; whose simple touch
    Is powerful to araise King Pippen, nay,
    To give great Charlemain a pen in's hand
    And write to her a love-line.

KING   What 'her' is this?

LAFEW
    Why, Doctor She! My lord, there's one arrived,

If you will see her. Now by my faith and honour,   80
If seriously I may convey my thoughts
In this my light deliverance, I have spoke
With one that in her sex, her years, profession,
Wisdom, and constancy hath amazed me more
Than I dare blame my weakness. Will you see her,
For that is her demand, and know her business?
That done, laugh well at me.

KING   Now, good Lafew,
Bring in the admiration, that we with thee
May spend our wonder too, or take off thine
By wondering how thou tookest it.

LAFEW   Nay, I'll fit you,   90
And not be all day neither.

          He goes to the door

KING
Thus he his special nothing ever prologues.

LAFEW
Nay, come your ways.

          Enter Helena

KING   This haste hath wings indeed.

LAFEW
Nay, come your ways.
This is his majesty: say your mind to him.
A traitor you do look like, but such traitors
His majesty seldom fears. I am Cressid's uncle
That dare leave two together. Fare you well.   *Exit*

KING
Now, fair one, does your business follow us?

HELENA
Ay, my good lord.   100
Gerard de Narbon was my father,
In what he did profess, well found.

KING   I knew him.

HELENA

    The rather will I spare my praises towards him;
    Knowing him is enough. On's bed of death
    Many receipts he gave me; chiefly one,
    Which, as the dearest issue of his practice,
    And of his old experience th'only darling,
    He bade me store up as a triple eye,
    Safer than mine own two, more dear; I have so,
110   And hearing your high majesty is touched
    With that malignant cause wherein the honour
    Of my dear father's gift stands chief in power,
    I come to tender it and my appliance,
    With all bound humbleness.

KING   We thank you, maiden,
    But may not be so credulous of cure,
    When our most learnèd doctors leave us, and
    The congregated college have concluded
    That labouring art can never ransom nature
    From her inaidible estate. I say we must not
120   So stain our judgement or corrupt our hope,
    To prostitute our past-cure malady
    To empirics, or to dissever so
    Our great self and our credit, to esteem
    A senseless help, when help past sense we deem.

HELENA

    My duty then shall pay me for my pains.
    I will no more enforce mine office on you,
    Humbly entreating from your royal thoughts
    A modest one to bear me back again.

KING

    I cannot give thee less, to be called grateful.
130   Thou thoughtest to help me, and such thanks I give
    As one near death to those that wish him live.
    But what at full I know, thou knowest no part;

I knowing all my peril, thou no art.

HELENA

What I can do can do no hurt to try,
Since you set up your rest 'gainst remedy.
He that of greatest works is finisher
Oft does them by the weakest minister.
So holy writ in babes hath judgement shown,
When judges have been babes; great floods have flown
From simple sources; and great seas have dried   140
When miracles have by the greatest been denied.
Oft expectation fails, and most oft there
Where most it promises, and oft it hits
Where hope is coldest and despair most fits.

KING

I must not hear thee. Fare thee well, kind maid.
Thy pains, not used, must by thyself be paid;
Proffers not took reap thanks for their reward.

HELENA

Inspirèd merit so by breath is barred.
It is not so with Him that all things knows
As 'tis with us that square our guess by shows;   150
But most it is presumption in us when
The help of heaven we count the act of men.
Dear sir, to my endeavours give consent.
Of heaven, not me, make an experiment.
I am not an impostor, that proclaim
Myself against the level of mine aim,
But know I think, and think I know most sure,
My art is not past power, nor you past cure.

KING

Art thou so confident? Within what space
Hopest thou my cure?

HELENA   The greatest grace lending grace,   160
Ere twice the horses of the sun shall bring

Their fiery torcher his diurnal ring,
Ere twice in murk and occidental damp
Moist Hesperus hath quenched her sleepy lamp,
Or four and twenty times the pilot's glass
Hath told the thievish minutes how they pass,
What is infirm from your sound parts shall fly,
Health shall live free and sickness freely die.

KING

Upon thy certainty and confidence
170 What darest thou venture?

HELENA   Tax of impudence,
A strumpet's boldness, a divulgèd shame;
Traduced by odious ballads my maiden's name;
Seared otherwise, ne worse of worst, extended
With vildest torture let my life be ended.

KING

Methinks in thee some blessèd spirit doth speak
His powerful sound within an organ weak;
And what impossibility would slay
In common sense, sense saves another way.
Thy life is dear, for all that life can rate
180 Worth name of life in thee hath estimate:
Youth, beauty, wisdom, courage – all
That happiness and prime can happy call.
Thou this to hazard needs must intimate
Skill infinite, or monstrous desperate.
Sweet practiser, thy physic I will try,
That ministers thine own death if I die.

HELENA

If I break time, or flinch in property
Of what I spoke, unpitied let me die,
And well deserved. Not helping, death's my fee;
190 But if I help, what do you promise me?

KING

Make thy demand.

HELENA   But will you make it even?

KING

Ay, by my sceptre and my hopes of heaven.

HELENA

Then shalt thou give me with thy kingly hand
What husband in thy power I will command:
Exempted be from me the arrogance
To choose from forth the royal blood of France
My low and humble name to propagate
With any branch or image of thy state;
But such a one, thy vassal, whom I know
Is free for me to ask, thee to bestow.   200

KING

Here is my hand; the premises observed,
Thy will by my performance shall be served.
So make the choice of thy own time, for I,
Thy resolved patient, on thee still rely.
More should I question thee, and more I must,
Though more to know could not be more to trust:
From whence thou camest, how tended on — but rest
Unquestioned welcome, and undoubted blessed.
Give me some help here, ho! If thou proceed
As high as word, my deed shall match thy deed.   210

                              Flourish. Exeunt

Enter the Countess and the Clown   II.2

COUNTESS Come on, sir. I shall now put you to the
    height of your breeding.

CLOWN I will show myself highly fed and lowly taught. I
    know my business is but to the court.

COUNTESS To the court! Why, what place make you special, when you put off that with such contempt? But to the court!

CLOWN Truly, madam, if God have lent a man any manners he may easily put it off at court. He that cannot make a leg, put off's cap, kiss his hand, and say nothing, has neither leg, hands, lip, nor cap; and indeed such a fellow, to say precisely, were not for the court. But for me, I have an answer will serve all men.

COUNTESS Marry, that's a bountiful answer that fits all questions.

CLOWN It is like a barber's chair that fits all buttocks: the pin-buttock, the quatch-buttock, the brawn-buttock, or any buttock.

COUNTESS Will your answer serve fit to all questions?

CLOWN As fit as ten groats is for the hand of an attorney, as your French crown for your taffety punk, as Tib's rush for Tom's forefinger, as a pancake for Shrove Tuesday, a morris for May-day, as the nail to his hole, the cuckold to his horn, as a scolding quean to a wrangling knave, as the nun's lip to the friar's mouth; nay, as the pudding to his skin.

COUNTESS Have you, I say, an answer of such fitness for all questions?

CLOWN From below your duke to beneath your constable, it will fit any question.

COUNTESS It must be an answer of most monstrous size that must fit all demands.

CLOWN But a trifle neither, in good faith, if the learned should speak truth of it. Here it is, and all that belongs to't. Ask me if I am a courtier; it shall do you no harm to learn.

COUNTESS To be young again, if we could! I will be a fool in question, hoping to be the wiser by your answer.

I pray you, sir, are you a courtier?

CLOWN O Lord, sir! – There's a simple putting off. More, 40
more, a hundred of them.

COUNTESS Sir, I am a poor friend of yours that loves you.

CLOWN O Lord, sir! – Thick, thick; spare not me.

COUNTESS I think, sir, you can eat none of this homely
meat.

CLOWN O Lord, sir! – Nay, put me to't, I warrant you.

COUNTESS You were lately whipped, sir, as I think.

CLOWN O Lord, sir! – Spare not me.

COUNTESS Do you cry 'O Lord, sir!' at your whipping,
and 'spare not me'? Indeed your 'O Lord, sir!' is very 50
sequent to your whipping: you would answer very well
to a whipping, if you were but bound to't.

CLOWN I ne'er had worse luck in my life in my 'O Lord,
sir!' I see things may serve long, but not serve ever.

COUNTESS
    I play the noble housewife with the time,
    To entertain it so merrily with a fool.

CLOWN
    O Lord, sir! – Why, there't serves well again.

COUNTESS
    An end, sir! To your business: give Helen this,
    And urge her to a present answer back.
    Commend me to my kinsmen and my son.   60
    This is not much.

CLOWN Not much commendation to them?

COUNTESS Not much employment for you. You understand me?

CLOWN Most fruitfully. I am there before my legs.

COUNTESS Haste you again.   *Exeunt*

II.3   *Enter Bertram, Lafew, and Parolles*

LAFEW They say miracles are past, and we have our
philosophical persons to make modern and familiar,
things supernatural and causeless. Hence is it that
we make trifles of terrors, ensconcing ourselves into
seeming knowledge when we should submit ourselves
to an unknown fear.

PAROLLES Why, 'tis the rarest argument of wonder that
hath shot out in our latter times.

BERTRAM And so 'tis.

10 LAFEW To be relinquished of the artists –

PAROLLES So I say – both of Galen and Paracelsus.

LAFEW Of all the learnèd and authentic fellows –

PAROLLES Right, so I say.

LAFEW That gave him out incurable –

PAROLLES Why, there 'tis, so say I too.

LAFEW Not to be helped.

PAROLLES Right, as 'twere a man assured of a –

LAFEW Uncertain life and sure death.

PAROLLES Just, you say well. So would I have said.

20 LAFEW I may truly say it is a novelty to the world.

PAROLLES It is indeed. If you will have it in showing, you
shall read it in what-do-ye-call there.

LAFEW A showing of a heavenly effect in an earthly actor.

PAROLLES That's it, I would have said the very same.

LAFEW Why, your dolphin is not lustier. Fore me, I speak
in respect –

PAROLLES Nay, 'tis strange, 'tis very strange, that is the
brief and the tedious of it; and he's of a most facinerious
spirit that will not acknowledge it to be the –

30 LAFEW Very hand of heaven.

PAROLLES Ay, so I say.

LAFEW In a most weak –

PAROLLES And debile minister, great power, great

transcendence, which should indeed give us a further
use to be made than alone the recovery of the King, as
to be –

LAFEW Generally thankful.

Enter the King, Helena, and Attendants

PAROLLES I would have said it, you say well. Here comes
the King.

LAFEW Lustique, as the Dutchman says. I'll like a maid   40
the better whilst I have a tooth in my head. Why, he's
able to lead her a coranto.

PAROLLES *Mor du vinager!* Is not this Helen?

LAFEW Fore God, I think so.

KING

Go, call before me all the lords in court.

Exit an Attendant

Sit, my preserver, by thy patient's side,
And with this healthful hand, whose banished sense
Thou hast repealed, a second time receive
The confirmation of my promised gift,
Which but attends thy naming.   50

Enter four Lords

Fair maid, send forth thine eye. This youthful parcel
Of noble bachelors stand at my bestowing,
O'er whom both sovereign power and father's voice
I have to use. Thy frank election make;
Thou hast power to choose, and they none to forsake.

HELENA

To each of you one fair and virtuous mistress
Fall, when love please! Marry, to each but one!

LAFEW

I'd give bay curtal and his furniture
My mouth no more were broken than these boys',
And writ as little beard.

KING   Peruse them well.   60

Not one of those but had a noble father.
Helena addresses the Lords

HELENA
Gentlemen,
Heaven hath through me restored the King to health.

ALL THE LORDS
We understand it, and thank heaven for you.

HELENA
I am a simple maid, and therein wealthiest
That I protest I simply am a maid.
Please it your majesty, I have done already.
The blushes in my cheeks thus whisper me:
'We blush that thou shouldst choose, but, be refused,
70   Let the white death sit on thy cheek for ever,
We'll ne'er come there again.'

KING   Make choice and see,
Who shuns thy love shuns all his love in me.

HELENA
Now, Dian, from thy altar do I fly,
And to imperial Love, that god most high,
Do my sighs stream. (*To First Lord*) Sir, will you hear
    my suit?

FIRST LORD
And grant it.

HELENA   Thanks, sir. All the rest is mute.

LAFEW I had rather be in this choice than throw ames-ace
for my life.

HELENA (*to Second Lord*)
The honour, sir, that flames in your fair eyes
80   Before I speak, too threateningly replies.
Love make your fortunes twenty times above
Her that so wishes, and her humble love!

SECOND LORD
No better, if you please.

HELENA   My wish receive,
  Which great Love grant. And so I take my leave.
LAFEW Do all they deny her? An they were sons of mine
  I'd have them whipped, or I would send them to th'Turk
  to make eunuchs of.
HELENA (*to Third Lord*)
  Be not afraid that I your hand should take;
  I'll never do you wrong, for your own sake.
  Blessing upon your vows, and in your bed   90
  Find fairer fortune if you ever wed!
LAFEW These boys are boys of ice; they'll none have her.
  Sure, they are bastards to the English; the French ne'er
  got 'em.
HELENA (*to Fourth Lord*)
  You are too young, too happy, and too good
  To make yourself a son out of my blood.
FOURTH LORD Fair one, I think not so.
LAFEW There's one grape yet. I am sure thy father drunk
  wine; but if thou beest not an ass, I am a youth of four-
  teen; I have known thee already.   100
HELENA (*to Bertram*)
  I dare not say I take you, but I give
  Me and my service, ever whilst I live,
  Into your guiding power. This is the man.
KING
  Why, then, young Bertram, take her, she's thy wife.
BERTRAM
  My wife, my liege! I shall beseech your highness,
  In such a business give me leave to use
  The help of mine own eyes.
KING   Knowest thou not, Bertram,
  What she has done for me?
BERTRAM   Yes, my good lord,
  But never hope to know why I should marry her.

KING

110   Thou knowest she has raised me from my sickly bed.

BERTRAM

But follows it, my lord, to bring me down
Must answer for your raising? I know her well:
She had her breeding at my father's charge.
A poor physician's daughter my wife! Disdain
Rather corrupt me ever!

KING

'Tis only title thou disdainest in her, the which
I can build up. Strange is it that our bloods,
Of colour, weight, and heat, poured all together,
Would quite confound distinction, yet stands off
120 In differences so mighty. If she be
All that is virtuous, save what thou dislikest –
A poor physician's daughter – thou dislikest
Of virtue for the name. But do not so.
From lowest place when virtuous things proceed,
The place is dignified by th'doer's deed.
Where great additions swell's and virtue none,
It is a dropsied honour. Good alone
Is good, without a name: vileness is so;
The property by what it is should go,
130 Not by the title. She is young, wise, fair;
In these to nature she's immediate heir,
And these breed honour; that is honour's scorn
Which challenges itself as honour's born
And is not like the sire. Honours thrive
When rather from our acts we them derive
Than our foregoers. The mere word's a slave,
Debauched on every tomb, on every grave
A lying trophy, and as oft is dumb
Where dust and damned oblivion is the tomb
140 Of honoured bones indeed. What should be said?

If thou canst like this creature as a maid,
I can create the rest. Virtue and she
Is her own dower; honour and wealth from me.

BERTRAM

I cannot love her nor will strive to do't.

KING

Thou wrongest thyself if thou shouldst strive to choose.

HELENA

That you are well restored, my lord, I'm glad.
Let the rest go.

KING

My honour's at the stake, which to defeat,
I must produce my power. Here, take her hand,
Proud, scornful boy, unworthy this good gift,   150
That dost in vile misprision shackle up
My love and her desert; that canst not dream
We, poising us in her defective scale,
Shall weigh thee to the beam; that wilt not know
It is in us to plant thine honour where
We please to have it grow. Check thy contempt.
Obey our will which travails in thy good.
Believe not thy disdain, but presently
Do thine own fortunes that obedient right
Which both thy duty owes and our power claims;   160
Or I will throw thee from my care for ever
Into the staggers and the careless lapse
Of youth and ignorance, both my revenge and hate
Loosing upon thee in the name of justice,
Without all terms of pity. Speak. Thine answer.

BERTRAM

Pardon, my gracious lord; for I submit
My fancy to your eyes. When I consider
What great creation and what dole of honour
Flies where you bid it, I find that she, which late

170 Was in my nobler thoughts most base, is now
The praisèd of the King; who, so ennobled,
Is as 'twere born so.

KING   Take her by the hand
And tell her she is thine; to whom I promise
A counterpoise, if not to thy estate,
A balance more replete.

BERTRAM   I take her hand.

KING

Good fortune and the favour of the King
Smile upon this contract, whose ceremony
Shall seem expedient on the now-born brief,
And be performed tonight. The solemn feast
180 Shall more attend upon the coming space,
Expecting absent friends. As thou lovest her
Thy love's to me religious; else, does err.

Exeunt all but Parolles and Lafew,
who stay behind, commenting on this wedding

LAFEW Do you hear, monsieur? A word with you.

PAROLLES Your pleasure, sir.

LAFEW Your lord and master did well to make his
recantation.

PAROLLES Recantation! My lord! My master!

LAFEW Ay. Is it not a language I speak?

PAROLLES A most harsh one, and not to be understood
190 without bloody succeeding. My master!

LAFEW Are you companion to the Count Rossillion?

PAROLLES To any Count, to all Counts, to what is man.

LAFEW To what is Count's man; Count's master is of
another style.

PAROLLES You are too old, sir; let it satisfy you, you are
too old.

LAFEW I must tell thee, sirrah, I write man, to which
title age cannot bring thee.

PAROLLES What I dare too well do, I dare not do.

LAFEW I did think thee for two ordinaries to be a pretty 200
wise fellow. Thou didst make tolerable vent of thy
travel; it might pass. Yet the scarfs and the bannerets
about thee did manifoldly dissuade me from believing
thee a vessel of too great a burden. I have now found
thee; when I lose thee again I care not. Yet art thou
good for nothing but taking up, and that thou'rt scarce
worth.

PAROLLES Hadst thou not the privilege of antiquity upon
thee —

LAFEW Do not plunge thyself too far in anger, lest thou 210
hasten thy trial; which if — Lord have mercy on thee for
a hen! So, my good window of lattice, fare thee well; thy
casement I need not open, for I look through thee. Give
me thy hand.

PAROLLES My lord, you give me most egregious in-
dignity.

LAFEW Ay, with all my heart; and thou art worthy of it.

PAROLLES I have not, my lord, deserved it.

LAFEW Yes, good faith, every dram of it, and I will not
bate thee a scruple. 220

PAROLLES Well, I shall be wiser.

LAFEW Even as soon as thou canst, for thou hast to pull at
a smack o'th'contrary. If ever thou beest bound in thy
scarf and beaten, thou shall find what it is to be proud of
thy bondage. I have a desire to hold my acquaintance
with thee, or rather my knowledge, that I may say, in the
default, 'He is a man I know.'

PAROLLES My lord, you do me most insupportable
vexation.

LAFEW I would it were hell-pains for thy sake, and my 230
poor doing eternal; for doing I am past, as I will by
thee, in what motion age will give me leave. *Exit*

PAROLLES Well, thou hast a son shall take this disgrace off me, scurvy, old, filthy, scurvy lord! Well, I must be patient, there is no fettering of authority. I'll beat him, by my life, if I can meet him with any convenience, an he were double and double a lord. I'll have no more pity of his age than I would have of — I'll beat him an if I could but meet him again.

Enter Lafew

240 LAFEW Sirrah, your lord and master's married, there's news for you; you have a new mistress.

PAROLLES I most unfeignedly beseech your lordship to make some reservation of your wrongs. He is my good lord: whom I serve above is my master.

LAFEW Who? God?

PAROLLES Ay, sir.

LAFEW The devil it is that's thy master. Why dost thou garter up thy arms o'this fashion? Dost make hose of thy sleeves? Do other servants so? Thou wert best set
250 thy lower part where thy nose stands. By mine honour, if I were but two hours younger I'd beat thee. Methinkst thou art a general offence and every man should beat thee. I think thou wast created for men to breathe themselves upon thee.

PAROLLES This is hard and undeserved measure, my lord.

LAFEW Go to, sir. You were beaten in Italy for picking a kernel out of a pomegranate. You are a vagabond and no true traveller. You are more saucy with lords and
260 honourable personages than the commission of your birth and virtue gives you heraldry. You are not worth another word, else I'd call you knave. I leave you. *Exit*

Enter Bertram

PAROLLES Good, very good, it is so then. Good, very good; let it be concealed awhile.

BERTRAM
    Undone and forfeited to cares for ever!
PAROLLES What's the matter, sweetheart?
BERTRAM
    Although before the solemn priest I have sworn,
    I will not bed her.
PAROLLES
    What, what, sweetheart?
BERTRAM
    O my Parolles, they have married me!   270
    I'll to the Tuscan wars and never bed her.
PAROLLES
    France is a dog-hole and it no more merits
    The tread of a man's foot. To th'wars!
BERTRAM
    There's letters from my mother: what th'import is
    I know not yet.
PAROLLES
    Ay, that would be known. To th'wars, my boy, to
        th'wars!
    He wears his honour in a box unseen
    That hugs his kicky-wicky here at home,
    Spending his manly marrow in her arms,
    Which should sustain the bound and high curvet   280
    Of Mars's fiery steed. To other regions!
    France is a stable, we that dwell in't jades.
    Therefore to th'war!
BERTRAM
    It shall be so. I'll send her to my house,
    Acquaint my mother with my hate to her
    And wherefore I am fled; write to the King
    That which I durst not speak. His present gift
    Shall furnish me to those Italian fields
    Where noble fellows strike. Wars is no strife

290   To the dark house and the detested wife.

PAROLLES

Will this capriccio hold in thee, art sure?

BERTRAM

Go with me to my chamber and advise me.
I'll send her straight away. Tomorrow
I'll to the wars, she to her single sorrow.

PAROLLES

Why, these balls bound, there's noise in it. 'Tis hard:
A young man married is a man that's marred.
Therefore away, and leave her bravely; go.
The King has done you wrong, but hush, 'tis so.

                         Exeunt

II.4   *Enter Helena and the Clown*

HELENA My mother greets me kindly. Is she well?

CLOWN She is not well, but yet she has her health; she's
very merry, but yet she is not well. But thanks be given
she's very well and wants nothing i'th'world; but yet she
is not well.

HELENA If she be very well, what does she ail that she's
not very well?

CLOWN Truly, she's very well indeed, but for two things.

HELENA What two things?

10 CLOWN One, that she's not in heaven, whither God send
her quickly! The other, that she's in earth, from whence
God send her quickly!

    Enter Parolles

PAROLLES Bless you, my fortunate lady.

HELENA I hope, sir, I have your good will to have mine
own good fortune.

PAROLLES You had my prayers to lead them on, and to
keep them on have them still. O, my knave! How does
my old lady?

CLOWN So that you had her wrinkles and I her money, I
would she did as you say.   20

PAROLLES Why, I say nothing.

CLOWN Marry, you are the wiser man, for many a man's
tongue shakes out his master's undoing. To say nothing,
to do nothing, to know nothing, and to have nothing, is
to be a great part of your title, which is within a very
little of nothing.

PAROLLES Away! Th'art a knave.

CLOWN You should have said, sir, 'Before a knave th'art
a knave'; that's 'Before me, th'art a knave.' This had
been truth, sir.   30

PAROLLES Go to, thou art a witty fool: I have found thee.

CLOWN Did you find me in your self, sir, or were you
taught to find me? The search, sir, was profitable; and
much fool may you find in you, even to the world's
pleasure and the increase of laughter.

PAROLLES
A good knave i'faith, and well fed.
Madam, my lord will go away tonight:
A very serious business calls on him.
The great prerogative and rite of love,
Which as your due time claims, he does acknowledge,   40
But puts it off to a compelled restraint;
Whose want and whose delay is strewed with sweets,
Which they distil now in the curbèd time,
To make the coming hour o'erflow with joy
And pleasure drown the brim.

HELENA   What's his will else?

PAROLLES
That you will take your instant leave o'th'King,
And make this haste as your own good proceeding,
Strengthened with what apology you think
May make it probable need.

HELENA   What more commands he?

PAROLLES

50   That, having this obtained, you presently
      Attend his further pleasure.

HELENA

      In everything I wait upon his will.

PAROLLES

      I shall report it so.   *Exit*

HELENA

      I pray you. Come, sirrah.   *Exeunt*

II.5   *Enter Lafew and Bertram*

LAFEW But I hope your lordship thinks not him a soldier.

BERTRAM Yes, my lord, and of very valiant approof.

LAFEW You have it from his own deliverance.

BERTRAM And by other warranted testimony.

LAFEW Then my dial goes not true: I took this lark for a
      bunting.

BERTRAM I do assure you, my lord, he is very great in
      knowledge, and accordingly valiant.

LAFEW I have then sinned against his experience and
10   transgressed against his valour, and my state that way is
      dangerous, since I cannot yet find in my heart to repent.
      Here he comes. I pray you make us friends; I will pursue
      the amity.

      Enter Parolles

PAROLLES (*to Bertram*) These things shall be done, sir.

LAFEW Pray you, sir, who's his tailor?

PAROLLES Sir!

LAFEW O, I know him well. Ay, sir, he, sir, 's a good
      workman, a very good tailor.

BERTRAM (*aside to Parolles*) Is she gone to the King?

20 PAROLLES She is.

BERTRAM Will she away tonight?

PAROLLES As you'll have her.

BERTRAM

    I have writ my letters, casketed my treasure,
    Given order for our horses; and tonight,
    When I should take possession of the bride,
    End ere I do begin.

LAFEW (*aside*) A good traveller is something at the latter
    end of a dinner; but one that lies three thirds and uses a
    known truth to pass a thousand nothings with, should
    be once heard and thrice beaten. (*Aloud*) God save you,   30
    captain!

BERTRAM Is there any unkindness between my lord and
    you, monsieur?

PAROLLES I know not how I have deserved to run into
    my lord's displeasure.

LAFEW You have made shift to run into't, boots and spurs
    and all, like him that leaped into the custard; and out of
    it you'll run again rather than suffer question for your
    residence.

BERTRAM It may be you have mistaken him, my lord.   40

LAFEW And shall do so ever, though I took him at's
    prayers. Fare you well, my lord, and believe this of me:
    there can be no kernel in this light nut. The soul of this
    man is his clothes. Trust him not in matter of heavy
    consequence. I have kept of them tame, and know their
    natures. Farewell, monsieur; I have spoken better of
    you than you have or will to deserve at my hand, but we
    must do good against evil.   *Exit*

PAROLLES An idle lord, I swear.

BERTRAM I think not so.   50

PAROLLES Why, do you not know him?

BERTRAM

    Yes, I do know him well, and common speech

Gives him a worthy pass. Here comes my clog.
Enter Helena

HELENA

I have, sir, as I was commanded from you,
Spoke with the King, and have procured his leave
For present parting; only he desires
Some private speech with you.

BERTRAM   I shall obey his will.
You must not marvel, Helen, at my course,
Which holds not colour with the time, nor does
60 The ministration and requirèd office
On my particular. Prepared I was not
For such a business, therefore am I found
So much unsettled. This drives me to entreat you
That presently you take your way for home,
And rather muse than ask why I entreat you;
For my respects are better than they seem,
And my appointments have in them a need
Greater than shows itself at the first view
To you that know them not. This to my mother.
He gives Helena a letter

70 'Twill be two days ere I shall see you, so
I leave you to your wisdom.

HELENA   Sir, I can nothing say
But that I am your most obedient servant.

BERTRAM

Come, come, no more of that.

HELENA   And ever shall
With true observance seek to eke out that
Wherein toward me my homely stars have failed
To equal my great fortune.

BERTRAM   Let that go.
My haste is very great. Farewell. Hie home.

HELENA

Pray, sir, your pardon.

BERTRAM   Well, what would you say?

HELENA

I am not worthy of the wealth I owe,
Nor dare I say 'tis mine – and yet it is;   80
But, like a timorous thief, most fain would steal
What law does vouch mine own.

BERTRAM   What would you have?

HELENA

Something, and scarce so much; nothing indeed.
I would not tell you what I would, my lord.
Faith, yes:
Strangers and foes do sunder and not kiss.

BERTRAM

I pray you, stay not, but in haste to horse.

HELENA

I shall not break your bidding, good my lord.
Where are my other men? Monsieur, farewell.   *Exit*

BERTRAM

Go thou toward home, where I will never come   90
Whilst I can shake my sword or hear the drum.
Away, and for our flight.

PAROLLES   Bravely. Coragio!   *Exeunt*

*

Flourish. Enter the Duke of Florence, and the two   III.1
French Lords, with a troop of Soldiers

DUKE

So that from point to point now have you heard
The fundamental reasons of this war,
Whose great decision hath much blood let forth,

And more thirsts after.

FIRST LORD   Holy seems the quarrel
Upon your grace's part, black and fearful
On the opposer.

DUKE
Therefore we marvel much our cousin France
Would in so just a business shut his bosom
Against our borrowing prayers.

SECOND LORD   Good my lord,
10 The reasons of our state I cannot yield,
But like a common and an outward man
That the great figure of a council frames
By self-unable motion; therefore dare not
Say what I think of it, since I have found
Myself in my incertain grounds to fail
As often as I guessed.

DUKE   Be it his pleasure.

FIRST LORD
But I am sure the younger of our nature
That surfeit on their ease will day by day
Come here for physic.

DUKE   Welcome shall they be,
20 And all the honours that can fly from us
Shall on them settle. You know your places well;
When better fall, for your avails they fell.
Tomorrow to the field.   *Flourish. Exeunt*

III.2   *Enter the Countess and the Clown*

COUNTESS It hath happened all as I would have had it,
save that he comes not along with her.

CLOWN By my troth, I take my young lord to be a very
melancholy man.

COUNTESS By what observance, I pray you?

CLOWN Why, he will look upon his boot and sing, mend
the ruff and sing, ask questions and sing, pick his teeth
and sing. I knew a man that had this trick of melancholy
hold a goodly manor for a song.

COUNTESS Let me see what he writes, and when he   10
means to come.

She opens the letter

CLOWN I have no mind to Isbel since I was at court. Our
old lings and our Isbels o'th'country are nothing like
your old ling and your Isbels o'th'court. The brains of
my Cupid's knocked out, and I begin to love as an old
man loves money, with no stomach.

COUNTESS What have we here?

CLOWN E'en that you have there.   *Exit*

COUNTESS (*reading the letter aloud*) *I have sent you a
daughter-in-law; she hath recovered the King and undone*   20
*me. I have wedded her, not bedded her, and sworn to make
the 'not' eternal. You shall hear I am run away; know it
before the report come. If there be breadth enough in the
world I will hold a long distance. My duty to you.*

                    Your unfortunate son,
                              Bertram.

This is not well, rash and unbridled boy,
To fly the favours of so good a King,
To pluck his indignation on thy head
By the misprizing of a maid too virtuous   30
For the contempt of empire.

Enter Clown

CLOWN O madam, yonder is heavy news within, between
two soldiers and my young lady.

COUNTESS What is the matter?

CLOWN Nay, there is some comfort in the news, some
comfort: your son will not be killed so soon as I thought
he would.

COUNTESS Why should he be killed?

CLOWN So say I, madam, if he run away, as I hear he
does. The danger is in standing to't; that's the loss of
men, though it be the getting of children. Here they
come will tell you more. For my part, I only hear your
son was run away.   *Exit*

Enter Helena and the two French Lords

FIRST LORD

Save you, good madam.

HELENA

Madam, my lord is gone, for ever gone.

SECOND LORD

Do not say so.

COUNTESS

Think upon patience. Pray you, gentlemen –
I have felt so many quirks of joy and grief
That the first face of neither on the start
Can woman me unto't. Where is my son, I pray you?

SECOND LORD

Madam, he's gone to serve the Duke of Florence.
We met him thitherward, for thence we came,
And, after some dispatch in hand at court,
Thither we bend again.

HELENA

Look on his letter, madam: here's my passport.
(*She reads the letter aloud*)
*When thou canst get the ring upon my finger, which never
shall come off, and show me a child begotten of thy body
that I am father to, then call me husband; but in such a
'then' I write a 'never'.*
This is a dreadful sentence.

COUNTESS Brought you this letter, gentlemen?

FIRST LORD Ay, madam, and for the contents' sake are
sorry for our pains.

COUNTESS

    I prithee, lady, have a better cheer.
    If thou engrossest all the griefs are thine
    Thou robbest me of a moiety. He was my son,
    But I do wash his name out of my blood
    And thou art all my child. Towards Florence is he?

SECOND LORD

    Ay, madam.

COUNTESS   And to be a soldier?

SECOND LORD

    Such is his noble purpose; and, believe't,   70
    The Duke will lay upon him all the honour
    That good convenience claims.

COUNTESS   Return you thither?

FIRST LORD

    Ay, madam, with the swiftest wing of speed.

HELENA (*reading*)

    Till I have no wife I have nothing in France.
    'Tis bitter.

COUNTESS   Find you that there?

HELENA   Ay, madam.

FIRST LORD 'Tis but the boldness of his hand, haply,
    which his heart was not consenting to.

COUNTESS

    Nothing in France until he have no wife!
    There's nothing here that is too good for him
    But only she, and she deserves a lord   80
    That twenty such rude boys might tend upon
    And call her, hourly, mistress. Who was with him?

FIRST LORD A servant only, and a gentleman which I
    have sometime known.

COUNTESS Parolles, was it not?

FIRST LORD Ay, my good lady, he.

COUNTESS

A very tainted fellow, and full of wickedness.
My son corrupts a well-derivèd nature
With his inducement.

FIRST LORD   Indeed, good lady,
90 The fellow has a deal of that too much
Which holds him much to have.

COUNTESS   Y'are welcome, gentlemen.
I will entreat you, when you see my son,
To tell him that his sword can never win
The honour that he loses. More I'll entreat you
Written to bear along.

SECOND LORD   We serve you, madam,
In that and all your worthiest affairs.

COUNTESS

Not so, but as we change our courtesies.
Will you draw near? *Exeunt the Countess and the Lords*

HELENA

'Till I have no wife I have nothing in France.'
100 Nothing in France until he has no wife!
Thou shalt have none, Rossillion, none in France,
Then hast thou all again. Poor lord, is't I
That chase thee from thy country, and expose
Those tender limbs of thine to the event
Of the none-sparing war? And is it I
That drive thee from the sportive court, where thou
Wast shot at with fair eyes, to be the mark
Of smoky muskets? O you leaden messengers,
That ride upon the violent speed of fire,
110 Fly with false aim, move the still-piecing air
That sings with piercing, do not touch my lord.
Whoever shoots at him, I set him there.
Whoever charges on his forward breast,
I am the caitiff that do hold him to't;

And though I kill him not, I am the cause
His death was so effected. Better 'twere
I met the ravin lion when he roared
With sharp constraint of hunger; better 'twere
That all the miseries which nature owes
Were mine at once. No, come thou home, Rossillion,   120
Whence honour but of danger wins a scar,
As oft it loses all. I will be gone;
My being here it is that holds thee hence.
Shall I stay here to do't? No, no, although
The air of paradise did fan the house
And angels officed all. I will be gone,
That pitiful rumour may report my flight
To consolate thine ear. Come, night; end, day!
For with the dark, poor thief, I'll steal away.   *Exit*

Flourish. Enter the Duke of Florence, Bertram,   III.3
drum and trumpets, Soldiers, Parolles

DUKE
The general of our horse thou art, and we,
Great in our hope, lay our best love and credence
Upon thy promising fortune.

BERTRAM   Sir, it is
A charge too heavy for my strength; but yet
We'll strive to bear it for your worthy sake
To th'extreme edge of hazard.

DUKE   Then go thou forth,
And fortune play upon thy prosperous helm
As thy auspicious mistress!

BERTRAM   This very day,
Great Mars, I put myself into thy file;
Make me but like my thoughts and I shall prove   10
A lover of thy drum, hater of love.   *Exeunt*

III.4   *Enter the Countess and the Steward*

COUNTESS

Alas! and would you take the letter of her?
Might you not know she would do as she has done
By sending me a letter? Read it again.

STEWARD (*reading*)

I am Saint Jaques' pilgrim, thither gone.
    Ambitious love hath so in me offended
That barefoot plod I the cold ground upon,
    With sainted vow my faults to have amended.
Write, write, that from the bloody course of war
    My dearest master, your dear son, may hie.
Bless him at home in peace, whilst I from far
    His name with zealous fervour sanctify.
His taken labours bid him me forgive;
    I, his despiteful Juno, sent him forth
From courtly friends, with camping foes to live
    Where death and danger dogs the heels of worth.
He is too good and fair for death and me;
    Whom I myself embrace to set him free.

COUNTESS

Ah, what sharp stings are in her mildest words!
Rynaldo, you did never lack advice so much
As letting her pass so. Had I spoke with her,
I could have well diverted her intents,
Which thus she hath prevented.

STEWARD   Pardon me, madam.
If I had given you this at overnight
She might have been o'erta'en; and yet she writes
Pursuit would be but vain.

COUNTESS   What angel shall
Bless this unworthy husband? He cannot thrive,
Unless her prayers, whom heaven delights to hear
And loves to grant, reprieve him from the wrath

Of greatest justice. Write, write, Rynaldo,
To this unworthy husband of his wife.   30
Let every word weigh heavy of her worth
That he does weigh too light. My greatest grief,
Though little he do feel it, set down sharply.
Dispatch the most convenient messenger.
When haply he shall hear that she is gone,
He will return; and hope I may that she,
Hearing so much, will speed her foot again,
Led hither by pure love. Which of them both
Is dearest to me I have no skill in sense
To make distinction. Provide this messenger.   40
My heart is heavy and mine age is weak;
Grief would have tears, and sorrow bids me speak.

                                                    Exeunt

A tucket afar off. Enter the old Widow of Florence,   III.5
   her daughter Diana, and Mariana, with other
   citizens

WIDOW Nay, come, for if they do approach the city, we
   shall lose all the sight.

DIANA They say the French Count has done most
   honourable service.

WIDOW It is reported that he has taken their greatest
   commander, and that with his own hand he slew the
   Duke's brother.
       Tucket
   We have lost our labour; they are gone a contrary way.
   Hark! You may know by their trumpets.

MARIANA Come, let's return again and suffice ourselves   10
   with the report of it. Well, Diana, take heed of this
   French Earl. The honour of a maid is her name, and no
   legacy is so rich as honesty.

WIDOW I have told my neighbour how you have been
solicited by a gentleman his companion.

MARIANA I know that knave, hang him! one Parolles; a
filthy officer he is in those suggestions for the young
Earl. Beware of them, Diana: their promises, entice-
ments, oaths, tokens, and all these engines of lust, are
20   not the things they go under. Many a maid hath been
seduced by them, and the misery is, example, that so
terrible shows in the wrack of maidenhood, cannot for
all that dissuade succession, but that they are limed with
the twigs that threatens them. I hope I need not to
advise you further; but I hope your own grace will keep
you where you are, though there were no further danger
known but the modesty which is so lost.

DIANA You shall not need to fear me.

          Enter Helena

WIDOW I hope so. Look, here comes a pilgrim. I know
30   she will lie at my house; thither they send one another.
I'll question her. God save you, pilgrim! Whither are
bound?

HELENA
To Saint Jaques le Grand.
Where do the palmers lodge, I do beseech you?

WIDOW
At the Saint Francis here beside the port.

HELENA
Is this the way?

          A march afar

WIDOW
Ay, marry, is't. Hark you, they come this way.
If you will tarry, holy pilgrim,
But till the troops come by,
40   I will conduct you where you shall be lodged;
The rather for I think I know your hostess

As ample as myself.

HELENA   Is it yourself?

WIDOW

If you shall please so, pilgrim.

HELENA

I thank you and will stay upon your leisure.

WIDOW

You came, I think, from France?

HELENA   I did so.

WIDOW

Here you shall see a countryman of yours
That has done worthy service.

HELENA   His name, I pray you?

DIANA

The Count Rossillion. Know you such a one?

HELENA

But by the ear, that hears most nobly of him;
His face I know not.

DIANA   Whatsome'er he is,   50
He's bravely taken here. He stole from France,
As 'tis reported, for the King had married him
Against his liking. Think you it is so?

HELENA

Ay, surely, mere the truth. I know his lady.

DIANA

There is a gentleman that serves the Count
Reports but coarsely of her.

HELENA   What's his name?

DIANA

Monsieur Parolles.

HELENA   O, I believe with him,
In argument of praise or to the worth
Of the great Count himself, she is too mean
To have her name repeated; all her deserving   60

Is a reservèd honesty, and that
I have not heard examined.

DIANA   Alas, poor lady!
'Tis a hard bondage to become the wife
Of a detesting lord.

WIDOW
I warrant, good creature, wheresoe'er she is,
Her heart weighs sadly. This young maid might do her
A shrewd turn if she pleased.

HELENA   How do you mean?
Maybe the amorous Count solicits her
In the unlawful purpose?

WIDOW   He does indeed,
70 And brokes with all that can in such a suit
Corrupt the tender honour of a maid;
But she is armed for him and keeps her guard
In honestest defence.

    *Drum and colours. Enter Bertram, Parolles, and the
    whole army*

MARIANA   The gods forbid else!

WIDOW
So, now they come.
That is Antonio, the Duke's eldest son;
That Escalus.

HELENA   Which is the Frenchman?

DIANA   He –
That with the plume. 'Tis a most gallant fellow.
I would he loved his wife; if he were honester
He were much goodlier. Is't not a handsome gentleman?

HELENA
80 I like him well.

DIANA
'Tis pity he is not honest. Yond's that same knave
That leads him to these places. Were I his lady

I would poison that vile rascal.

HELENA   Which is he?

DIANA That jackanapes with scarfs. Why is he melancholy?

HELENA Perchance he's hurt i'th'battle.

PAROLLES Lose our drum! Well!

MARIANA He's shrewdly vexed at something. Look, he
has spied us.

WIDOW Marry, hang you!   90

MARIANA And your courtesy, for a ring-carrier!

                    Exeunt Bertram, Parolles, and the army

WIDOW

The troop is past. Come, pilgrim, I will bring you
Where you shall host. Of enjoined penitents
There's four or five, to great Saint Jaques bound,
Already at my house.

HELENA   I humbly thank you.
Please it this matron and this gentle maid
To eat with us tonight; the charge and thanking
Shall be for me, and, to requite you further,
I will bestow some precepts of this virgin,
Worthy the note.

WIDOW *and* MARIANA

                    We'll take your offer kindly.   *Exeunt*   100

Enter Bertram and the two French Lords   III.6

FIRST LORD Nay, good my lord, put him to't, let him
have his way.

SECOND LORD If your lordship find him not a hilding,
hold me no more in your respect.

FIRST LORD On my life, my lord, a bubble.

BERTRAM Do you think I am so far deceived in him?

FIRST LORD Believe it, my lord, in mine own direct

knowledge, without any malice, but to speak of him as
my kinsman, he's a most notable coward, an infinite and
endless liar, an hourly promise-breaker, the owner of no
one good quality worthy your lordship's entertainment.

SECOND LORD It were fit you knew him; lest, reposing
too far in his virtue which he hath not, he might at some
great and trusty business in a main danger fail you.

BERTRAM I would I knew in what particular action to try
him.

SECOND LORD None better than to let him fetch off his
drum, which you hear him so confidently undertake to
do.

FIRST LORD I, with a troop of Florentines, will suddenly
surprise him; such I will have whom I am sure he
knows not from the enemy. We will bind and hoodwink
him so, that he shall suppose no other but that he is
carried into the leaguer of the adversaries when we
bring him to our own tents. Be but your lordship present
at his examination. If he do not for the promise of his
life, and in the highest compulsion of base fear, offer to
betray you and deliver all the intelligence in his power
against you, and that with the divine forfeit of his soul
upon oath, never trust my judgement in anything.

SECOND LORD O, for the love of laughter, let him fetch
his drum; he says he has a stratagem for't. When your
lordship sees the bottom of his success in't, and to what
metal this counterfeit lump of ore will be melted, if you
give him not John Drum's entertainment your inclining
cannot be removed. Here he comes.

Enter Parolles

FIRST LORD O, for the love of laughter, hinder not the
honour of his design; let him fetch off his drum in any
hand.

BERTRAM How now, monsieur! This drum sticks sorely
in your disposition.

SECOND LORD A pox on't! Let it go, 'tis but a drum.

PAROLLES But a drum! Is't but a drum? A drum so lost!
There was excellent command: to charge in with our
horse upon our own wings and to rend our own soldiers!

SECOND LORD That was not to be blamed in the command of the service; it was a disaster of war that Caesar
himself could not have prevented if he had been there to
command.

BERTRAM Well, we cannot greatly condemn our success;   50
some dishonour we had in the loss of that drum, but it is
not to be recovered.

PAROLLES It might have been recovered.

BERTRAM It might, but it is not now.

PAROLLES It is to be recovered. But that the merit of
service is seldom attributed to the true and exact performer, I would have that drum or another, or *hic jacet*.

BERTRAM Why, if you have a stomach, to't, monsieur! If
you think your mystery in stratagem can bring this
instrument of honour again into his native quarter, be   60
magnanimious in the enterprise and go on. I will grace
the attempt for a worthy exploit. If you speed well in it
the Duke shall both speak of it and extend to you what
further becomes his greatness, even to the utmost
syllable of your worthiness.

PAROLLES By the hand of a soldier, I will undertake it.

BERTRAM But you must not now slumber in it.

PAROLLES I'll about it this evening, and I will presently
pen down my dilemmas, encourage myself in my certainty, put myself into my mortal preparation; and by   70
midnight look to hear further from me.

BERTRAM May I be bold to acquaint his grace you are
gone about it?

PAROLLES I know not what the success will be, my lord,
but the attempt I vow.

BERTRAM I know th'art valiant, and to the possibility of
thy soldiership will subscribe for thee. Farewell.

PAROLLES I love not many words.   *Exit*

FIRST LORD No more than a fish loves water. Is not this a
80   strange fellow, my lord, that so confidently seems to
undertake this business, which he knows is not to be
done, damns himself to do, and dares better be damned
than to do't.

SECOND LORD You do not know him, my lord, as we do.
Certain it is that he will steal himself into a man's
favour and for a week escape a great deal of discoveries,
but when you find him out you have him ever after.

BERTRAM Why, do you think he will make no deed at all
of this that so seriously he does address himself unto?

90 FIRST LORD None in the world, but return with an invention, and clap upon you two or three probable lies.
But we have almost embossed him. You shall see his
fall tonight; for indeed he is not for your lordship's
respect.

SECOND LORD We'll make you some sport with the fox
ere we case him. He was first smoked by the old Lord
Lafew. When his disguise and he is parted tell me what a
sprat you shall find him; which you shall see this very
night.

100 FIRST LORD I must go look my twigs. He shall be caught.

BERTRAM Your brother, he shall go along with me.

FIRST LORD As't please your lordship. I'll leave you.

                                            Exit

BERTRAM
Now will I lead you to the house and show you
The lass I spoke of.

SECOND LORD   But you say she's honest.

BERTRAM
That's all the fault. I spoke with her but once

And found her wondrous cold, but I sent to her
By this same coxcomb that we have i'th'wind
Tokens and letters which she did re-send,
And this is all I have done. She's a fair creature;
Will you go see her?

SECOND LORD   With all my heart, my lord. *Exeunt* 110

Enter Helena and the Widow   III.7

HELENA
If you misdoubt me that I am not she,
I know not how I shall assure you further
But I shall lose the grounds I work upon.

WIDOW
Though my estate be fallen, I was well born,
Nothing acquainted with these businesses,
And would not put my reputation now
In any staining act.

HELENA   Nor would I wish you.
First give me trust the Count he is my husband,
And what to your sworn counsel I have spoken
Is so from word to word, and then you cannot,   10
By the good aid that I of you shall borrow,
Err in bestowing it.

WIDOW   I should believe you,
For you have showed me that which well approves
Y'are great in fortune.

HELENA   Take this purse of gold,
And let me buy your friendly help thus far,
Which I will over-pay, and pay again
When I have found it. The Count he woos your daughter,
Lays down his wanton siege before her beauty,
Resolved to carry her; let her in fine consent
As we'll direct her how 'tis best to bear it.   20

Now his important blood will naught deny
That she'll demand. A ring the County wears
That downward hath succeeded in his house
From son to son some four or five descents
Since the first father wore it. This ring he holds
In most rich choice, yet, in his idle fire,
To buy his will it would not seem too dear,
Howe'er repented after.

WIDOW   Now I see
The bottom of your purpose.

HELENA

30   You see it lawful then. It is no more
But that your daughter, ere she seems as won,
Desires this ring; appoints him an encounter;
In fine, delivers me to fill the time,
Herself most chastely absent. After,
To marry her I'll add three thousand crowns
To what is passed already.

WIDOW   I have yielded.
Instruct my daughter how she shall persever
That time and place with this deceit so lawful
May prove coherent. Every night he comes

40   With musics of all sorts, and songs composed
To her unworthiness. It nothing steads us
To chide him from our eaves, for he persists
As if his life lay on't.

HELENA   Why then tonight
Let us assay our plot, which, if it speed,
Is wicked meaning in a lawful deed,
And lawful meaning in a lawful act,
Where both not sin, and yet a sinful fact.
But let's about it.   *Exeunt*

*

Enter the First French Lord, with five or six other   IV.I
Soldiers in ambush

FIRST LORD He can come no other way but by this hedge-
corner. When you sally upon him speak what terrible
language you will; though you understand it not yourselves, no matter; for we must not seem to understand
him, unless some one among us, whom we must produce
for an interpreter.

FIRST SOLDIER Good captain, let me be th'interpreter.

FIRST LORD Art not acquainted with him? Knows he
not thy voice?

FIRST SOLDIER No, sir, I warrant you.   10

FIRST LORD But what linsey-woolsey hast thou to speak
to us again?

FIRST SOLDIER E'en such as you speak to me.

FIRST LORD He must think us some band of strangers
i'th'adversary's entertainment. Now he hath a smack of
all neighbouring languages, therefore we must every one
be a man of his own fancy, not to know what we speak
one to another; so we seem to know is to know straight
our purpose – choughs' language, gabble enough and
good enough. As for you, interpreter, you must seem   20
very politic. But couch, ho! Here he comes to beguile
two hours in a sleep, and then to return and swear the
lies he forges.

Enter Parolles

PAROLLES Ten o'clock. Within these three hours 'twill be
time enough to go home. What shall I say I have done?
It must be a very plausive invention that carries it. They
begin to smoke me, and disgraces have of late knocked
too often at my door. I find my tongue is too foolhardy,
but my heart hath the fear of Mars before it and of his
creatures, not daring the reports of my tongue.   30

FIRST LORD This is the first truth that e'er thine own
tongue was guilty of.

PAROLLES What the devil should move me to undertake
the recovery of this drum, being not ignorant of the
impossibility, and knowing I had no such purpose? I
must give myself some hurts, and say I got them in
exploit. Yet slight ones will not carry it: they will say
'Came you off with so little?' And great ones I dare not
give. Wherefore, what's the instance? Tongue, I must
40   put you into a butter-woman's mouth, and buy myself
another of Bajazeth's mule, if you prattle me into these
perils.

FIRST LORD Is it possible he should know what he is, and
be that he is?

PAROLLES I would the cutting of my garments would
serve the turn, or the breaking of my Spanish sword.

FIRST LORD We cannot afford you so.

PAROLLES Or the baring of my beard, and to say it was in
stratagem.

50   FIRST LORD 'Twould not do.

PAROLLES Or to drown my clothes and say I was stripped.

FIRST LORD Hardly serve.

PAROLLES Though I swore I leaped from the window of
the citadel —

FIRST LORD How deep?

PAROLLES Thirty fathom.

FIRST LORD Three great oaths would scarce make that be
believed.

PAROLLES I would I had any drum of the enemy's; I
60   would swear I recovered it.

FIRST LORD You shall hear one anon.

PAROLLES A drum now of the enemy's —
      Alarum within

FIRST LORD *Throca movousus, cargo, cargo, cargo.*

ALL *Cargo, cargo, cargo, villianda par corbo, cargo.*

> *They seize him*

PAROLLES

O, ransom, ransom!

> *They blindfold him*

               Do not hide mine eyes.

FIRST SOLDIER *Boskos thromuldo boskos.*

PAROLLES

I know you are the Muskos' regiment,
And I shall lose my life for want of language.
If there be here German, or Dane, Low Dutch,
Italian, or French, let him speak to me,   70
I'll discover that which shall undo the Florentine.

FIRST SOLDIER *Boskos vauvado.* I understand thee, and
can speak thy tongue. *Kerelybonto.* Sir, betake thee to
thy faith, for seventeen poniards are at thy bosom.

PAROLLES O!

FIRST SOLDIER O, pray, pray, pray! *Manka revania
dulche.*

FIRST LORD *Oscorbidulchos volivorco.*

FIRST SOLDIER

The General is content to spare thee yet,
And, hoodwinked as thou art, will lead thee on   80
To gather from thee. Haply thou mayst inform
Something to save thy life.

PAROLLES   O, let me live,
And all the secrets of our camp I'll show,
Their force, their purposes; nay, I'll speak that
Which you will wonder at.

FIRST SOLDIER   But wilt thou faithfully?

PAROLLES

If I do not, damn me.

FIRST SOLDIER   *Acordo linta.*

Come on, thou art granted space.

Exit with Parolles guarded

A short alarum within

FIRST LORD

Go tell the Count Rossillion and my brother

We have caught the woodcock and will keep him muffled

90 Till we do hear from them.

SECOND SOLDIER   Captain, I will.

FIRST LORD

'A will betray us all unto ourselves:

Inform on that.

SECOND SOLDIER

So I will, sir.

FIRST LORD

Till then I'll keep him dark and safely locked. *Exeunt*

IV.2   *Enter Bertram and Diana*

BERTRAM

They told me that your name was Fontybell.

DIANA

No, my good lord, Diana.

BERTRAM   Titled goddess,

And worth it, with addition! But, fair soul,

In your fine frame hath love no quality?

If the quick fire of youth light not your mind

You are no maiden but a monument.

When you are dead you should be such a one

As you are now; for you are cold and stern,

And now you should be as your mother was

10 When your sweet self was got.

DIANA

She then was honest.

BERTRAM   So should you be.

DIANA   No.
My mother did but duty, such, my lord,
As you owe to your wife.

BERTRAM   No more o'that!
I prithee do not strive against my vows.
I was compelled to her, but I love thee
By love's own sweet constraint, and will for ever
Do thee all rights of service.

DIANA   Ay, so you serve us
Till we serve you; but when you have our roses,
You barely leave our thorns to prick ourselves,
And mock us with our bareness.

BERTRAM   How have I sworn!   20

DIANA
'Tis not the many oaths that makes the truth,
But the plain single vow that is vowed true.
What is not holy, that we swear not by,
But take the highest to witness. Then, pray you, tell
   me:
If I should swear by Love's great attributes
I loved you dearly, would you believe my oaths
When I did love you ill? This has no holding,
To swear by him whom I protest to love
That I will work against him. Therefore your oaths
Are words, and poor conditions but unsealed –   30
At least in my opinion.

BERTRAM   Change it, change it.
Be not so holy-cruel. Love is holy,
And my integrity ne'er knew the crafts
That you do charge men with. Stand no more off,
But give thyself unto my sick desires,
Who then recovers. Say thou art mine, and ever
My love as it begins shall so persever.

DIANA

> I see that men make vows in such a flame
> That we'll forsake ourselves. Give me that ring.

BERTRAM

40   I'll lend it thee, my dear, but have no power
> To give it from me.

DIANA   Will you not, my lord?

BERTRAM

> It is an honour 'longing to our house,
> Bequeathèd down from many ancestors,
> Which were the greatest obloquy i'th'world
> In me to lose.

DIANA   Mine honour's such a ring;
> My chastity's the jewel of our house,
> Bequeathèd down from many ancestors,
> Which were the greatest obloquy i'th'world
> In me to lose. Thus your own proper wisdom

50   Brings in the champion Honour on my part
> Against your vain assault.

BERTRAM   Here, take my ring.
> My house, mine honour, yea, my life be thine,
> And I'll be bid by thee.

DIANA

> When midnight comes, knock at my chamber window;
> I'll order take my mother shall not hear.
> Now will I charge you in the band of truth,
> When you have conquered my yet maiden bed,
> Remain there but an hour, nor speak to me.
> My reasons are most strong and you shall know them

60   When back again this ring shall be delivered.
> And on your finger in the night I'll put
> Another ring, that what in time proceeds
> May token to the future our past deeds.
> Adieu till then; then, fail not. You have won

A wife of me, though there my hope be done.

BERTRAM

A heaven on earth I have won by wooing thee.   *Exit*

DIANA

For which live long to thank both heaven and me!
You may so in the end.
My mother told me just how he would woo
As if she sat in's heart. She says all men   70
Have the like oaths. He had sworn to marry me
When his wife's dead; therefore I'll lie with him
When I am buried. Since Frenchmen are so braid,
Marry that will, I live and die a maid.
Only, in this disguise, I think't no sin
To cozen him that would unjustly win.   *Exit*

Enter the two French Lords, and two or three Soldiers   IV.3

FIRST LORD You have not given him his mother's letter?

SECOND LORD I have delivered it an hour since. There is
something in't that stings his nature, for on the reading
it he changed almost into another man.

FIRST LORD He has much worthy blame laid upon him
for shaking off so good a wife and so sweet a lady.

SECOND LORD Especially he hath incurred the ever-
lasting displeasure of the King, who had even tuned his
bounty to sing happiness to him. I will tell you a thing,
but you shall let it dwell darkly with you.   10

FIRST LORD When you have spoken it 'tis dead, and I am
the grave of it.

SECOND LORD He hath perverted a young gentlewoman
here in Florence, of a most chaste renown, and this
night he fleshes his will in the spoil of her honour. He
hath given her his monumental ring, and thinks himself
made in the unchaste composition.

FIRST LORD Now, God delay our rebellion! As we are ourselves, what things are we!

20 SECOND LORD Merely our own traitors. And as in the common course of all treasons we still see them reveal themselves till they attain to their abhorred ends, so he that in this action contrives against his own nobility, in his proper stream o'erflows himself.

FIRST LORD Is it not meant damnable in us to be trumpeters of our unlawful intents? We shall not then have his company tonight?

SECOND LORD Not till after midnight, for he is dieted to his hour.

30 FIRST LORD That approaches apace. I would gladly have him see his company anatomized, that he might take a measure of his own judgements wherein so curiously he had set this counterfeit.

SECOND LORD We will not meddle with him till he come, for his presence must be the whip of the other.

FIRST LORD In the meantime, what hear you of these wars?

SECOND LORD I hear there is an overture of peace.

FIRST LORD Nay, I assure you, a peace concluded.

40 SECOND LORD What will Count Rossillion do then? Will he travel higher, or return again into France?

FIRST LORD I perceive by this demand you are not altogether of his counsel.

SECOND LORD Let it be forbid, sir; so should I be a great deal of his act.

FIRST LORD Sir, his wife some two months since fled from his house. Her pretence is a pilgrimage to Saint Jaques le Grand; which holy undertaking with most austere sanctimony she accomplished; and there resid-
50 ing, the tenderness of her nature became as a prey to her

grief; in fine, made a groan of her last breath, and now
she sings in heaven.

SECOND LORD How is this justified?

FIRST LORD The stronger part of it by her own letters,
which makes her story true even to the point of her
death. Her death itself, which could not be her office to
say is come, was faithfully confirmed by the rector of
the place.

SECOND LORD Hath the Count all this intelligence?

FIRST LORD Ay, and the particular confirmations, point   60
from point, to the full arming of the verity.

SECOND LORD I am heartily sorry that he'll be glad of
this.

FIRST LORD How mightily sometimes we make us comforts of our losses!

SECOND LORD And how mightily some other times we
drown our gain in tears! The great dignity that his
valour hath here acquired for him shall at home be
encountered with a shame as ample.

FIRST LORD The web of our life is of a mingled yarn, good   70
and ill together. Our virtues would be proud if our faults
whipped them not, and our crimes would despair if they
were not cherished by our virtues.

Enter a Messenger

How now? Where's your master?

MESSENGER He met the Duke in the street, sir, of whom
he hath taken a solemn leave: his lordship will next
morning for France. The Duke hath offered him letters
of commendations to the King.

SECOND LORD They shall be no more than needful there,
if they were more than they can commend.   80

Enter Bertram

FIRST LORD They cannot be too sweet for the King's

tartness. Here's his lordship now. How now, my lord?
Is't not after midnight?

BERTRAM I have tonight dispatched sixteen businesses a
month's length apiece. By an abstract of success: I have
congied with the Duke, done my adieu with his nearest,
buried a wife, mourned for her, writ to my lady mother
I am returning, entertained my convoy, and between
these main parcels of dispatch effected many nicer
90 needs; the last was the greatest, but that I have not ended
yet.

SECOND LORD If the business be of any difficulty, and
this morning your departure hence, it requires haste of
your lordship.

BERTRAM I mean, the business is not ended, as fearing to
hear of it hereafter. But shall we have this dialogue
between the Fool and the Soldier? Come, bring forth
this counterfeit module has deceived me like a double-
meaning prophesier.

100 SECOND LORD Bring him forth.

Exeunt the Soldiers

Has sat i'th'stocks all night, poor gallant knave.

BERTRAM No matter. His heels have deserved it in usurping his spurs so long. How does he carry himself?

SECOND LORD I have told your lordship already: the
stocks carry him. But to answer you as you would be
understood, he weeps like a wench that had shed her
milk. He hath confessed himself to Morgan, whom he
supposes to be a friar, from the time of his remembrance
to this very instant disaster of his setting i'th'stocks.
110 And what think you he hath confessed?

BERTRAM Nothing of me, has 'a?

SECOND LORD His confession is taken, and it shall be
read to his face; if your lordship be in't, as I believe you
are, you must have the patience to hear it.

Enter Parolles guarded, with the First Soldier as his interpreter

BERTRAM A plague upon him! Muffled! He can say nothing of me.

FIRST LORD (*aside to Bertram*) Hush, hush! Hoodman comes. (*Aloud*) Portotartarossa.

FIRST SOLDIER He calls for the tortures. What will you say without 'em?   120

PAROLLES I will confess what I know without constraint. If ye pinch me like a pasty I can say no more.

FIRST SOLDIER *Bosko chimurcho.*

FIRST LORD *Boblibindo chicurmurco.*

FIRST SOLDIER You are a merciful general. Our General bids you answer to what I shall ask you out of a note.

PAROLLES And truly, as I hope to live.

FIRST SOLDIER (*reading*) *First demand of him how many horse the Duke is strong*. What say you to that?

PAROLLES Five or six thousand, but very weak and un-   130
serviceable. The troops are all scattered and the commanders very poor rogues, upon my reputation and credit, and as I hope to live.

FIRST SOLDIER Shall I set down your answer so?

PAROLLES Do. I'll take the sacrament on't, how and which way you will.

BERTRAM All's one to him. What a past-saving slave is this!

FIRST LORD Y'are deceived, my lord; this is Monsieur Parolles, the gallant militarist – that was his own phrase   140
– that had the whole theoric of war in the knot of his scarf, and the practice in the chape of his dagger.

SECOND LORD I will never trust a man again for keeping his sword clean, nor believe he can have everything in him by wearing his apparel neatly.

FIRST SOLDIER Well, that's set down.

PAROLLES 'Five or six thousand horse' I said – I will say
    true – 'or thereabouts' set down, for I'll speak truth.

FIRST LORD He's very near the truth in this.

150 BERTRAM But I con him no thanks for't, in the nature he
    delivers it.

PAROLLES 'Poor rogues' I pray you say.

FIRST SOLDIER Well, that's set down.

PAROLLES I humbly thank you, sir. A truth's a truth, the
    rogues are marvellous poor.

FIRST SOLDIER (*reading*) *Demand of him of what strength*
    they are a-foot. What say you to that?

PAROLLES By my troth, sir, if I were to live this present
    hour, I will tell true. Let me see: Spurio, a hundred and
160 fifty; Sebastian, so many; Corambus, so many; Jaques,
    so many; Guiltian, Cosmo, Lodowick, and Gratii, two
    hundred fifty each; mine own company, Chitopher,
    Vaumond, Bentii, two hundred fifty each; so that the
    muster-file, rotten and sound, upon my life, amounts
    not to fifteen thousand poll; half of the which dare not
    shake the snow from off their cassocks lest they shake
    themselves to pieces.

BERTRAM What shall be done to him?

FIRST LORD Nothing but let him have thanks. Demand
170 of him my condition, and what credit I have with the
    Duke.

FIRST SOLDIER Well, that's set down. (*Reading*) *You*
    shall demand of him whether one Captain Dumaine be
    i'th'camp, a Frenchman; what his reputation is with the
    Duke, what his valour, honesty, and expertness in wars;
    or whether he thinks it were not possible with well-weighing
    sums of gold to corrupt him to a revolt. What say you to
    this? What do you know of it?

PAROLLES I beseech you, let me answer to the particular
180 of the inter'gatories. Demand them singly.

FIRST SOLDIER Do you know this Captain Dumaine?

PAROLLES I know him: 'a was a botcher's prentice in
Paris, from whence he was whipped for getting the
shrieve's fool with child, a dumb innocent that could not
say him nay.

BERTRAM Nay, by your leave, hold your hands – though
I know his brains are forfeit to the next tile that falls.

FIRST SOLDIER Well, is this captain in the Duke of
Florence's camp?

PAROLLES Upon my knowledge he is, and lousy.   190

FIRST LORD Nay, look not so upon me; we shall hear of
your lordship anon.

FIRST SOLDIER What is his reputation with the Duke?

PAROLLES The Duke knows him for no other but a poor
officer of mine, and writ to me this other day to turn
him out o'th'band. I think I have his letter in my pocket.

FIRST SOLDIER Marry, we'll search.

PAROLLES In good sadness, I do not know; either it is
there or it is upon a file with the Duke's other letters in
my tent.   200

FIRST SOLDIER Here 'tis; here's a paper. Shall I read it
to you?

PAROLLES I do not know if it be it or no.

BERTRAM Our interpreter does it well.

FIRST LORD Excellently.

FIRST SOLDIER (reading)
Dian, the Count's a fool, and full of gold.

PAROLLES That is not the Duke's letter, sir; that is an
advertisement to a proper maid in Florence, one Diana,
to take heed of the allurement of one Count Rossillion, a
foolish idle boy, but for all that very ruttish. I pray you,   210
sir, put it up again.

FIRST SOLDIER Nay, I'll read it first by your favour.

PAROLLES My meaning in't, I protest, was very honest in

the behalf of the maid; for I knew the young Count to
be a dangerous and lascivious boy, who is a whale to
virginity, and devours up all the fry it finds.

BERTRAM Damnable both-sides rogue!

FIRST SOLDIER (*reading*)

> *When he swears oaths, bid him drop gold, and take it;*
> *After he scores he never pays the score.*
220 *Half-won is match well made; match, and well make it.*
> *He ne'er pays after-debts, take it before.*
> *And say a soldier, Dian, told thee this:*
> *Men are to mell with, boys are not to kiss;*
> *For count of this, the Count's a fool, I know it,*
> *Who pays before, but not when he does owe it.*
>> *Thine, as he vowed to thee in thine ear,*
>> *Parolles.*

BERTRAM He shall be whipped through the army, with
this rhyme in's forehead.

230 SECOND LORD This is your devoted friend, sir, the
manifold linguist, and the armipotent soldier.

BERTRAM I could endure anything before but a cat, and
now he's a cat to me.

FIRST SOLDIER I perceive, sir, by the General's looks,
we shall be fain to hang you.

PAROLLES My life, sir, in any case! Not that I am afraid
to die, but that, my offences being many, I would
repent out the remainder of nature. Let me live, sir, in a
dungeon, i'th'stocks, or anywhere, so I may live.

240 FIRST SOLDIER We'll see what may be done, so you
confess freely. Therefore once more to this Captain
Dumaine: you have answered to his reputation with
the Duke and to his valour; what is his honesty?

PAROLLES He will steal, sir, an egg out of a cloister. For
rapes and ravishments he parallels Nessus. He professes
not keeping of oaths; in breaking 'em he is stronger than

Hercules. He will lie, sir, with such volubility that you
would think truth were a fool. Drunkenness is his best
virtue, for he will be swine-drunk, and in his sleep he
does little harm, save to his bedclothes about him; but   250
they know his conditions and lay him in straw. I have
but little more to say, sir, of his honesty: he has everything that an honest man should not have; what an
honest man should have, he has nothing.

FIRST LORD I begin to love him for this.

BERTRAM For this description of thine honesty? A pox
upon him! For me, he's more and more a cat.

FIRST SOLDIER What say you to his expertness in war?

PAROLLES Faith, sir, has led the drum before the English
tragedians – to belie him I will not – and more of his   260
soldiership I know not, except in that country he had
the honour to be the officer at a place there called Mile-
end, to instruct for the doubling of files. I would do the
man what honour I can, but of this I am not certain.

FIRST LORD He hath out-villained villainy so far that the
rarity redeems him.

BERTRAM A pox on him! He's a cat still.

FIRST SOLDIER His qualities being at this poor price, I
need not to ask you if gold will corrupt him to revolt.

PAROLLES Sir, for a cardecue he will sell the fee-simple   270
of his salvation, the inheritance of it, and cut th'entail
from all remainders, and a perpetual succession for it
perpetually.

FIRST SOLDIER What's his brother, the other Captain
Dumaine?

SECOND LORD Why does he ask him of me?

FIRST SOLDIER What's he?

PAROLLES E'en a crow o'th'same nest; not altogether so
great as the first in goodness, but greater a great deal in
evil. He excels his brother for a coward, yet his brother   280

is reputed one of the best that is. In a retreat he outruns any lackey; marry, in coming on he has the cramp.

FIRST SOLDIER If your life be saved will you undertake to betray the Florentine?

PAROLLES Ay, and the captain of his horse, Count Rossillion.

FIRST SOLDIER I'll whisper with the General and know his pleasure.

PAROLLES I'll no more drumming. A plague of all
290   drums! Only to seem to deserve well, and to beguile the supposition of that lascivious young boy, the Count, have I run into this danger. Yet who would have suspected an ambush where I was taken?

FIRST SOLDIER There is no remedy, sir, but you must die. The General says you that have so traitorously discovered the secrets of your army, and made such pestiferous reports of men very nobly held, can serve the world for no honest use; therefore you must die. Come, headsman, off with his head.

300 PAROLLES O Lord, sir, let me live, or let me see my death!

FIRST SOLDIER That shall you, and take your leave of all your friends.

    He removes the blindfold

So: look about you. Know you any here?

BERTRAM Good morrow, noble captain.

SECOND LORD God bless you, Captain Parolles.

FIRST LORD God save you, noble captain.

SECOND LORD Captain, what greeting will you to my Lord Lafew? I am for France.

FIRST LORD Good captain, will you give me a copy of the
310   sonnet you writ to Diana in behalf of the Count Rossillion? An I were not a very coward I'd compel it of you; but fare you well.

    Exeunt Bertram and the Lords

FIRST SOLDIER You are undone, captain – all but your
    scarf; that has a knot on't yet.

PAROLLES Who cannot be crushed with a plot?

FIRST SOLDIER If you could find out a country where
    but women were that had received so much shame, you
    might begin an impudent nation. Fare ye well, sir. I am
    for France too; we shall speak of you there.

                            Exeunt the Soldiers

PAROLLES

Yet am I thankful. If my heart were great   320
'Twould burst at this. Captain I'll be no more,
But I will eat and drink and sleep as soft
As captain shall. Simply the thing I am
Shall make me live. Who knows himself a braggart,
Let him fear this; for it will come to pass
That every braggart shall be found an ass.
Rust, sword; cool, blushes; and Parolles live
Safest in shame; being fooled, by foolery thrive.
There's place and means for every man alive.
I'll after them.   *Exit* 330

    Enter Helena, the Widow, and Diana   IV.4

HELENA

That you may well perceive I have not wronged you
One of the greatest in the Christian world
Shall be my surety; fore whose throne 'tis needful,
Ere I can perfect mine intents, to kneel.
Time was, I did him a desirèd office,
Dear almost as his life, which gratitude
Through flinty Tartar's bosom would peep forth
And answer thanks. I duly am informed
His grace is at Marcellus, to which place
We have convenient convoy. You must know   10

I am supposèd dead. The army breaking,
My husband hies him home, where, heaven aiding,
And by the leave of my good lord the King,
We'll be before our welcome.

WIDOW   Gentle madam,
You never had a servant to whose trust
Your business was more welcome.

HELENA   Nor you, mistress,
Ever a friend whose thoughts more truly labour
To recompense your love. Doubt not but heaven
Hath brought me up to be your daughter's dower,
20   As it hath fated her to be my motive
And helper to a husband. But, O strange men!
That can such sweet use make of what they hate,
When saucy trusting of the cozened thoughts
Defiles the pitchy night; so lust doth play
With what it loathes for that which is away.
But more of this hereafter. You, Diana,
Under my poor instructions yet must suffer
Something in my behalf.

DIANA   Let death and honesty
Go with your impositions, I am yours,
30   Upon your will to suffer.

HELENA   Yet, I pray you.
But with the word the time will bring on summer,
When briars shall have leaves as well as thorns
And be as sweet as sharp. We must away;
Our wagon is prepared, and time revives us.
All's well that ends well; still the fine's the crown.
Whate'er the course, the end is the renown.   *Exeunt*

IV.5   *Enter the Countess, Lafew, and the Clown*
LAFEW No, no, no, your son was misled with a snipped-

taffeta fellow there, whose villainous saffron would have
made all the unbaked and doughy youth of a nation in
his colour. Your daughter-in-law had been alive at this
hour, and your son here at home, more advanced by the
King than by that red-tailed humble-bee I speak of.

COUNTESS I would I had not known him; it was the
death of the most virtuous gentlewoman that ever
nature had praise for creating. If she had partaken of my
flesh and cost me the dearest groans of a mother I   10
could not have owed her a more rooted love.

LAFEW 'Twas a good lady, 'twas a good lady. We may pick
a thousand sallets ere we light on such another herb.

CLOWN Indeed, sir, she was the sweet-marjoram of the
sallet, or, rather, the herb of grace.

LAFEW They are not herbs, you knave, they are nose-
herbs.

CLOWN I am no great Nabuchadnezzar, sir, I have not
much skill in grass.

LAFEW Whether dost thou profess thyself, a knave or a   20
fool?

CLOWN A fool, sir, at a woman's service, and a knave at a
man's.

LAFEW Your distinction?

CLOWN I would cozen the man of his wife and do his
service.

LAFEW So you were a knave at his service indeed.

CLOWN And I would give his wife my bauble, sir, to do
her service.

LAFEW I will subscribe for thee, thou art both knave and   30
fool.

CLOWN At your service.

LAFEW No, no, no.

CLOWN Why, sir, if I cannot serve you I can serve as great
a prince as you are.

LAFEW Who's that? A Frenchman?

CLOWN Faith, sir, 'a has an English name; but his fisnomy is more hotter in France than there.

LAFEW What prince is that?

40 CLOWN The Black Prince, sir, alias the prince of darkness, alias the devil.

LAFEW Hold thee, there's my purse. I give thee not this to suggest thee from thy master thou talkest of; serve him still.

CLOWN I am a woodland fellow, sir, that always loved a great fire, and the master I speak of ever keeps a good fire. But sure he is the prince of the world; let his nobility remain in's court. I am for the house with the narrow gate, which I take to be too little for pomp to 50 enter; some that humble themselves may, but the many will be too chill and tender, and they'll be for the flowery way that leads to the broad gate and the great fire.

LAFEW Go thy ways. I begin to be aweary of thee, and I tell thee so before, because I would not fall out with thee. Go thy ways. Let my horses be well looked to, without any tricks.

CLOWN If I put any tricks upon 'em, sir, they shall be jades' tricks, which are their own right by the law of 60 nature.   *Exit*

LAFEW A shrewd knave and an unhappy.

COUNTESS So 'a is. My lord that's gone made himself much sport out of him; by his authority he remains here, which he thinks is a patent for his sauciness; and indeed he has no pace, but runs where he will.

LAFEW I like him well, 'tis not amiss. And I was about to tell you, since I heard of the good lady's death and that my lord your son was upon his return home, I moved

the King my master to speak in the behalf of my
daughter; which, in the minority of them both, his 70
majesty out of a self-gracious remembrance did first
propose. His highness hath promised me to do it; and to
stop up the displeasure he hath conceived against your
son there is no fitter matter. How does your ladyship
like it?

COUNTESS With very much content, my lord, and I wish
it happily effected.

LAFEW His highness comes post from Marcellus, of as
able body as when he numbered thirty. 'A will be here
tomorrow, or I am deceived by him that in such 80
intelligence hath seldom failed.

COUNTESS It rejoices me that I hope I shall see him ere I
die. I have letters that my son will be here tonight. I
shall beseech your lordship to remain with me till they
meet together.

LAFEW Madam, I was thinking with what manners I
might safely be admitted.

COUNTESS You need but plead your honourable privilege.

LAFEW Lady, of that I have made a bold charter, but, I
thank my God, it holds yet. 90

Enter Clown

CLOWN O madam, yonder's my lord your son with a patch
of velvet on's face; whether there be a scar under't or no,
the velvet knows, but 'tis a goodly patch of velvet. His
left cheek is a cheek of two pile and a half, but his right
cheek is worn bare.

LAFEW A scar nobly got, or a noble scar, is a good livery
of honour; so belike is that.

CLOWN But it is your carbonadoed face.

LAFEW Let us go see your son, I pray you. I long to talk
with the young noble soldier. 100

CLOWN Faith, there's a dozen of 'em with delicate fine
hats, and most courteous feathers which bow the head
and nod at every man.   *Exeunt*

*

V.1   *Enter Helena, the Widow, and Diana, with two*
Attendants

HELENA

But this exceeding posting day and night
Must wear your spirits low. We cannot help it;
But since you have made the days and nights as one
To wear your gentle limbs in my affairs,
Be bold you do so grow in my requital
As nothing can unroot you.
        Enter a Gentleman, Astringer to the King
                                In happy time!
This man may help me to his majesty's ear,
If he would spend his power. God save you, sir!

GENTLEMAN

And you.

HELENA

10   Sir, I have seen you in the court of France.

GENTLEMAN

I have been sometimes there.

HELENA

I do presume, sir, that you are not fallen
From the report that goes upon your goodness;
And therefore, goaded with most sharp occasions
Which lay nice manners by, I put you to
The use of your own virtues, for the which
I shall continue thankful.

GENTLEMAN   What's your will?

HELENA

   That it will please you
   To give this poor petition to the King,
   And aid me with that store of power you have   20
   To come into his presence.

GENTLEMAN

   The King's not here.

HELENA   Not here, sir?

GENTLEMAN   Not indeed.

   He hence removed last night, and with more haste
   Than is his use.

WIDOW   Lord, how we lose our pains!

HELENA

   All's well that ends well yet,
   Though time seem so adverse and means unfit.
   I do beseech you, whither is he gone?

GENTLEMAN

   Marry, as I take it, to Rossillion;
   Whither I am going.

HELENA   I do beseech you, sir,
   Since you are like to see the King before me,   30
   Commend the paper to his gracious hand,
   Which I presume shall render you no blame,
   But rather make you thank your pains for it.
   I will come after you with what good speed
   Our means will make us means.

GENTLEMAN   This I'll do for you.

HELENA

   And you shall find yourself to be well thanked,
   Whate'er falls more. We must to horse again.
   Go, go, provide.   *Exeunt*

V.2   *Enter the Clown and Parolles*

PAROLLES Good Master Lavatch, give my Lord Lafew
this letter. I have ere now, sir, been better known to
you, when I have held familiarity with fresher clothes;
but I am now, sir, muddied in Fortune's mood, and
smell somewhat strong of her strong displeasure.

CLOWN Truly, Fortune's displeasure is but sluttish if it
smell so strongly as thou speakest of. I will henceforth
eat no fish of Fortune's buttering. Prithee, allow the
wind.

10 PAROLLES Nay, you need not to stop your nose, sir. I
spake but by a metaphor.

CLOWN Indeed, sir, if your metaphor stink I will stop my
nose, or against any man's metaphor. Prithee, get thee
further.

PAROLLES Pray you, sir, deliver me this paper.

CLOWN Foh! Prithee stand away. A paper from Fortune's
close-stool, to give to a nobleman! Look, here he comes
himself.

        Enter Lafew

Here is a pur of Fortune's, sir, or of Fortune's cat, but
20 not a musk-cat, that has fallen into the unclean fishpond
of her displeasure and, as he says, is muddied withal.
Pray you, sir, use the carp as you may, for he looks like a
poor, decayed, ingenious, foolish, rascally knave. I do
pity his distress in my similes of comfort, and leave him
to your lordship.   *Exit*

PAROLLES My lord, I am a man whom Fortune hath
cruelly scratched.

LAFEW And what would you have me to do? 'Tis too late
to pare her nails now. Wherein have you played the
30 knave with Fortune that she should scratch you, who of
herself is a good lady and would not have knaves thrive
long under her? There's a cardecue for you. Let the

justices make you and Fortune friends; I am for other
business.

PAROLLES I beseech your honour to hear me one single
word.

LAFEW You beg a single penny more. Come, you shall
ha't, save your word.

PAROLLES My name, my good lord, is Parolles.

LAFEW You beg more than 'word' then. Cox my passion!   40
Give me your hand. How does your drum?

PAROLLES O my good lord, you were the first that found
me.

LAFEW Was I, in sooth? And I was the first that lost thee.

PAROLLES It lies in you, my lord, to bring me in some
grace, for you did bring me out.

LAFEW Out upon thee, knave! Dost thou put upon me at
once both the office of God and the devil? One brings
thee in grace and the other brings thee out.

Trumpets sound

The King's coming; I know by his trumpets. Sirrah,   50
inquire further after me. I had talk of you last night.
Though you are a fool and a knave you shall eat. Go to,
follow.

PAROLLES I praise God for you.   *Exeunt*

Flourish. Enter the King, the Countess, Lafew, the   V.3
two French Lords, with Attendants

KING
   We lost a jewel of her, and our esteem
   Was made much poorer by it; but your son,
   As mad in folly, lacked the sense to know
   Her estimation home.

COUNTESS   'Tis past, my liege,
   And I beseech your majesty to make it

Natural rebellion done i'th'blade of youth,
When oil and fire, too strong for reason's force,
O'erbears it and burns on.

KING   My honoured lady,
I have forgiven and forgotten all,
10   Though my revenges were high bent upon him
And watched the time to shoot.

LAFEW   This I must say –
But first I beg my pardon – the young lord
Did to his majesty, his mother, and his lady
Offence of mighty note, but to himself
The greatest wrong of all. He lost a wife
Whose beauty did astonish the survey
Of richest eyes, whose words all ears took captive,
Whose dear perfection hearts that scorned to serve
Humbly called mistress.

KING   Praising what is lost
20   Makes the remembrance dear. Well, call him hither;
We are reconciled, and the first view shall kill
All repetition. Let him not ask our pardon;
The nature of his great offence is dead,
And deeper than oblivion we do bury
Th'incensing relics of it. Let him approach
A stranger, no offender; and inform him
So 'tis our will he should.

ATTENDANT   I shall, my liege.   *Exit*

KING
What says he to your daughter? Have you spoke?

LAFEW
All that he is hath reference to your highness.

KING
30   Then shall we have a match. I have letters sent me
That sets him high in fame.
        Enter Bertram

LAFEW   He looks well on't.

KING

I am not a day of season,
For thou mayst see a sunshine and a hail
In me at once. But to the brightest beams
Distracted clouds give way; so stand thou forth:
The time is fair again.

BERTRAM   My high-repented blames,
Dear sovereign, pardon to me.

KING   All is whole.
Not one word more of the consumèd time.
Let's take the instant by the forward top;
For we are old, and on our quickest decrees   40
Th'inaudible and noiseless foot of time
Steals ere we can effect them. You remember
The daughter of this lord?

BERTRAM

Admiringly, my liege. At first
I stuck my choice upon her, ere my heart
Durst make too bold a herald of my tongue;
Where, the impression of mine eye infixing,
Contempt his scornful perspective did lend me,
Which warped the line of every other favour,
Scorned a fair colour or expressed it stolen,   50
Extended or contracted all proportions
To a most hideous object. Thence it came
That she whom all men praised, and whom myself,
Since I have lost, have loved, was in mine eye
The dust that did offend it.

KING   Well excused.
That thou didst love her, strikes some scores away
From the great compt; but love that comes too late,
Like a remorseful pardon slowly carried,
To the great sender turns a sour offence,

60   Crying 'That's good that's gone.' Our rash faults
      Make trivial price of serious things we have,
      Not knowing them until we know their grave.
      Oft our displeasures, to ourselves unjust,
      Destroy our friends and after weep their dust;
      Our own love waking cries to see what's done,
      While shameful hate sleeps out the afternoon.
      Be this sweet Helen's knell, and now forget her.
      Send forth your amorous token for fair Maudlin.
      The main consents are had, and here we'll stay
70   To see our widower's second marriage-day.

COUNTESS

      Which better than the first, O dear heaven, bless!
      Or, ere they meet, in me, O nature, cesse!

LAFEW

      Come on, my son, in whom my house's name
      Must be digested, give a favour from you
      To sparkle in the spirits of my daughter,
      That she may quickly come.

            Bertram gives Lafew a ring

                              By my old beard
      And every hair that's on't, Helen that's dead
      Was a sweet creature; such a ring as this,
      The last that e'er I took her leave at court,
80   I saw upon her finger.

BERTRAM   Hers it was not.

KING

      Now pray you let me see it; for mine eye,
      While I was speaking, oft was fastened to't.
      This ring was mine, and when I gave it Helen
      I bade her, if her fortunes ever stood
      Necessitied to help, that by this token
      I would relieve her. Had you that craft to reave her
      Of what should stead her most?

BERTRAM   My gracious sovereign,
  Howe'er it pleases you to take it so,
  The ring was never hers.
COUNTESS   Son, on my life,
  I have seen her wear it, and she reckoned it   90
  At her life's rate.
LAFEW   I am sure I saw her wear it.
BERTRAM
  You are deceived, my lord, she never saw it.
  In Florence was it from a casement thrown me,
  Wrapped in a paper which contained the name
  Of her that threw it. Noble she was, and thought
  I stood ingaged; but when I had subscribed
  To mine own fortune, and informed her fully
  I could not answer in that course of honour
  As she had made the overture, she ceased
  In heavy satisfaction, and would never   100
  Receive the ring again.
KING   Plutus himself,
  That knows the tinct and multiplying medicine,
  Hath not in nature's mystery more science
  Than I have in this ring. 'Twas mine, 'twas Helen's,
  Whoever gave it you; then if you know
  That you are well acquainted with yourself,
  Confess 'twas hers, and by what rough enforcement
  You got it from her. She called the saints to surety
  That she would never put it from her finger
  Unless she gave it to yourself in bed,   110
  Where you have never come, or sent it us
  Upon her great disaster.
BERTRAM   She never saw it.
KING
  Thou speakest it falsely, as I love mine honour,
  And makest conjectural fears to come into me

Which I would fain shut out. If it should prove
That thou art so inhuman – 'twill not prove so,
And yet I know not; thou didst hate her deadly,
And she is dead; which nothing but to close
Her eyes myself could win me to believe,
More than to see this ring. Take him away.
My fore-past proofs, howe'er the matter fall,
Shall tax my fears of little vanity,
Having vainly feared too little. Away with him.
We'll sift this matter further.

BERTRAM   If you shall prove
This ring was ever hers, you shall as easy
Prove that I husbanded her bed in Florence,
Where yet she never was.   *Exit, guarded*

KING

I am wrapped in dismal thinkings.

   Enter a Gentleman (the Astringer)

GENTLEMAN   Gracious sovereign,
Whether I have been to blame or no, I know not:
Here's a petition from a Florentine
Who hath for four or five removes come short
To tender it herself. I undertook it,
Vanquished thereto by the fair grace and speech
Of the poor suppliant, who, by this, I know,
Is here attending. Her business looks in her
With an importing visage, and she told me,
In a sweet verbal brief, it did concern
Your highness with herself.

KING (*reading the letter*) *Upon his many protestations to
marry me when his wife was dead, I blush to say it, he
won me. Now is the Count Rossillion a widower; his vows
are forfeited to me and my honour's paid to him. He stole
from Florence, taking no leave, and I follow him to his
country for justice. Grant it me, O King! In you it best*

lies; otherwise a seducer flourishes, and a poor maid is
undone.

                           Diana Capilet.

LAFEW I will buy me a son-in-law in a fair, and toll for
  this. I'll none of him.

KING

  The heavens have thought well on thee, Lafew,   150
  To bring forth this discovery. Seek these suitors.
  Go speedily, and bring again the Count.

                        Exeunt some Attendants

  I am afeard the life of Helen, lady,
  Was foully snatched.

COUNTESS   Now justice on the doers!

  Enter Bertram, guarded

KING

  I wonder, sir, since wives are monsters to you,
  And that you fly them as you swear them lordship,
  Yet you desire to marry.

  Enter the Widow and Diana

                   What woman's that?

DIANA

  I am, my lord, a wretched Florentine,
  Derivèd from the ancient Capilet.
  My suit, as I do understand, you know,   160
  And therefore know how far I may be pitied.

WIDOW

  I am her mother, sir, whose age and honour
  Both suffer under this complaint we bring,
  And both shall cease, without your remedy.

KING

  Come hither, Count. Do you know these women?

BERTRAM

  My lord, I neither can nor will deny
  But that I know them. Do they charge me further?

DIANA

Why do you look so strange upon your wife?

BERTRAM

She's none of mine, my lord.

DIANA   If you shall marry

170   You give away this hand, and that is mine,
You give away heaven's vows, and those are mine,
You give away myself, which is known mine;
For I by vow am so embodied yours
That she which marries you must marry me –
Either both or none.

LAFEW Your reputation comes too short for my daughter;
you are no husband for her.

BERTRAM

My lord, this is a fond and desperate creature
Whom sometime I have laughed with. Let your highness
180   Lay a more noble thought upon mine honour
Than for to think that I would sink it here.

KING

Sir, for my thoughts, you have them ill to friend
Till your deeds gain them; fairer prove your honour
Than in my thought it lies!

DIANA   Good my lord,
Ask him upon his oath if he does think
He had not my virginity.

KING

What sayst thou to her?

BERTRAM   She's impudent, my lord,
And was a common gamester to the camp.

DIANA

He does me wrong, my lord; if I were so
190   He might have bought me at a common price.
Do not believe him. O behold this ring
Whose high respect and rich validity

Did lack a parallel; yet for all that
He gave it to a commoner o'th'camp,
If I be one.

COUNTESS   He blushes and 'tis hit.
Of six preceding ancestors, that gem
Conferred by testament to th'sequent issue,
Hath it been owed and worn. This is his wife:
That ring's a thousand proofs.

KING   Methought you said
You saw one here in court could witness it.   200

DIANA
I did, my lord, but loath am to produce
So bad an instrument: his name's Parolles.

LAFEW
I saw the man today, if man he be.

KING
Find him and bring him hither.   *Exit an Attendant*

BERTRAM   What of him?
He's quoted for a most perfidious slave
With all the spots o'th'world taxed and debauched,
Whose nature sickens but to speak a truth.
Am I or that or this for what he'll utter,
That will speak anything?

KING   She hath that ring of yours.

BERTRAM
I think she has. Certain it is I liked her   210
And boarded her i'th'wanton way of youth.
She knew her distance and did angle for me,
Madding my eagerness with her restraint,
As all impediments in fancy's course
Are motives of more fancy; and in fine
Her infinite cunning with her modern grace
Subdued me to her rate. She got the ring,
And I had that which any inferior might

At market-price have bought.

DIANA   I must be patient.

220   You that have turned off a first so noble wife
May justly diet me. I pray you yet –
Since you lack virtue I will lose a husband –
Send for your ring, I will return it home,
And give me mine again.

BERTRAM   I have it not.

KING

What ring was yours, I pray you?

DIANA   Sir, much like
The same upon your finger.

KING

Know you this ring? This ring was his of late.

DIANA

And this was it I gave him, being abed.

KING

The story then goes false you threw it him
230   Out of a casement?

DIANA   I have spoke the truth.

Enter Parolles

BERTRAM

My lord, I do confess the ring was hers.

KING

You boggle shrewdly; every feather starts you. –
Is this the man you speak of?

DIANA   Ay, my lord.

KING

Tell me, sirrah – but tell me true I charge you,
Not fearing the displeasure of your master,
Which on your just proceeding I'll keep off –
By him and by this woman here what know you?

PAROLLES So please your majesty, my master hath been

an honourable gentleman. Tricks he hath had in him,
which gentlemen have.   240

KING Come, come, to th'purpose. Did he love this
woman?

PAROLLES Faith, sir, he did love her; but how?

KING How, I pray you?

PAROLLES He did love her, sir, as a gentleman loves a
woman.

KING How is that?

PAROLLES He loved her, sir, and loved her not.

KING As thou art a knave and no knave. What an equivocal
companion is this!   250

PAROLLES I am a poor man, and at your majesty's
command.

LAFEW He's a good drum, my lord, but a naughty orator.

DIANA Do you know he promised me marriage?

PAROLLES Faith, I know more than I'll speak.

KING But wilt thou not speak all thou knowest?

PAROLLES Yes, so please your majesty. I did go between
them as I said; but more than that, he loved her, for
indeed he was mad for her and talked of Satan and of
Limbo and of furies and I know not what; yet I was in   260
that credit with them at that time that I knew of their
going to bed and of other motions, as promising her
marriage and things which would derive me ill will to
speak of; therefore I will not speak what I know.

KING Thou hast spoken all already, unless thou canst say
they are married. But thou art too fine in thy evidence —
therefore, stand aside.

This ring you say was yours?

DIANA   Ay, my good lord.

KING
Where did you buy it? Or who gave it you?

DIANA

270   It was not given me, nor I did not buy it.

KING

Who lent it you?

DIANA   It was not lent me neither.

KING

Where did you find it then?

DIANA   I found it not.

KING

If it were yours by none of all these ways

How could you give it him?

DIANA   I never gave it him.

LAFEW This woman's an easy glove, my lord; she goes off
and on at pleasure.

KING

This ring was mine; I gave it his first wife.

DIANA

It might be yours or hers for aught I know.

KING

Take her away, I do not like her now.

280   To prison with her. And away with him.

Unless thou tellest me where thou hadst this ring

Thou diest within this hour.

DIANA   I'll never tell you.

KING

Take her away.

DIANA   I'll put in bail, my liege.

KING

I think thee now some common customer.

DIANA

By Jove, if ever I knew man 'twas you.

KING

Wherefore hast thou accused him all this while?

DIANA

    Because he's guilty and he is not guilty.

    He knows I am no maid, and he'll swear to't;

    I'll swear I am a maid and he knows not.

    Great king, I am no strumpet; by my life   290

    I am either maid or else this old man's wife.

KING

    She does abuse our ears. To prison with her.

DIANA

    Good mother, fetch my bail. Stay, royal sir;

                           Exit the Widow

    The jeweller that owes the ring is sent for

    And he shall surety me. But for this lord

    Who hath abused me as he knows himself,

    Though yet he never harmed me, here I quit him.

    He knows himself my bed he hath defiled,

    And at that time he got his wife with child.

    Dead though she be she feels her young one kick.   300

    So there's my riddle: one that's dead is quick.

    And now behold the meaning.

    Enter the Widow, with Helena

KING   Is there no exorcist

    Beguiles the truer office of mine eyes?

    Is't real that I see?

HELENA   No, my good lord,

    'Tis but the shadow of a wife you see,

    The name and not the thing.

BERTRAM   Both, both. O pardon!

HELENA

    O my good lord, when I was like this maid

    I found you wondrous kind. There is your ring,

    And, look you, here's your letter. This it says:

    When from my finger you can get this ring . . .   310

And is by me with child, etc. This is done.
Will you be mine now you are doubly won?

BERTRAM

If she, my liege, can make me know this clearly
I'll love her dearly, ever, ever dearly.

HELENA

If it appear not plain and prove untrue
Deadly divorce step between me and you!
O my dear mother, do I see you living?

LAFEW

Mine eyes smell onions, I shall weep anon.
(*To Parolles*) Good Tom Drum, lend me a handkercher.
320   So, I thank thee. Wait on me home, I'll make sport with
thee. Let thy curtsies alone, they are scurvy ones.

KING

Let us from point to point this story know
To make the even truth in pleasure flow.
(*To Diana*) If thou beest yet a fresh uncroppèd flower
Choose thou thy husband and I'll pay thy dower;
For I can guess that by thy honest aid
Thou keptest a wife herself, thyself a maid.
Of that and all the progress more and less
Resolvèdly more leisure shall express.
330   All yet seems well, and if it end so meet,
The bitter past, more welcome is the sweet.
    Flourish

EPILOGUE

Spoken by the King
The King's a beggar, now the play is done.
All is well ended if this suit be won,
That you express content; which we will pay
With strife to please you, day exceeding day.

Ours be your patience then and yours our parts;
Your gentle hands lend us and take our hearts. *Exeunt*

An Account of the Text

Our only authoritative text of *All's Well That Ends Well* was published in 1623 – seven years after Shakespeare's death – in the volume now known as the first Folio. The plays included in the first Folio present many different kinds of textual problem, and the first question to be considered with each is its provenance. It has to be remembered that the text of a Shakespeare play once existed in a number of forms, among which there might be interrelationship. There were two major forms. One source was 'foul papers', the name given to the author's own draft or drafts of a play, before they were regularized for use in the theatre. This is a class of text that is regarded as distinctively authentic and indicative of authorial intention. The second source was 'prompt-copy', the manuscript of the play as used in the theatre by actors – a source for a text that would be likely to give a version 'cleaner', more coherent, and more regular than the former.

There is a fair consensus of opinion that the text of *All's Well That Ends Well* is based on foul papers or authorial manuscript, and may even record quite early stages of composition, during which the author was still working things out. Some signs of authorial indecisiveness are as follows. There are a good many cases of inconsistent speech-prefixes (for example, in the course of the play the Countess appears as *Coun.*, *Old Coun.*, *Mo.* and *La.*, for *Countess*, *Old Countess*, *Mother* and *Lady*) which may reflect the way in which various attributes of a character would, scene by scene, present themselves to the author. Such inconsistency would necessarily prove inconvenient in prompt-copy, and would have been regularized. Similar evidence of foul papers is the fact that certain characters in the play start off by being named according to their type (for example, the Widow, the Clown, the Steward, the French Lords) and only acquire their individual names at a later stage in the action (when they become Widow Capilet, Lavatch, Rynaldo, the brothers Dumaine). The last named, the brothers Dumaine, form a textual problem in themselves. In the Folio text there appear to be (at least) *two* sets of paired Lords: one pair, who are attached to the French King, Shakespeare refers to as *E* and *G*, while the other pair, who are attached to the Duke of Florence, he calls *1* and *2*. It looks as though, at some point in his work, Shakespeare decided to fuse these two pairs (who would probably have been played by the same actors) into one pair. In the process of fusion certain mistakes seem to have occurred so that, for example, there is uncertainty about which Lord helps Bertram woo Diana and which one helps him to fool Parolles. Modern editors have to simplify the situation and eliminate the inconsistency. There are other signs of foul papers. Certain stage directions in the Folio text seem to suggest an attitude of permissiveness on the part of the author, where prompt-copy would probably have been more specific: for example, *Enter 3 or 4 Lords* (II.3.50). There are other stage directions in the Folio text which are equally hard to assign to prompt-copy: for example, that at II.3.61, *She addresses her to a Lord* (whereupon she in fact says *Gentlemen . . .*), or that at II.3.182, *Parolles and Lafew stay behind, commenting of this wedding* (where the nature of the two men's talk is made immediately apparent by what they say). It has been suggested that these are not true stage directions at all: they are in fact some kind of author's note or reminder, perhaps left on breaking off composition, such as would have no place in prompt-copy.

The textual situation can be summarized, then, by saying that the compositors of the Folio text were almost certainly working on foul papers, which perhaps incorporated quite early drafts of the play. In so far as they reproduced their manuscript, their text deserves high respect for its authenticity. On the other hand, there is also evidence that the manuscript was not at all clear and easy to read. The Folio text of *All's Well That Ends Well* is not, in short, a very good one. Minor errors are frequent; punctuation is poor; major cruxes are (for this type of textual situation, where there is only one authoritative text) unusually high in number. It may be that the printer, faced by bad handwriting or confused copy, sometimes found the play too difficult and too original for his guesses: the complex syntax baffled him and the striking turns of phrase left him behind.

Whatever the reasons for it, a modern edition must depart in a good many ways from the Folio text. Such departures are listed below in the tables of collations. The collations include only major departures, such as affect the sense of the text. They do not include such minor details as obvious misprints, mislineations, and so on, nor do they list any details of the modernization of spelling and punctuation – except those which affect the sense of the text. As part of such modernization, *and* meaning 'if' is reduced to *an* throughout, and contracted second person singular endings and superlatives are in general extended to their fuller form.

The names of persons and places have *not* been modernized, since this might obscure their pronunciation. Also, since even those editions which do modernize names always retain the form *Parolles* (which should, strictly, be modernized to 'Paroles'), it seems preferable to retain the old forms throughout: *Lafew* not 'Lafeu', *Lavatch* not 'Lavache', and so on. This applies also to place names: *Rossillion* not 'Rousillon', and *Marcellus* not 'Marseilles'.

COLLATIONS

1

Text

Below are listed major departures in the present text from that of the first Folio (F), whose readings are given – unmodernized except for the 'long s' (ſ) – on the right of the square bracket. A few of these alterations were made in one of the seventeenth-century reprints of F (F2, F3 and F4) and are so indicated. Most of the others were made by eighteenth- and nineteenth-century editors. Those made by twentieth-century editors of the play are acknowledged.

The Characters in the Play] *not in* F
I.1

   1 COUNTESS] *Mother.*

3, 31, 34,

   57 BERTRAM] *Ros.*
   51 have't.] (*this editor*); haue –
   73 BERTRAM] *Ro.*
   86 me.] me
  156 wear] were

I.2

  3, 9, 18 FIRST LORD] 1.*Lo.G.*
  15, 67 SECOND LORD] 2.*Lo.E.*
   18 Rossillion] *Rosignoll*

I.3

   42 madam; e'en] Madam in
   84 but one] but ore
  110 level; Dian no queen] leuell, Queene
  166 loneliness] louelinesse
  172 it t'one to th'other] it 'ton tooth to th'other
  197 intenable] (*C. J. Sisson, 1956*); intemible

II.1

   3 gain all,] gaine, all
   15 wed it. When] wed it, when
   16 shrinks, find] shrinkes: finde
   18 FIRST LORD] *L.G.*
 24, 34, 38 FIRST LORD] 1.*Lo.G.*
 25, 35, 39 SECOND LORD] 2.*Lo.E.*
   43 with his cicatrice, an emblem] his sicatrice, with an
     Embleme
   46 FIRST LORD] *Lo.G.*
   49 Stay: the King] (F2); Stay the King
   62 sue] see
  109 two, more dear; I] two: more dear I
  144 fits] shifts
  155 impostor] (F3); Impostrue
  171 shame;] shame
  172 ballads my maiden's name;] (*this editor*); ballads: my
     maidens name
  173 worst, extended] (*C. J. Sisson, 1956*); worst extended

192 heaven] helpe

II.2

   1 COUNTESS] *Lady* (*Lady or La. throughout scene*)

  37 could!] could:

  58 An end, sir! To] And end sir to

II.3

   1 LAFEW] *Ol. Laf.* (*so to* 183; *except* 37, 58, 92: *Old Laf.*;
     98: *Ol. Lord*)

  69 but, be refused,] but be refused;

  95 HELENA] *La.*

 124 place when] place, whence

 128 good, without a name: vileness] good without a name?
     Vilenesse

 137 grave] graue:

139–40 tomb | Of . . . indeed. What] Tombe. | Of . . . indeed,
     what

 167 eyes. When] eies, when

 169 it,] it:

 200 ordinaries to] (F3); ordinaries: to

 290 detested] detected

II.4

  33 find me? The] finde me? *Clo.* The

II.5

  26 End] And

  50 not so] so

III.1

   9 SECOND LORD] *French E.*

  17 FIRST LORD] *Fren. G.*

III.2

   8 knew] know

 10, 17 COUNTESS] *Lad.* (*La. throughout scene, except* 64: *Old
     La.*)

  18 E'en] In

  44 FIRST LORD] *French E.* (*so throughout scene, except* 62:
     1.G.)

  46 SECOND LORD] *French G.* (*so throughout scene*)

 110 still-piecing] still-peering

III.4

  18 COUNTESS] *not in* F

III.5

> 33 le] (F3); la
> 65 I warrant] I write

III.6

>   1 FIRST LORD] *Cap. E.* (*so to* 102)
>   3 SECOND LORD] *Cap. G.* (*so to* 102)
> 33 his] this
> 34 ore] ours
> 58 stomach, to't, monsieur! If] stomacke, too't Monsieur:
>   if
> 102 FIRST LORD As't . . . lordship. I'll . . . you.] *Cap. G.*
>   As't . . . lordship, Ile . . . you.
> 104, 110 SECOND LORD] *Cap. E.*

III.7

> 19 Resolved] Resolue
> 34 After,] (*G. K. Hunter, 1959*); after

IV.1

>   1 FIRST LORD] *1. Lord E.* (*so – Lor. E., Lo.E., L.E. –*
>   *throughout scene*)
> 66 FIRST SOLDIER] *Inter.* (*so throughout scene, except* 72,
>   79: *Int.*)
> 67 Muskos'] *Muskos*
> 87 art] (F3); are

IV.2

> 25 Love's] Ioues
> 30 words, and poor conditions] (*G. K. Hunter, 1959*); words
>   and poore conditions,
> 38 make vows . . . flame] (*this editor*); make rope's . . .
>   scarre

IV.3

>   1 FIRST LORD] *Cap. G.* (*so throughout scene*)
>   2 SECOND LORD] *Cap. E.* (*so throughout scene, except* 305,
>   307: *Lo.E*)
> 43 counsel] councell
> 75 MESSENGER] *Ser.*
> 81 FIRST LORD] *Ber.*
> 116–17 me. FIRST LORD (*aside to Bertram*) Hush, hush!
>   Hoodman] me: hush, hush. *Cap. G.* Hoodman
> 119 FIRST SOLDIER] *Inter.* (*so – Int., Interp. – throughout scene*)

136–7 will. BERTRAM All's . . . him. What] will: all's . . . him.
        Ber. What
    192 lordship] Lord
    234 the] (F3); your
    257 him!] (*P. Alexander, 1951*); him
    259 has] ha's

IV.4

      3 fore] (F2); for
      9 Marcellus] (*G. K. Hunter, 1959*); *Marcellæ*
     16 you] (F4); your

IV.5

     19 grass] grace
     37 name] maine

V.2

      1 Master] Mr
     19 Here] *Clo.* Heere
     20 musk-cat] Muscat
     24 similes] smiles
     32 under her] (F2); vnder

V.3

     27 ATTENDANT] *Gent.*
     44 Admiringly, my liege.] Admiringly my Liege,
     71 COUNTESS Which] Which
    155 sir, since] sir, sir,
    183 them; fairer] them fairer.
    207 truth.] truth,
    216 infinite cunning] insuite comming

Act and scene divisions

Act divisions are marked in F, but of scene divisions there is only
'*Actus primus. Scæna Prima*' at the opening of the play. The present
text follows the traditional scene numberings used by editors.

Stage directions

Stage directions in the present edition are based on those in F.
Emendations and additions have been made where necessary to clarify
the action. Indications of persons to whom speeches are addressed,
and such directives as *aside* and *aloud*, have been silently added to the
text. The forms of name by which the hero and heroine appear in
stage directions in F (*Bertram, Rossillion* and *Count Rossillion, Helena*

and *Hellen*) have been regularized to the more traditional usage in each case: *Bertram* and *Helena*. Other significant departures from, or additions to, F stage directions are listed below. The reading of the present edition is to the left of the square bracket.

I.1

    72 *Exit*] (F2); *not in* F
    77 *Exeunt Bertram and Lafew*] *not in* F
  184 *Exit*] *not in* F
  211 *Exit*] (F2); *not in* F

I.2

    76 *Exeunt*] *Exit*

I.3

    0 *Enter the Countess, Rynaldo her Steward, and Lavatch her Clown*] *Enter Countesse, Steward, and Clowne*

II.1

    0 *Enter the King . . . Bertram and Parolles; Attendants.*] *Enter the King . . . Count, Rosse, and Parrolles*
   23 (*To some Attendants*)] *not in* F
     He withdraws] *not in* F
   46 *Exeunt the Lords*] *not in* F
   60 *The King comes forward*] (*G. K. Hunter, 1959*); *not in* F
   61 (*kneeling*)] *not in* F
   91 *He goes to the door*] (*G. K. Hunter, 1959*); *not in* F
  210 *Exeunt*] *Exit*

II.3

   45 *Exit an Attendant*] *not in* F
   50 *Enter four Lords*] *Enter 3 or 4 Lords*
   61 *Helena addresses the Lords*] *She addresses her to a Lord*
  182 *Exeunt all but Parolles and Lafew, who stay behind, commenting on this wedding*] *Exeunt | Parolles and Lafew stay behind, commenting of this wedding*

II.4

   54 *Exeunt*] *Exit*

II.5

   48 *Exit*] *not in* F
   69 *He gives Helena a letter*] *not in* F
   92 *Exeunt*] *not in* F

III.1

    0 *and the two French Lords*] *the two Frenchmen*

  23 *Flourish. Exeunt*] *Flourish*

III.2

  19 *(reading the letter aloud)*] *A Letter*

  43 *Exit*] *not in* F

      Enter Helena and the two French Lords] *Enter Hellen and two Gentlemen*

  55 *(She reads the letter aloud)*] *not in* F

  74 *(reading)*] *not in* F

  98 *Exeunt the Countess and the Lords*] *Exit*

III.3

  11 *Exeunt*] *Exeunt omnes*

III.4

   4 STEWARD *(reading)*] *Letter*

III.5

    0 *her daughter Diana, and Mariana, with other citizens*] *her daughter, Violenta and Mariana, with other Citizens*

   7 *Tucket*] *not in* F

  91 *Exeunt Bertram, Parolles, and the army*] *Exit*

III.6

    0 *Enter Bertram and the two French Lords*] *Enter Count Rossillion and the Frenchmen, as at first*

 102 *Exit*] *not in* F

III.7

  48 *Exeunt*] *not in* F

IV.1

    0 *Enter the First French Lord*] *Enter one of the Frenchmen*

 64, 65 *They seize him . . . They blindfold him*] (G. K. Hunter, *1959*); *not in* F

  87 *Exit with Parolles guarded*] *Exit*

  94 *Exeunt*] *Exit*

IV.2

    0 *Enter Bertram and Diana*] *Enter Bertram, and the Maide called Diana*

  66 *Exit*] *not in* F

IV.3

    0 *Enter the two French Lords, and two or three Soldiers*]

Enter the two French Captaines, and some two or three
Souldiours

100 *Exeunt the Soldiers] not in* F

114 *Enter Parolles guarded, with the First Soldier as his inter-
preter] Enter Parolles with his Interpreter*

128, 156,

172, 206 *(reading)] not in* F

218 FIRST SOLDIER *(reading)] Int. Let.*

302 *He removes the blindfold] not in* F

312 *Exeunt Bertram and the Lords] Exeunt*

319 *Exeunt the Soldiers] Exit*

IV.5

0 *Enter the Countess, Lafew, and the Clown] Enter Clowne,
old Lady, and Lafew.*

V.1

6 *Enter a Gentleman, Astringer to the King] Enter a gentle
Astringer.*

38 *Exeunt] not in* F

V.2

25 *Exit] not in* F

49 *Trumpets sound] not in* F

54 *Exeunt] not in* F

V.3

0 *Enter the King, the Countess] Enter King, old Lady*

27 *Exit] not in* F

76 *Bertram gives Lafew a ring] not in* F

127 *Exit, guarded] not in* F

128 *Enter a Gentleman (the Astringer)] Enter a Gentleman*

139 KING *(reading the letter)] A Letter*

152 *Exeunt some Attendants] not in* F

154 *Enter Bertram, guarded] Enter Bertram (after 152)*

157 *Enter the Widow and Diana] Enter Widdow, Diana, and
Parrolles (after 'that')*

204 *Exit an Attendant] not in* F

293 *Exit the Widow] not in* F

Epilogue

6 *Exeunt] Exeunt omn.*

2

The following are some of the more interesting and important
variant readings and proposed emendations *not* accepted in the
present text. They derive from F2, F3 and F4, or have been made
or conjectured in other editions of the play. To the left of the
square brackets are the readings of the present text, and to the
right of them the suggested emendations. Where there are several
citations they are separated by semi-colons.

I.1

  55–8 COUNTESS If . . . mortal. BERTRAM Madam . . . wishes.
    LAFEW How . . . that?] COUNTESS If . . . mortal. LAFEW
    How . . . that? BERTRAM Madam . . . wishes; COUNTESS
    How . . . that? If . . . mortal. BERTRAM Madam . . .
    wishes

  114–15 valiant, in the defence] valiant in the defence,

   145 ten year . . . two] the year . . . two; two years . . . two;
    ten months . . . two; one year . . . two

I.3

   84 but one] but or; but o'er; but for; before

   244 day, an] day, and (F3)

II.1

   62 sue] fee

   76 Pippen] Pepin

   162 torcher] coacher

   164 her] his

   173 Seared otherwise, ne worse of] Seard otherwise, no worse
    of (F2); Sear'd otherwise; nay, worse of; Sear'd other-
    wise; nay worse – of; Seared; otherwise – ne worse of
    worst, extended] worst extended,

II.2

   37 could!] could,

   58 An end, sir! To] And end; sir to; An end, Sir; to

II.3

  7–9 PAROLLES Why . . . times. BERTRAM And so 'tis] Why
    . . . times. PAROLLES And so 'tis

  11–12 PAROLLES So . . . Paracelsus. LAFEW Of all] PAROLLES

So I say. LAFEW Both . . . Paracelsus. PAROLLES So I
say. LAFEW Of all

22 what-do-ye-call there] what-do-ye-call't there; what-
do-ye-call't here; what do you call these

23 A showing . . . actor] *A showing . . . actor*

32–7 LAFEW In . . . weak – PAROLLES And . . . be – LAFEW
Generally thankful] LAFEW In . . . weak – PAROLLES
Ay, so I say. LAFEW And debile . . . as to be (*after a
pause*) generally thankful; LAFEW In . . . weak and
debile . . . King, as to be generally thankful

128 good, without a name: vileness] good, without a name
vileness

II.4

33 find me? The] find me? PAROLLES In myself. CLOWN
The; find me? (*Parolles shakes his head*) The; find me?
. . . The

II.5

89 Where . . . men? Monsieur, farewell] BERTRAM Where
. . . men, Monsieur? – farewell; BERTRAM Where . . .
men? HELENA Monsieur, farewell

III.1

17 nature] Nation

III.2

9 hold] sold

110 still-piecing] still-piercing; still-'pearing; still-pairing

III.5

65 I warrant] I right (F2); Ah! right; A right; I weet

III.6

102 FIRST LORD As't . . . lordship. I'll . . . you] SECOND
LORD As't . . . Lordship, I'll . . . you; FRENCH
GENTLEMAN As't . . . lordship. FRENCH ENVOY I'll .
. . you

104, 110 SECOND LORD] FIRST LORD

III.7

34 After,] after this

IV.1

41 Bajazeth's mule] Bajazet's mute; Balaam's mule;
Bajazet's mate

IV.2

    25 Love's] God's

  28, 29 him] Him

    30 words, and poor conditions] words and poor, conditions

    38 make vows in such a flame] make Hopes . . . Affairs; make hopes . . . scene; make rapes . . . scour; may grope's . . . scarre; may cope's . . . stir; may rope's . . . snare

IV.3

    18 delay] allay; lay

   158 live] die; leave

      this] but this

IV.4

    9 Marcellus] Marseilles

 30–31 pray you. | But with the word the] pray you, | Bear with the word: the; pay you | But with the word; the; pray you . . . | But with the word, that; pray you; | But with the word: 'the

IV.5

    16 not herbs] not Sallet-Herbs; knot-herbs

    78 Marcellus] Marseilles

V.2

    1 Master] Monsieur

    4 mood] moat

    23 ingenious] ingenuous; ingenerous

V.3

    6 blade] blaze

    96 ingaged] engag'd; ungag'd

   195 hit] his; it

Commentary

Only the more substantial emendations to the Folio edition of Shakespeare's plays (1623; referred to as F) are discussed here (see also An Account of the Text). Biblical references are to the Bishops' Bible (1568, etc.), the version that was probably best known to Shakespeare.

I.1

  0 *Rossillion*: Three syllables, with the accent on the second; pronounced Ross-ill-yon. The F and probably Shakespeare's spelling of Rousillon, once a province of south-western France.

    Lafew: The name possibly means '*le feu*', 'the late' – a direct enough way of referring to his age.

    all in black: The characters are in mourning for the late Count, Bertram's father; they make a strangely sombre opening tableau for a comedy.

1–2 *In delivering my son from me, I bury a second husband*: The Countess opens with a riddle matched and reversed by one very near the end: *one that's dead is quick* (V.3.301). She quibbles on 'delivers', which means 'sending away', 'freeing' and 'giving birth to', word-play close to the heart of the play; as is her association of birth and death, and her statement of the complex relationship of youth and age.

  5 *to whom I am now in ward*: Whose ward I am now. The death of Bertram's father makes him technically an orphan, and the King guardian of the Rossillion estates,

until Bertram comes of age; his age is unclear but his wardship directs our attention to his youth.

6 *of*: In the person of.

7 *generally*: To all men, without respect of persons.

8 *hold his virtue*: Continue to be good.

8–10 *whose worthiness would stir . . . such abundance*: Your merits are such as to call forth kindness even from one not usually possessed of it; you will hardly then fail to meet it in one so bountifully kind as the King.

13–14 *under whose practices he hath persecuted time with hope*: Under whose professional attentions he has wasted his days hoping.

17–18 *O that 'had', how sad a passage 'tis*: The felicity of this remark arises principally from the complex quibbles in *passage*, which includes the meanings 'expression, phrase', 'event', 'transition', and 'death'.

19 *honesty*: Honour, integrity.

33 *fistula*: A species of ulcer.

38–44 *I have those hopes of her good . . . achieves her goodness*: The courtly diction of the Countess here makes her topic (one vital to the play) sound more difficult and unfamiliar than it is. She is talking about what we and the Elizabethans call Nature and Nurture (or Heredity and Environment), and the Countess calls *dispositions* [*which*] *she inherits* and *education*.

38–40 *I have those hopes . . . makes fair gifts fairer*: I believe she may come to great good, for her upbringing has added to her inborn gifts, improving fine qualities as it so often does.

40 *unclean mind*: Bad character (inherent, not acquired).

41 *virtuous qualities*: Skills and accomplishments (acquired, not inherent).

42 *they are virtues and traitors too*: Such skills and accomplishments prove treacherous to the self and to others when they serve evil not good.

43 *simpleness*: Purity, unmixed quality.

43–4 *She derives her honesty and achieves her goodness*: She inherits her honour and succeeds in being good by her own efforts.

46 *season*: Preserve in salt (a domestic image frequently used by Shakespeare in metaphorical senses).

49 *livelihood*: The Countess's meaning here is halfway between two senses of the word: 'liveliness or animation', and 'means of life or nourishment'.

50 *go to*: Come, come.

51 *affect*: Both the Countess and Helena play on the Elizabethan sense, 'to be in love with', as well as on the continuing modern sense of 'feign'.

have't: F reads *haue* –, which many editors emend to either 'have.' or 'have it'. It seems unlikely that either could have been misread for the F version; yet equally unlikely that the F reading, implying that Helena interrupts the Countess, can be correct. The contracted *have't* avoids both these objections, and is perhaps supported by the large number of contractions that mark this text elsewhere.

52 *I do affect a sorrow indeed, but I have it too*: We later (78–97) learn that Helena is only feigning her sorrow for her father but feels real grief on account of Bertram. When uttered this remark (like much that she says in this first scene) is enigmatic and riddling, which makes Helena's first appearance in the play curiously like Hamlet's in his.

55–6 *If the living . . . soon mortal*: If grief is firmly resisted, it will soon wear itself out by its own violence. Lafew and the Countess are getting themselves launched into a traditional topic, the proper conduct of grief.

58 *How understand we that*: The exact significance of Lafew's remark is not clear, and some editors have altered its position or assigned it to the Countess. Lafew can hardly fail to understand the bearing of either the Countess's last remark (a language which he seemed himself very well to understand) or Bertram's simple interjection, asking for his mother's blessing so that he can leave. It may be that Shakespeare wishes to draw attention to Bertram's rudeness and abrupt impatience to leave, and uses Lafew's surprise as a means of doing this.

60 *manners*: Moral behaviour.

60 *Thy*: May your.

61–2 *thy goodness | Share with thy birthright*: May the goodness of behaviour you have learned share the rule of your life with the goodness of nature you have inherited!

63–4 *Be able for thine enemy | Rather in power than use*: Make sure you are potentially as strong as your enemy, but do not use this power.

64–5 *keep thy friend | Under thy own life's key*: Quibbling on the double sense of *keep*: 'to retain' and 'to protect': keep your friend as close as your own life; protect your friend's life even at the cost of your own.

66 *taxed*: Blamed.

69 *unseasoned*: Immature, unready.

70–71 *He cannot want the best | That shall attend his love*: The sense of this is not clear. Lafew is probably uttering a deliberately and suitably vague phrase of courtly courtesy, meaning, 'Things are bound to go splendidly for him if he is a good, loving boy.' *want* means 'lack'.

74 *comfortable*: Comforting.

76–7 *hold the credit of your father*: Maintain your father's good name.

79–80 *these great tears grace his remembrance more | Than those I shed for him*: Helena's soliloquy opens with a line and a half as opaque and inward as her earlier remark to the Countess (52). She is here presumably speaking only of her father, as Bertram is not introduced by name until 82. The point seems to be that her present fierce grief is not aroused by her father, but does him more honour *indirectly* (by contrasting him with the cause of it, perhaps?) than did her tears of grief directly aroused by his death. Cf. Bertram on a similar subject, I.2.48–51.

82 *favour*: Face (with a quibble on 'love-token').

87 *collateral*: Parallel. Helena is talking in the language of the old astronomy: she and Bertram must move like two stars describing concentric but separated circles, one (Bertram) above the other, and never side by side, or in one *sphere*.

93 *hawking*: Hawk-like, sharp.

94 *table*: Board or other flat surface for drawing and painting on.

94–5 *capable | Of*: Susceptible to, retentive of.

95 *trick of his sweet favour*: Characteristic expression of his dear face.

96 *fancy*: Love or imagination.

97 *Parolles*: His name is the French word '*paroles*', 'words', clearly in the sense of '*mere* words'; and it has been suggested that there is play also on the word 'parole', 'word of honour'. It is in three syllables, accented on the second.

100 *a great way fool, solely a coward*: Largely a fool and wholly a coward.

102 *take place*: A disputed phrase, which seems to mean 'successfully claim first place, take precedence' (over virtue, with its *steely bones*). The image here is of Parolles wearing his ineradicable faults (*fixed evils*) as though they were smart well-fitting new clothes, bustling forward and pushing out of his way a far more virtuous man.

102–3 *virtue's steely bones | Looks bleak i'th'cold wind*: This phrase seems to be based on one in Juvenal: '*Probitas laudatur et alget*', 'Virtue is praised and is freezing cold' (*Satires*, I.74). (See the relevant chapter in A. P. Rossiter's *Angel with Horns*, mentioned in Further Reading.) Shakespeare's *steely* admirably fuses ideas of harshness, coldness, steadiness and purity. Good is seen here by Helena as lacking not only the bright clothes of evil on Parolles but even the warmth of flesh and blood. See Introduction, 'The desiring body' and 'Honour and blood'.

103 *Looks*: A third person plural of the verb ending in 's' was quite commonly used in Shakespeare's time.
Withal: Besides.

104 *superfluous*: Luxurious, overdressed; unnecessary; immoderate.

105 *Save*: God save.

108 *And no*: And no more am I a queen (than you are a monarch).

109 *Are you meditating on virginity*: See Introduction, 'Helena', for a discussion of this exchange between Parolles and Helena.

110 *stain*: Tinge, tincture, dash. The word usually has a pejorative sense in Shakespeare.

117 *setting down before*: Laying siege to.

118 *blow you up*: Parolles, playing with the meanings 'explode' and 'make you pregnant', here begins a series of bawdy quibbles that utilize the old analogy between sex and warfare.

123 *be blown up*: A bawdy quibble: 'reach orgasm'.

126 *rational increase*: Parolles is arguing sophistically for the 'rationality' of sexual licence by saying that the result of the sexual act is an increase in the number of rational beings.

127 *got*: Begotten.

128 *mettle*: Elizabethan spelling made no distinction between *mettle* and 'metal'. The word thus plays on the meanings 'temperament, disposition' and metal (through the image of minting coins).

132 *stand . . . die*: Bawdy quibbles. See Introduction, 'Helena'.

134 *in't*: For it.

137–8 *He that hangs himself is a virgin; virginity murders itself*: A suicide is no less and no more of a self-destroyer than a virgin who refuses to give life to children (who are virgins).

139 *sanctified limit*: Consecrated ground.

141–2 *feeding his own stomach*: Sacrificing to its own pride.

143–4 *inhibited sin in the canon*: Prohibited sin in the Scriptures.

144 *Keep*: Hoard (a series of commercial metaphors follows).

145 *Out with't*: Put it out, invest it, to gain interest!

145–6 *Within ten year . . . a goodly increase*: Many emendations have been made of the F text, on the ground that the rate of increase quoted – which was the allowed rate of interest at the time – does not sound like a *goodly increase*. But the mistake, if any, seems to be Shakespeare's. The F reading is therefore retained.

150 *Marry*: A mild oath, originally referring to the Virgin
    Mary; here meaning 'to be sure'.

150–51 *ill, to like him that ne'er it likes*: A virgin must do ill (if
    she is to lose her virginity to her liking) and must like
    a man who does not like virginity. The ironic refer-
    ence to Helena and Bertram is unmistakable.

151 *lying*: The primary meaning is 'lying unused', but there
    may be a further ironic reference to the lying (in the
    sense of 'telling lies') to come.

153 *vendible*: Saleable.

155 *unsuitable*: Unfashionable.

156 *wear not now*: Are not now in fashion.
    Your date: His primary meaning concerns the fruit,
    with *Your* used loosely in the verbal gesture known as
    'ethic dative'; but there is a quibble on the sense 'your
    age', which (he argues) undesirably reveals itself in
    time in a withered *cheek* (157).

162 *Not my virginity, yet . . .*: The fact that this is a half-
    line, followed by what seems to many an abrupt tran-
    sition of thought, has made some editors conclude that
    there is textual corruption at this point. A passage may
    have been omitted, but it is not necessary to suppose
    so. It is usually assumed that by *There* at 163 Helena
    means the court, even though she does not mention the
    court until 174; and that she is meditating anxiously on
    the romantic encounters which the inexperienced
    Bertram is likely to have there. But the transition may
    be less abrupt than this. The discussion of virginity
    has, for Helena, had bearing only on her feeling for
    Bertram and her possible relation to him. She may, in
    this speech, be continuing to pursue this train of
    thought: that is, she is allowing herself to imagine a
    romantic and consummated love between them.
    Certainly this is not explicit. But Helena is character-
    ized by self-communing and elliptical disclosures.
    Interpreted in this way, the *There* of 163 is elliptical
    and secretive: perhaps meaning 'in the surrendering of
    a woman's virginity'.

164–72 *A mother, and a mistress . . . Cupid gossips*: Helena alludes

to the language of contemporary love poetry, which is
characterized by oxymoron.

165 *phoenix*: A unique, immortal, and fabulous bird; hence,
'a wonder'.

170 *disaster*: Unlucky star.

171–2 *fond, adoptious christendoms | That blinking Cupid
gossips*: Foolish loving nicknames given when blind
Cupid is the godfather (*gossips*) at the christening.

180 *Whose baser stars*: Referring to the malevolent aspect
of stars at their birth, which doomed them to a 'base'
or poor life.

192 *under*: In a bad way, in an inferior position.

194–5 *predominant . . . retrograde*: In the ascendant . . . moving
backward (astrological terms).

199 *proposes*: Brings to notice.

200 *composition*: Fusion of personal characteristics (perhaps
with a quibble on the meaning 'truce', 'surrender').

201 *of a good wing*: Swift in flight. This is praise when
applied to a bird, less so when said of a soldier. *wing*
can also mean 'a flap on clothing', hence Helena's
wear that follows in the same sentence, meaning
'fashion'.

205 *naturalize*: Familiarize.

206–7 *capable . . . understand . . . thrust . . . diest*: Parolles is
explicitly and implicitly here reiterating his earlier
advice on virginity (with bawdy quibbles).

209–10 *When thou hast leisure . . . remember thy friends*: The
sense of this undoubtedly cynical utterance is debatable. Parolles seems to be saying that prayers are good
for filling in the gaps of an empty existence, but that
friends should be relied on for practical purposes.

213 *The fated sky*: The sky that directs and destines us, or
that we think of as doing so.

218–19 *The mightiest space . . . kiss like native things*: Even those
immensely far apart in fortune and other such condi-
tioning can come together quite naturally like identical
things, and kiss like creatures closely related.

221 *That weigh their pains in sense*: A difficult passage:
each of the words *weigh*, *their*, *pains* and *sense* carries

at least two different meanings. Either 'who estimate
the pains they are willing to take in terms of what
they may suffer as a result', or 'who consider the
difficulties (of *strange attempts*) with a common-
sensical level-headedness'.

223 *miss*: Fail to achieve.

I.2

0 *Flourish*: Fanfare.

1 *Senoys*: Sienese, people of Siena.
by th'ears: Quarrelling.

3 *braving war*: War of challenges.

5 *cousin*: A courtesy title used by a sovereign when
addressing or mentioning another.

6 *move*: Appeal to, urge.

8 *Prejudicates*: Judges in advance, prejudices.

10 *Approved*: Demonstrated.

11 *armed our answer*: Persuaded me to give a hostile
answer.

15 *stand on either part*: Serve on either side.

16 *nursery*: School, training-ground.

16–17 *sick | For breathing and exploit*: This probably means
'longing for exercise and adventure', but it may mean
'sick for lack of exercise, etc.'.

20 *Frank*: Generous, open, without disguise.
curious: Careful, skilful and precise.

26–7 *He did look far | Into the service of the time*: He had
penetrating insight into the art of war.

27–8 *was | Discipled of the bravest*: This probably means
'had the bravest men as his pupils and followers', but
it may mean 'had been taught by the bravest'.

30 *wore us out of act*: Wore us down into inactivity.
repairs: Refreshes.

34 *Till their own scorn return to them unnoted*: Until at last
people cease to give their derisive remarks any attention at all, except a scornful dismissal.

35 *Ere they can hide their levity in honour*: Sooner than they
can make up for their light ways with noble actions
(such as Bertram's father carried out).

36 *like a courtier*: The late Count of Rossillion was truly

'courteous'; 'gentle' in his ways as well as 'gentle' born. His son's angry concern with his standing and his rights will prove him, as his mother has said, an *unseasoned courtier* (I.1.69).

37-8 *if they were, | His equal had awaked them*: If they (contempt and bitterness) were aroused, it was only by his social equals (and not by those beneath him in rank, as the speech goes on to clarify).

40 *Exception*: Disapproval.

41 *His tongue obeyed his hand*: As the clapper (*tongue*) of a bell rings when directed by the movement of the clock's hand, so were his words directed by his (exact and true) sense of honour.

Who: Those who.

42 *another place*: A different rank (perhaps an understated form of 'an equal or higher rank').

43-5 *And bowed his eminent top . . . he humbled*: An elliptical and paradoxical description of *noblesse oblige* in action. The general sense is that Bertram's father made those socially beneath him proud of the way he humbled himself before them in praising them. A 'which' is understood after *humility* at 44.

50-51 *So in approof lives not his epitaph | As in*: Nothing proves the truth of his epitaph so fully as does.

53 *plausive*: Fit to be applauded, deserving of high praise.

57 *On the catastrophe and heel of pastime*: At the conclusion and end of pleasure.

58 *out*: Over, finished. (There may be a reference back to *heel* at 57, which makes a kind of quibble out of *out*, or there may be a reference forward to the image of the *flame* at 59, already present in Shakespeare's mind.)

59 *snuff*: Burnt-out part of a wick (which if not trimmed off makes the lower part of the wick (*younger spirits*) smoulder).

60 *apprehensive*: Quick to perceive or learn.

61-2 *whose judgements are | Mere fathers of their garments*: Whose severest mental efforts are expended on their clothes.

64 *I, after him, do after him wish too*: I, surviving him,
agree with him in wishing that.

65–7 *Since I nor wax nor honey ... labourers room*: The King
is using the image of the beehive to acknowledge his
own sense of being socially useless: he suggests that, as
an unproductive worker, he could be easily dispensed
with in order to make room for more productive
workers. (Queen bees – or king-bees, as they were
thought of in Shakespeare's time – are of course not
workers.)

68 *They that least lend it you shall lack you first*: Those who
love you least will be first to feel the loss of you.

73–4 *The rest have worn me out | With several applications*:
That is, each doctor has his own idea of the proper
treatment for the King, who has had to endure them
all.

1.3

3–7 *Madam, the care ... we publish them*: These highly
rhetorical lines express the Steward's wish that his
concern for her should be self-evident from his actions,
since if he were to recall his good record to the Countess
himself he would damage his standing. He is, of course,
implicitly making such reference to his own virtue
through this speech.

3–4 *even your content*: Act to your full satisfaction, come up
to your expectations.

4 *calendar*: Record.

9 *sirrah*: Form of address used to inferiors.

18 *go to the world*: Get married.

19 *do as we may*: Get on as well as we can (probably with
a bawdy quibble on *do*).

23 *In Isbel's case*: The Clown begins to quibble on *case* as
sexual organ.

23–4 *Service is no heritage*: This was a proverb, meaning that
a servant's life does not give a man much to leave his
children; balanced by the Clown's second wise proverb,
that *barnes are blessings* (25–6) or 'Children are poor
men's riches'. There may be a bawdy undertone to
Service, which could have a sexual meaning.

29–30 *he must needs go that the devil drives*: Another proverb.

32–3 *holy reasons, such as they are*: The words *holy reasons* form a double bawdy quibble, with *holy* punning on 'hole' and *reasons* punning on 'raising' in the sense of tumescence. The Clown is also gravely alluding to the fact that procreation is recommended in the marriage service.

36–7 *I do marry that I may repent*: Alluding to another proverb, 'Marry in haste and repent at leisure.'

40 *for my wife's sake*: On account of my wife.

42 *Y'are shallow*: You take a superficial view.
madam; e'en: Some modern editors retain F's *Madam in*. This may be correct, though the phrase *shallow . . . in* is unusual and elliptical. But F (or Shakespeare) so frequently spells 'e'en' as 'in' that it seems likely that it has done so here, and 'e'en' is the true reading. The Clown is answering the Countess by doggedly laying stress on his own definition of friendship.

44–9 *He that ears my land spares my team . . . he that kisses my wife is my friend*: The Clown's ironical argument is probably traditional. Something like it is found in Shakespeare's Sonnet 42, 'That thou hast her, it is not all my grief.'

44 *ears*: Ploughs.

45 *in*: Bring in, harvest.
cuckold: Deceived husband.

50 *what they are*: That is, cuckolds.

51–4 *for young Charbon the puritan . . . they may jowl horns together like any deer i'th'herd*: There is a meeting-ground for all men, however divided superficially, on the common ground of their being cuckolds (who traditionally wear horns on their heads to show their humiliation); young and old, puritan and papist (eaters of flesh – or '*chair bonne*' – and eaters of fish – or '*poisson*' are all alike in this.

54 *jowl*: Dash, knock.

57–8 *the next way*: The nearest way, directly. He is probably suggesting that, like the prophets, he is directly and divinely inspired.

62 *by kind*: According to nature, by a natural instinct.

63 *anon*: Soon.

68–77 *Was this fair face the cause, quoth she . . . There's yet one good in ten*: This song or fragment of song is hardly among the best in Shakespeare's plays. It is in fact less like the beautiful lyrics usually found in the comedies than the harsh scraps of ballad quoted in *King Lear* by the Fool for the light they throw on the situation. The song is presumably prompted by the Countess's mention of *Helen* at 67, since Helen of Troy is the owner of the *fair face* in the song's first line. Helen's Trojan lover, Paris, the son of Priam, may be *King Priam's joy* at 71, and the subject of *quoth she* in the first line is probably Hecuba, mother of Paris and wife of Priam.

No music seems to have survived for the song, if indeed there is a song behind Lavatch's rhyme. He seems throughout the play to be reciting rather than singing his ballads.

70 *fond*: Foolishly.

74 *sentence*: Maxim, wise saying.

78 *corrupt the song*: Make the song worse than it was. The original song must have said something like, 'If one be bad among nine good, | There's yet one bad in ten.' The Clown answers the Countess by saying that the song referred to men and he is referring to women; and to find *One good woman in ten* is, if anything, an over-generous estimate.

82 *tithe-woman*: Tenth-woman. The tithe was the tenth-part of the parish produce sent to the parson as his due.

83 *quoth 'a*: Says he.
   An: If.

84 *but one*: F has *but ore*. Mistakes involving the letter 'r' are several times found in this text; and the Clown is likely to be repeating his rhetorically important word *one* to create a ludicrous yet vivid image of the rarity of female decency.

86 *pluck*: Draw (as from a pack of cards).

89–90 *That man should be . . . no hurt done*: It is usually assumed that there is a bawdy undertone to this remark, and that the *hurt* in question implies a sexual encounter.

90–92 *Though honesty be no puritan . . . a big heart*: The Clown may here be making a pregnant general utterance; or referring obliquely to Helena (in which case *honesty* means 'chastity'); or saying (perhaps with irony) of his own frank nature that though it has no great pretensions to virtue, yet it does no real harm – he controls his proud nature and keeps the laws. The allusion is to certain Puritan clergymen who obeyed the law by wearing the surplice, but placed it over the black Geneva gown.

97–101 *Her father bequeathed her to me . . . demand*: The image is of Helena as a sum of money, to which interest (*advantage*) accrues. In the next sentence she is imagined as simultaneously this capital sum and a claimant to money herself: even without addition of the interest accrued (her positive qualities) she has the right to claim more (love and duty) than is actually being spent on her, and that more will be spent regardless of her modest demands. The Countess's last point – that she will indeed be paid more than she lays claim to – is also both ironic (in that she is about to lay claim to so much) and prophetic (since, in renouncing her demand, she is finally paid more than she asks in love and duty).

98 *without other advantage*: Even without having accrued any interest.

102 *late*: Lately.

105–6 *touched not any stranger sense*: Reached no one's ears but her own.

107–8 *Fortune, she said, was no goddess . . . two estates*: The difference between people's station and place in life, or *estates*, is an accidental thing, not a matter of essential importance, and not therefore a question for divinities; so Fortune or Chance is no goddess.

109 *only*: Except.

109–10 *where qualities were level*: Where two people were of the same rank.

111 *knight*: Any chaste devotee of Diana, of either sex.

113 *touch*: Pang.

115 *withal*: With.

    sithence: Since.

120–21 *Stall this*: Keep this close.

122 *Enter Helena*: Helena enters some time before the Countess actually addresses her. In performance this makes a strong visual effect which brings out the affinities and also the separateness of the two women.

124 *these*: These troubles, these difficulties.

126 *Our blood to us, this to our blood is born*: This plays on the multiple meanings of *blood* as physical substance and metaphor for both social degree and passion, 'as our blood is a natural part of our body from birth, so suffering is also part of our natural inheritance'; 'as we are born into a particular social rank, so we are also born into suffering'; and 'as we are born with passionate desires, so suffering is a natural part of passionate desire'.

128 *impressed*: As wax by a seal.

130 *or then we thought them none*: Or rather things that then we did not call faults.

140–41 *and choice breeds | A native slip to us from foreign seeds*: We choose a cutting that has grown from seeds foreign to us, graft it on and let it grow, and it becomes native to us.

146 *distempered*: Disturbed, inclement.

147 *The many-coloured Iris*: Iris was goddess of the rainbow; Helena's tears are iridescent.

148 *That I am not*: When the Countess speaks of *daughters* and *mothers* Helena thinks of daughters-in-law and mothers-in-law, which gives ambiguity to the whole dialogue that follows.

152 *No note upon my parents*: No fame attaches to my family.

157 *So that*: Provided that.

158 *both our mothers*: The mother of both of us.

159 *I care no more for than I do for heaven*: A dense and difficult close to a speech uttered in a state of confused desperation. Helena is trying to say both 'I wouldn't mind (*care for*) that at all' and 'In fact I should like (*care*

for) that as much as I should like heaven' and produces
a statement that compresses the two together.

160 *Can't no other*: Can it not be otherwise.

163 *shield*: Forbid.

163–4 *'Daughter' and 'mother'* | *So strive upon your pulse*: You
seem to be so upset and nervous when a daughter or
mother is mentioned. The Countess may be playing on
the word *mother*, which could mean 'hysteria, nervous
condition'.

165 *fondness*: The word can mean both 'foolishness' and
'love'.

167 *head*: Source (of a stream or river).
      gross: Obvious, palpable.

168–9 *Invention is ashamed* | *Against*: Your capacity for making
up excuses is ashamed, in the face of.

174 *in their kind*: In their own way, after their own fashion.

176 *suspected*: Brought under suspicion, made doubtful.

177 *you have wound a goodly clew*: This is proverbial. A *clew*
is a ball of thread. Cf. the well-known couplet from
Scott's *Marmion*:

> Oh what a tangled web we weave,
> When first we practise to deceive!

183 *Go not about*: Don't be evasive.

186 *appeached*: Informed against you.

190 *friends*: Relatives, 'people'.

192–3 *I follow him not* | *By any token of presumptuous suit*:
This sounds like a general statement of intention, 'I
shall not pursue him with signs of a presumptuous
love', but Helena may be merely saying, as G. K.
Hunter suggests in his edition, that she has not commu-
nicated with Bertram since he left Rossillion.

197 *this captious and intenable sieve*: The sieve is described
by F as *intemible*, which is emended or modernized by
most modern editors into either 'intenible' or
'inteemable'. The word may be one difficult to do literal
justice to, since the Elizabethans often had the same
spelling for words of slightly different meaning. For it

seems possible that this word is a dense pun that works
on exactly the same ground as *captious*. *captious* is really
a Shakespearian conflation of 'captious' (meaning
'deceiving', 'sophistical', 'erroneous in argument') with
'capacious' (meaning 'roomy', 'all-consuming') so as
to produce a third term meaning 'deceitfully and decep-
tively all-embracing', 'leading to large errors', 'seeming
roomier than it is' and so on. *intenable* is a similarly
compound pun. It means 'intenable' in both its literal
and metaphorical senses: the thing can't 'be held', it is
hard to hold on to, and also it is intellectually impossible, an error. *intenable* also means 'intenible': it won't
hold water, it loses whatever is put into it. Helena is in
fact condensing into two extraordinarily dense and
witty words what Orsino takes nearly five lines to say
in *Twelfth Night* (I.1.10–14):

> . . . notwithstanding thy capacity
> Receiveth as the sea, naught enters there,
> Of what validity and pitch soe'er,
> But falls into abatement and low price
> Even in a minute.

sieve: The sieve, used here as an emblem of hopeless
love, is more frequently found as an emblem of chastity;
it is so used in the portrait of Queen Elizabeth I now
in Siena (reproduced in Roy Strong's *Portraits of Queen
Elizabeth I* (1963) as Plate X).

199 *lack not to lose still*: A dense phrase, expressive of a rich
desperation. Helena never ceases to lose her love, and
never ceases to have more love to lose.

Indian-like: She is probably thinking of the American
Indians.

203 *encounter with*: Have a hostile encounter with.

205 *cites*: Is evidence of.

207–8 *Wish chastely . . . both herself and love*: *Wish chastely*
and *love dearly* are near-paradoxes, leading to the final
true paradox of the fusion of Diana, the goddess of
chastity, with Venus, the goddess of love. *Wish* has the

sense of 'desire', and *dearly* carries, as often, the subordinate sense of 'painfully, grievously'.

211 *that*: That which, what.

212 *riddle-like lives sweetly where she dies*: Helena sees herself, perhaps, as a 'wonder' of love, confounding reason, like the Phoenix in Shakespeare's own 'The Phoenix and the Turtle'.

218 *manifest experience*: Expertise that is well known, plain to all.

219 *For general sovereignty*: As panaceas, universal cures.

220 *In heedfullest reservation to bestow them*: To put them away and keep them extremely carefully (for an emergency).

221–2 *As notes whose faculties . . . they were in note*: As prescriptions more powerful than they were generally reported to be.

223 *approved*: Tested, tried out.

225 *rendered lost*: Said to be dying.

229 *conversation of my thoughts*: Active process of my thinking.

236–7 *Embowelled of their doctrine . . . itself*: Emptied of all their scientific knowledge, have abandoned the deadly threat as incurable and left it to itself.

239 *receipt*: Prescription, cure.

242 *try success*: Test the outcome.

242–3 *I'd venture | The well-lost life of mine*: I would willingly risk losing my life, and think it worth it.

245 *knowingly*: Not just believe, but know.

II.1

1–2 *lords . . . lords*: Many editors emend these words to the singular. It is likely, however, that the young men are in two groups, according to which side they are to support in the war.

6 *After well-entered soldiers*: After becoming experienced soldiers (a Latin construction).

9 *he owes*: It owns.

12 *higher Italy*: The curious word *higher* is probably simply geographical in connotation and signifies 'northerly'; the King is referring to Tuscany.

13–14 *Those bated that inherit but the fall | Of the last monarchy*:

A difficult passage. *bated* probably means 'excepted'; but it may mean 'abated', that is weakened, fallen off, decadent. *the last monarchy* may refer to the Holy Roman Empire or the house of the Medici.

16 *questant*: Seeker.

21–2 *Beware of being captives | Before you serve*: *captives* and *serve* are both quibbles: each word has an amatory and a military sense.

23 *To some Attendants*: F has no stage direction here. But the *Come* at 23 must have some force; and it must be addressed to another, or others, than Bertram, Parolles and the two Lords, who cannot simply ignore the King. He must be terminating this passage, and moving somewhat apart to address others, continuing that conversation up stage throughout what follows; and then turns down stage again as Lafew enters to him.

25 *spark*: Smart or foppish young man. Parolles plays on the word at 41.

27 *commanded here*: Ordered to stay here.
   kept a coil: Fussed, pestered.

29 *An*: If.

30 *the forehorse to a smock*: The leader in a team of horses driven by a woman.

31 *Creaking my shoes on the plain masonry*: Squeaking my shoes on the smooth floor.

36–7 *our parting is a tortured body*: Separating myself from you is as painful as being torn apart is to a man being tortured. Shakespeare's depiction of 'court life' takes the form of some remarkably mannered speech on the part of the young men, of which this of Bertram's is one of the most striking examples.

41 *metals*: Meaning both 'swords' or 'swordsmen', and 'mettles' or 'brave hearts'.

43 *Spurio*: His name is the Italian word for 'false, counterfeit, spurious'.
   cicatrice: Scar.

44 *sinister*: Left.

47 *Mars dote on you for his novices*: May the god of war look after you tenderly, as his pupils.

49   *Stay: the King*: F, followed by some modern editors,
      has the phrase *Stay the King*, and those who retain this
      punctuation interpret as 'Support the King'. Bertram's
      phrase is punctuated here as in the second Folio, and
      is interpreted as an advertisement that the King is
      approaching; though it could mean 'Stay, for reasons
      depending on the King'.

51   *list*: The selvage of cloth; hence, 'limit', 'boundary'.

53   *wear themselves in the cap of the time*: Are prominent
      and to be taken note of. Shakespeare uses the metaphor
      of the cap to emphasize high visibility and social success
      elsewhere; see, for example, *Hamlet*: 'On Fortune's cap
      we are not the very button' (II.2.228); 'A very riband
      in the cap of youth' (IV.7.76).

53-4 *muster true gait*: Display the true art of dignified move-
      ment.

55   *received*: Fashionable.

56   *measure*: Dance.

57   *dilated*: Extended, more lengthy.

62   *sue*: F reads *see*, which is possibly correct, but makes a
      clumsy and unidiomatic phrase when followed by an
      infinitive. Most modern editors emend to 'fee'. But *sue*
      has a good deal more point (and could easily have been
      misprinted as 'see' by attraction to *thee* following).
      Lafew 'sues for pardon': the King, with a ludicrous and
      ironical courtesy, 'sues him to get up'. A closely similar
      exchange occurs in *Richard II* (V.3.128-9); to King
      Henry's 'Good aunt, stand up' the Duchess of York
      replies: 'I do not sue to stand. | Pardon is all the suit
      I have in hand.'

66   *pate*: Head.

67   *across*: Lafew's word is from the language of tilting,
      which perhaps sharpens the sense of the elderliness of
      the combatants engaged in this slow-motion verbal
      passage of arms. A blow *across* is a bad hit, almost a
      miss: the man is trying the easy blow of a sidewise
      swipe across the body instead of the point head-on
      through the body.

69-70 *O, will you eat | No grapes, my royal fox*: The allu-

sion is to Aesop's fable of the fox who, being unable
to reach some grapes, declared them sour. Lafew
misunderstands the King's dry *No* at 69, which meant
'No, I shall not be cured', as 'No, I do not want to
be cured'; and then suggests that the King, like the
fox, does not want to be cured because he thinks it
impossible.

71 *My noble grapes, and if my royal fox*: A play on words:
both *noble* and *royal* are the names of coins. The first
two words of the line carry the main stress.

74 *Quicken*: Give life to.
canary: A lively Spanish dance.

75–8 *whose simple touch* | *Is powerful . . . And write to her a*
love-line: There is probably a sexual allusiveness in these
lines, less a matter of mere bawdy quibbles than a
conjuring up of the beauty, vitality and potency which
Helena is seen to carry with her.

75 *simple*: Mere (but the word is also probably suggested
by its relationship to *medicine* at 72: 'simples' are medic-
inal herbs).

76 *Pippen*: Pepin, the eighth-century King of France.

77 *in's*: In his.

82 *this my light deliverance*: These my jesting words.
He is presumably referring to his slightly improper
remarks at 75–8 on the nature of Helena's medical
capacity.

83 *profession*: Claim to have skilled knowledge.

84–5 *more* | *Than I dare blame my weakness*: In a way that I
cannot merely ascribe to my partiality for her, or my
elderly weakness of mind.

88 *admiration*: Wonder.

89 *take off*: Reduce.

90 *tookest it*: Came to conceive it (as wonderful).
fit: Satisfy.

91 *He goes to the door*: F does not have an exit here for
Lafew, nor an entry for him at 93, where Helena there
enters alone; so presumably Lafew meets her at the
stage-door and leads her in.

97 *Cressid's uncle*: Pandarus, who acted as go-between for

Cressida and Troilus, and became the prototypical pander.

102 *In what he did profess, well found*: Found to be skilled at what he professed, medicine.

106–7 *as the dearest issue . . . th'only darling*: The one and only beloved pet child of years of hard work and long experience.

108 *triple*: Third.

110–11 *touched | With that malignant cause*: Suffering from that deadly disease.

111–12 *wherein the honour . . . stands chief in power*: With which my beloved father's honoured gift has most power to deal.

113 *tender*: Offer.
appliance: The word covers both the doctor's services and the means of treatment he offers.

117 *The congregated college*: This is probably a reference to the assembled College of Physicians.

118 *labouring art*: The endeavours of human art and skill.

120 *stain*: Taint.
corrupt our hope: By basing it on an irrational foundation.

122 *empirics*: Quacks (accented on the first syllable).

122–4 *to dissever so . . . when help past sense we deem*: To act in a way so unlike what my reputation would lead men to expect of me, as to put trust in a cure too improbable to be believed, when it is impossible to have rational belief in a cure at all.

125 *My duty*: The respect I owe to and feel for you.

128 *A modest one*: A moderate thought. She is asking the King not to be angry with her, not to laugh at her and not to think her immodest.

135 *set up your rest*: Stake your all (a gambling term).

136–7 *He that of greatest works . . . weakest minister*: An echo of such texts as 1 Corinthians 1:27: 'God hath chosen the weak things of the world, to confound things which are mighty.'

138–9 *So holy writ in babes hath judgement shown, | When judges have been babes*: The best-known of the scriptural infant judges is Daniel, who gave Susanna justice against the Elders.

139–40 *great floods have flown* | *From simple sources*: There is possibly an allusion here to the miracle of Moses's striking water from the rock, Exodus 17.

140–41 *great seas have dried . . . been denied*: The sea in question is probably the Red Sea, dried to permit the passage of the Israelites from Egypt; the *greatest* may refer to Pharaoh, or the whole line may have a more general and unspecific reference.

144 *fits*: F has *shifts*. The lack of end-rhyme is strange; and if *fits* was written 'ffitts' (as it could have been) the confusibility of 'f' with the old long-tailed 's' (ʃ) would explain the mistake.

147 *thanks*: That is, nothing but thanks; Helena's *pains* and *Proffers*, not being taken up and put into creative use, can earn her nothing but a polite gratitude.

148 *Inspirèd merit*: Grace given by the spirit (breath) of God. *breath*: Human breath (that is, human speech).

150 *square our guess by shows*: Base our conjectures on appearances.

155–8 *I am not an impostor, that proclaim . . . nor you past cure*: I am not a charlatan, proclaiming my marksmanship before I take aim – I know exactly what I think – that my skill has the power of curing you.

160–68 *The greatest grace lending grace . . . Health shall live free and sickness freely die*: The somewhat stiff couplets of the later exchanges between the King and Helena develop at this point into an old-fashioned fustian, which helps to express Helena's incantatory intensity.

162 *diurnal ring*: Daily round, daily circuit.

164 *Hesperus*: The evening star.

165 *glass*: Hour-glass.

170–74 *Tax of impudence . . . let my life be ended*: Helena's verbal style becomes strained and dense in this speech; and the oracular nature of her utterance makes it hard to be certain what Shakespeare's exact intentions were at this textually difficult point. The present text departs from the punctuation of most modern editions at 171,

172 and 173, following two suggestions by eighteenth-century editors, as this seems to make Helena's statements at least a little clearer.

170 *Tax*: Accusation.

172 *Traduced*: Slandered.

173 *Seared*: Branded, blighted.

ne worse of worst: An almost impossible phrase. If textually correct, it is a deliberate archaism, with *ne* meaning 'nor'; the sense of the whole phrase would be 'nor would this, a death racked by savage torture, be *worse* than those other *worst* things, shame and slander'.

extended: Stretched out (as on a rack).

174 *vildest*: Most savage.

178 *sense saves*: Makes sense.

179 *rate*: Reckon, consider.

180 *estimate*: Value.

182 *prime*: Springtime (a metaphor for 'youth').

185 *physic*: Medicine.

187 *flinch in property*: Fall short in any respect.

189 *Not helping*: If I do not help.

191 *make it even*: Meet it fully.

192 *heaven*: F has *helpe*. The break in the rhyme would be obtrusive, prepared for as it is by *even*; and it is hard to see any reason for such a break. Hence the traditional emendation.

198 *branch or image*: G. K. Hunter in his edition suggests that the figure is that of a genealogical tree, with portraits or *images* of the persons involved.

204 *still*: Always.

II.2

1–2 *put you to the height of*: Make you show all.

3 *highly fed and lowly taught*: Alluding to the proverb 'Better fed than taught', descriptive – roughly – of a rich person's spoiled child.

6 *put off*: Dismiss, brush aside.

9 *put it off*: Palm it off (or perhaps 'sell it').

10 *make a leg*: Make obeisance (by bending one leg and drawing back the other).

16 *like a barber's chair*: Proverbial.

17 *quatch-buttock*: The word *quatch* does not seem to occur elsewhere but clearly means something like 'squat', 'fat'.

20 *ten groats*: The usual fee for an attorney at this time.

21 *French crown*: A play on words that is an all too frequent joke of the time: a *crown* is a coin, a *French crown* is the balding of the head caused by syphilis, called the 'French disease'.

 taffety punk: Finely dressed prostitute.

22 *rush*: Ring made of rush, once exchanged in mock-marriages. Obvious sexual double meanings underlie the pairings of ring and forefinger, nail and hole, pudding and skin.

23 *morris*: Country dance.

24 *quean*: Loose woman.

26 *pudding*: Sausage.

33 *But a trifle neither*: Nothing but a trifle.

40 *O Lord, sir*: A smart and silly catchphrase of the time. It is hard to know exactly how funny the passage that follows is meant to be, and whether the Countess speaks ironically or seriously at 55–6.

43 *Thick*: Quickly.

46 *put me to't*: Force or challenge me to do it.

50–51 *is very sequent to*: Follows (or 'would follow') very closely after.

51 *answer*: The Countess is quibbling in a somewhat menacing way: her answer means both 'reply to' and 'be suited to', just as her *bound to't* at 52 means both 'bound on oath to answer' and 'bound to a whipping-post'.

59 *present*: Immediate.

65 *fruitfully*: The Clown picks up the Countess's *understand*, makes it bawdy, and tosses back a bawdy answer. The reference to 'standing' then suggests *legs*: the Clown means 'I am in Paris already' and also perhaps 'I understand you quicker than my legs can move'.

66 *again*: Back again.

II.3

0 *Enter Bertram, Lafew, and Parolles*: The relationship between these three persons in the exchanges that follow

is a slightly curious one. The fact that Bertram utters
only one remark (and that a meek one) and that Parolles
– perhaps uncharacteristically – gains the upper hand
in fooling with Lafew has worried some editors into
proposing textual changes that eliminate these aspects
of the action. But the characters in this play do have
odd angles: the youth Bertram has his meekness and
the fool Parolles has his moments of strength.

2 *modern*: Everyday, commonplace.

3 *causeless*: Outside the ordinary course of nature.

4–6 *ensconcing ourselves . . . unknown fear*: Sheltering within
the illusion of knowledge when we should give
ourselves up to what we most fear, the unknown.

7 *argument*: Topic of conversation.

8 *shot out*: Suddenly appeared (like a comet).

10 *relinquished of the artists*: Abandoned by the profes-
sionals.

11 *both of Galen and Paracelsus*: That is, both 'parties' of
medical opinion, the former representing the Ancients,
the latter, the Moderns. Galen and Paracelsus were two
famous physicians, the first a Greek of the second
century AD, the second a Swiss of the sixteenth century.

12 *authentic fellows*: Authorized, qualified practitioners.
(This is, perhaps, like the mention of the *congregated
college*, a reference to the Fellows of the Royal College
of Physicians.)

21 *in showing*: Before your eyes, in print, in a picture.

23 *A showing of a heavenly effect in an earthly actor*: Most
modern editors regard this as the title of a broadsheet
ballad, referred to in the *what-do-ye-call there* of
Parolles and read aloud by Lafew. This may well
be correct; but it is as possible that the point lies in
Lafew's misunderstanding, or only half-hearing or half-
listening to, what Parolles means by *showing*, and
himself using the word gravely to mean 'showing-
forth', 'manifestation'.

25 *dolphin*: A symbol of love and lust.
   Fore me: An exclamation like 'upon my soul', 'upon my
   word'. Though spoken with the greatest seriousness,

the context of what goes before it and what follows it
on Lafew's lips makes it highly comical.

27–8 *the brief and the tedious of it*: A mannered way of
saying 'the long and the short of it'.

28 *facinerious*: Wicked, villainous.

33 *debile*: Weak.

40 *Lustique*: Sportive, frolicsome, lusty.
Dutchman: German.

41 *a tooth in my head*: A taste for the pleasures of the
senses (cf. 'a sweet tooth').

42 *coranto*: A lively dance.

43 *Mor du vinager*: A meaningless pseudo-French oath.
The words sound like 'death of vinegar' and may have,
like many oaths, some vague and blasphemous reference to the Crucifixion.

44 *Fore God, I think so*: Lafew cannot be, like Parolles,
surprised, since it was he who introduced Helena to
the King. He may be speaking in a proud understatement, or he may be watching the King and musing
happily on his recovery.

48 *repealed*: Called back from exile or banishment.

50 *Enter four Lords*: F's reading *Enter 3 or 4 Lords* is the
kind of tentative or permissive stage direction that
probably derives from the author's manuscript copy:
he had not yet decided – though he very soon did so
– how many Lords were to speak. A copy prepared in
the theatre would have had exact specifications.

51 *parcel*: Small group.

52 *at my bestowing*: The King had the right to marry his
wards to whom he pleased, provided he did not make
them marry a commoner. It seems unclear whether
Shakespeare wishes this latter condition to provide
Bertram with grounds for recalcitrance; but he makes
his King speak with an almost tyrannical rage at 148–65.

54 *frank election*: Free choice.

58 *bay curtal and his furniture*: My bay horse with the
docked tail, and his trappings.

59 *broken*: Lafew is wishing he were still young: he may
be speaking literally, and wishing he had all his teeth,

or metaphorically, and wishing he had not yet been 'broken to the bit', like a young horse.

60 *writ*: Claimed to have, laid claim to.

61 *Helena addresses the Lords*: F reads here *She addresses her to a Lord*, which may mean 'she moves over and stands in front of a Lord'. This is hard to make sense of, followed as it is by the plural *Gentlemen*, and it is often dropped by editors. It may be a simple survival from the author's manuscript copy, giving evidence of an uncancelled change of plan. Or the phrase may be a mere note (rather than an actual stage direction) left by Shakespeare in his manuscript at a pause in composition, to remind himself how he should proceed when he returned to it.

69 *choose, but, be refused*: F punctuates *choose, but be refused;* and this may be only a matter of 'rhetorical' punctuation, which tends to punctuate heavily after words which should be stressed or require a pause after them.

77 *ames-ace*: Two aces, the lowest throw at dice. If Lafew were dicing with his life at stake, this throw would certainly lose it, unless his opponent threw the same. He must therefore be speaking with an ironical understatement, since what he means is that he would give a very great deal to be *in this choice*.

79 *honour*: Some scholars gloss *honour* here as 'admiration' (that is, willingness to accept Helena's offer of marriage); the term *threateningly* at 80, however, would seem to make it more likely that *honour* here, as so frequently in this play and elsewhere, means 'noble birth' and that Helena sees rejection written in this lord's expression.

83 *No better, if you please*: I wish for nothing better than your humble love.

85 *Do they all deny her*: It has usually been assumed that the four young Lords' professions are sincere, and that Lafew's comment is a misunderstanding of what happens, due to his somewhat removed position on the stage. But Joseph Price (in *The Unfortunate Comedy,*

1984) convincingly argued that Lafew, who is usually a trustworthy choric commentator, is so here: the Lords' words are no more than a frigid formality, performed in obedience to the King.

98–9 *There's one grape yet. I am sure thy father drunk wine*: There's one product of a good stock left still. I am sure your father had good red blood in his veins.

100 *known*: Probably means 'found you out'.

110 *sickly bed*: Sick bed.

113 *breeding*: Upbringing.

114–15 *Disdain | Rather corrupt me ever*: Sooner (than be ruined by marriage to her) let my disdain of her ruin me (or my fortunes) for ever.

116 *title*: That is, lack of title.

117–20 *Strange is it that our bloods . . . In differences so mighty*: It is strange that different men's blood would be quite indistinguishable in respect of colour, weight and heat, if it were all poured together, and yet such great distinctions are based on the concept of 'blood'.

126 *great additions swell's*: Great titles inflate us.

127 *dropsied*: Swollen, inflated (the dropsy was a sickness characterized by water retention).

127–8 *Good alone | Is good, without a name*: Goodness is goodness because of its own essential nature, no matter what we call it. (F has *Good a lone, | Is good without a name?* The punctuation here is rhetorical – the comma and the question mark indicate emphasis given to the words they succeed, rather than a syntactical point.)

129–30 *The property by what it is should go, | Not by the title*: The particular quality that gives a thing its essential nature should decide how we think of it, and not the mere name it happens to carry.

131 *immediate heir*: One who inherits directly from another (and not circuitously, as honour for instance is inherited from nature through ancestors).

132–4 *that is honour's scorn . . . like the sire*: The truly honourable feel only contempt for one who claims to be honourable by birth and yet does not act with the honour of his forefathers.

137–40 *grave . . . indeed*: F has a colon after *grave*, a full stop
        after *tomb* at 139 and only a comma after *indeed* at 140.
        Since this makes sense – though a simpler one – of the
        passage, it may be that the printer was puzzled by the
        complexity of the syntax here.

   142 *she*: That is, all the good qualities of Helena that cannot
        be included in the strictly moral *Virtue*.

   148 *at the stake*: When he uses this phrase, Shakespeare
        usually seems to be fusing the term 'at the stake' from
        bear-baiting, in which the animal was tied to a stake
        and harried by dogs, with the term 'at stake' from the
        language of gaming, meaning 'at hazard'.
        which to defeat: And to overcome this threatened danger.

   151 *misprision*: The word here means both 'contempt' and
        'error', and may have an underlying quibbling allusion
        to the idea of 'false imprisonment'.

152–4 *that canst not dream . . . to the beam*: Who cannot grasp
        that when once the weight of my balanced judgement is
        added to her case, making up for whatever deficiencies
        are in it, your light objections fly up and away in a moment.

   157 *travails*: Labours.

   158 *presently*: Immediately.

   159 *obedient right*: Right of obedience.

   162 *staggers*: Literally, a horse-disease. Here, 'giddy behav-
        iour', or possibly 'sick confusion'.
        lapse: Fall.

   165 *Without all terms of pity*: Without pity in any form.

   167 *fancy*: Love, amorous inclinations. (He will 'see with
        the King's eyes'.)

   168 *dole*: Share, portion.

174–5 *if not to thy estate, | A balance more replete*: The King
        means here either that he will give a counterpoise which,
        if it will not be the size of Bertram's estate, at least will
        make Helena's and Bertram's estates more equal; or,
        just possibly, that he will give something at least the
        size of Bertram's estate and perhaps rather better.

177–8 *whose ceremony | Shall seem expedient on the now-born
        brief*: A much-discussed passage, whose uncertainty
        arises from the unclear meanings of *expedient* and *brief*.

The probable sense is 'and the ceremony shall follow swiftly, as is right and proper, on the slightly abridged contract we have just taken part in'.

180–81 *Shall more attend upon the coming space,* | *Expecting absent friends*: Can wait until a little time has passed, and friends now absent have joined us.

182 *religious*: Devoted.

Exeunt all but Parolles and Lafew, who stay behind, commenting on this wedding: The stage direction is closely based on that in F; it can hardly be said to afford actors any real direction, since the nature of the colloquy is immediately apparent. Like the F stage directions at 50 and 61 above, this helps to indicate a textual source in manuscript copy rather than in a copy prepared in the theatre; and, like *She addresses her to a Lord*, may represent an author's self-directed remark.

190 *bloody succeeding*: Bloodshed in consequence.

192–3 PAROLLES *To any Count, to all Counts, to what is man.* LAFEW *To what is Count's man*: Parolles is using *man* in the sense 'manly' or even 'human'; Lafew uses *man* in the sense 'servant'.

197 *write man*: Call myself a man, claim manhood.

199 *What I dare too well do, I dare not do*: What I have only too much physical courage for, I am prevented from by moral and social restraints.

200 *ordinaries*: Meal-times.

201–2 *make tolerable vent of thy travel*: Tell passable traveller's tales.

202 *scarfs*: It was the fashion for military men to wear scarfs as an adornment of their person.

204 *burden*: Capacity.

204–5 *I have now found thee; when I lose thee again I care not*: *found* has the sense 'found out'; *lose* perhaps has the sense 'forget', as well as the obvious one.

206 *taking up*: As well as the literal sense of 'picking up' – as one picks up a dropped thing – *taking up* here carries several hostile meanings: 'arresting', 'opposing', 'rebuking' and perhaps also 'levying as a soldier, as cannon-fodder'.

208 *antiquity*: Old age.

212 *window of lattice*: Parolles is easy to see through; his
     drapery of scarfs is like lattice-work; and he is as
     commonplace as an alehouse sign, which was a red
     lattice-window.

219–20 *I will not bate thee a scruple*: I will not reduce the indig-
     nity by the minutest particle.

222–3 *thou hast to pull at a smack o'th'contrary*: You have to
     drink down a quite different mouthful (that is, he will
     have to become aware of his own lack of wisdom).

224–5 *proud of thy bondage*: Lafew means that, as Parolles is
     proud of his scarves, so, when they become the objects
     that bind him, he will by implication become proud of
     that bondage.

226–7 *in the default*: When you default.

231 *doing*: Lafew is perhaps joking on the bawdy sense of
     this word.

231–2 *as I will by thee*: As I will pass by you (a neat and rapid
     exit-line belying Lafew's *antiquity*).

238 *I would have of —*: The *mot juste* is always escaping this
     'man of words'.
     an if: If.

247–9 *Why dost thou garter up thy arms o'this fashion? Dost
     make hose of thy sleeves*: Lafew is mocking Parolles's
     scarves again, comparing the way he has them tied
     around his arms to the way garters would be strapped
     around hose.

253–4 *breathe themselves upon*: Take exercise on.

257–9 *for picking a kernel out of a pomegranate*: Even for this
     ludicrous, and ludicrously small, crime.

258–9 *You are a vagabond and no true traveller*: Elizabethan
     travellers were required to carry a species of passport,
     otherwise were mere 'vagabonds'.

260–61 *than the commission of your birth and virtue gives you
     heraldry*: Than is warranted by your birth and virtue –
     in neither of which are you a gentleman.

278 *kicky-wicky*: The word, which does not occur else-
     where, obviously means 'girlfriend', and is probably
     bawdy.

280 *curvet*: A horse's leap in which all four legs are momentarily extended and off the ground (accented on the second syllable).

282 *jades*: Broken-backed nags.

290 *To*: Compared to.
the *dark house*: Perhaps 'the dismal house'; perhaps specifically 'the madhouse', since madmen were at this time confined in darkness.

291 *capriccio*: Caprice. The word probably indicates Italianate affectation on Parolles's part.

295 *these balls bound, there's noise in it*: Now you're talking.

297 *bravely*: Besides the modern meaning of 'courageously', the term can also mean 'gaily, splendidly' or 'worthily'. There is obvious irony in this play on words, underlining the degree to which Bertram's supposed bravery in going to war is in fact a cowardly running away from his responsibilities.

II.4

2 *She is not well*: The Clown picks up Helena's use of *well* in its simple sense of 'in health' and introduces play on its Elizabethan sense by which the dead were said to be *well*, in the sense of well rid of their bodies and well off in being in heaven.

16–17 *You had my prayers to lead them on, and to keep them on have them still*: The first two uses of *them* here refer to Helena's *good fortune*, as though it were a plural word, possibly by attraction to *prayers*.

20 *did as you say*: Editors note the possibility of a pun on *did*/'died', but there is no real evidence that they were ever so close in pronunciation. Susan Snyder, in the Oxford edition of the play, suggests that *did* is instead picking up on Parolles's *my old lady*, so that the Clown is expressing the wish that the Countess were both old and belonging to Parolles, so long as Parolles owned her wrinkles and the Clown her money.

22–3 *you are the wiser man . . . his master's undoing*: The Clown, like Parolles and Lafew in the previous scene, quibbles on the double sense of *man*, meaning both 'human being' and 'servant'.

25 *title*: Claim to possessions or other allotment in life.

29 *Before me*: An exclamation, like 'upon my word', 'upon my soul'.

31 *found thee*: Found you out.

32 *in*: *in* could mean both 'within' and 'by'.

32–3 *were you taught to find me? The search, sir, was profitable*: F follows *me?* with another speech-prefix for the Clown. A speech from Parolles may have dropped out; or what follows may have been a later insertion, written at the margin and incorrectly added; or it may be a simple mistake of the printer, continuing after a pause.

36 *well fed*: An echo of the Clown's own *highly fed and lowly taught* at II.2.3 earlier, with the proverb 'Better fed than taught' behind it.

41 *puts it off to*: Delays it in accordance with.

41–5 *a compelled restraint . . . And pleasure drown the brim*: An elaborate and false-sounding figure taken from the making of perfume. *restraint*, *want* and *delay* distil *sweets*, or sweet-scented flowers, in their still, the *curbèd time*.

47 *make this haste as your own good proceeding*: Represent the urgency as your own way of proceeding.

49 *probable need*: Likely necessity.

II.5

2 *valiant approof*: Proved valour.

5 *dial*: Timepiece or compass.

5–6 *I took this lark for a bunting*: I underestimated him. Lafew is drily reversing the proverb 'to take a bunting for a lark', meaning 'to overestimate someone worthless'.

8 *accordingly*: Correspondingly.

15 *Pray you, sir, who's his tailor*: Lafew is probably here behaving like Kent in *King Lear*, who teases Oswald by pretending to mistake him for a tailor's dummy (II.2.50–52).

27–8 *A good traveller is something at the latter end of a dinner*: Lafew continues his meditations on Parolles initiated in the earlier scene, II.3.200; if not a tailor's dummy, Parolles is a mere teller of tales.

36 *made shift*: Contrived, managed.

37 *like him that leaped into the custard*: A clown's leaping into a giant custard was a famous turn at Lord Mayor's Feasts at this period – an early association of fools with custard pies.

38–9 *suffer question for your residence*: Stand being asked why you are there.

41–2 *though I took him at's prayers*: Lafew picks up Bertram's *mistaken* and lets it mean 'mis-taken' or 'taken amiss': if he found Parolles praying, he would still take him amiss, or think some ill of him.

45 *I have kept of them tame*: I have had some such creatures as pets.

47–8 *we must do good against evil*: Cf. 1 Thessalonians 5:15: 'See that none recompense evil for evil unto any man: but ever follow that which is good.'

49 *idle*: Stupid, empty, crazy.

50 *I think not so*: F has *I think so*, which can be explained as an essentially hesitant and doubting agreement, such as to provoke Parolles's surprised and annoyed rejoinder. But it is more likely that the *not* in the next line confused the printer into thinking the first a slip and omitting it.

53 *Gives him a worthy pass*: Reputes him a good man.
clog: A cruel word. A *clog* is a block of wood tied to man or beast to stop him straying.

58–69 *You must not marvel, Helen, at my course . . . To you that know them not*: Bertram's lies emerge as conspicuously null rhetoric: his language is here quite devoid of vitality and savour.

59 *Which holds not colour with the time*: Which is not very well suited to the happy day (his wedding-day).

59–61 *nor does . . . my particular*: My course of action forces me to omit my personal duties and responsibilities as a husband.

66 *my respects*: The circumstances which prompt me.

67 *appointments*: Purposes.

74 *observance*: Dutiful service, respect.
eke out: Add to.

75 *homely stars*: The fate of being born of simple, humble family.

79 *owe*: Own.

89 *Where are my other men? Monsieur, farewell*: Some editors have found it hard to believe that Helena speaks these words, and have given either the whole line or the first part of it to Bertram. This text follows F.

92 *Coragio*: Courage (assimilated Italian).

III.1

3–4 *Whose great decision hath much blood let forth, | And more thirsts after*: Deciding the great issue involved in the war has caused the spilling of much blood and will cause more.

7 *cousin*: Title used by one sovereign of another.

9 *our borrowing prayers*: The King expressed his intended denial of the Duke of Florence's request for aid at I.2.4–12.

10–13 *The reasons of our state I cannot yield . . . By self-unable motion*: I cannot speak with authority on state policy, only give my views like a commoner who from outside the council chamber creates an image of what great affairs go on within, out of sketchy and subjective fantasies.

17 *nature*: Temperament, type. It is possible that this word is an error for 'nation', but *nature* makes sense as it stands.

18 *That surfeit on their ease*: Who find a life of ease too much for them (in the sense of sickening, and needing the *physic* or blood-letting of war to bring them back to health).

22 *When better fall, for your avails they fell*: When better places become available, you shall have them.

III.2

3 *troth*: Faith.

7 *ruff*: This usually means the neck-frill of the period, or a ruffled cuff on the sleeve, but here it seems to mean the same as one meaning of 'ruffle', the cuff or turned-over portion at the top of a boot.

8 *knew*: F has *know*. Some change is necessary in this sentence to bring *know* and *hold* into grammatical

concord. Some editors follow the third Folio and emend *hold* to *sold*, bearing in mind the proverb 'sold for a song'. This proposes a printer's slip less frequent than the familiar 'o'/'e' misreading of 'know'/'knew'; and the grammatical lack of concord between 'know' and *had* gives the impression that the error lies there, not later.

9   *hold*: Offer as a wager.

13 *old lings*: The *ling* was a long, slender fish of the cod family, so that the bawdy implication, as with 'eel', is obvious. 'Old ling' is the salted fish.

16 *stomach*: Keenness of appetite.

18 *E'en*: F has *In*, which is a common spelling for 'e'en' in Shakespeare.

22 *'not'*: There is possibly a quibble on 'knot' in the sense of 'marriage-tie'.

30 *misprizing*: Despising.

31 *For the contempt of empire*: For even emperors to despise.

40–41 *The danger is . . . getting of children*: The contrasting effects of *standing to't* in a bawdy sense (maintaining an erection) and in an orthodox military sense (standing firm, resisting attack) form a frequently treated topic in the literature of this period. The play on 'death' as both orgasm and death in battle is inherent in this paradox, which also draws on the contemporary notion that frequent orgasm weakened a man and hastened his death.

49 *on the start*: Suddenly appearing.

50 *Can woman me unto't*: Can make me behave in the conventional 'womanly' way, and weep.

54 *bend again*: Return.

55 *passport*: Licence to wander on a specified route as a beggar.

65 *If thou engrossest all the griefs are thine*: If you monopolize all the grief that is yours.

66 *moiety*: Share.

68 *thou art all my child*: Only you are my child, you are my only child.

68 *Towards*: Heading for.

72 *convenience*: Fitness, propriety.

76 *haply*: Perhaps.

89 *With his inducement*: By his (Parolles's) misleading example, his temptation.

90–91 *The fellow has a deal of that too much | Which holds him much to have*: He has too much of that quality (the power of inducement) that brings him so much advantage.

97 *Not so, but as we change our courtesies*: Only if the service is mutual (and you allow me to serve you).

101 *Rossillion*: Helena gives Bertram his formal title, which makes a dramatic point economically. She is withdrawing any private claims or any proprietary interest, and giving back to Bertram his independence and his important public status.

104 *event*: Outcome.

108 *leaden messengers*: Bullets.

110 *still*: Always, ever.

   still-piecing: F reads *still-peering*, which makes sense, though a difficult and very debatable sense. Numerous emendations have been proposed, of which *still-piecing* is the most widely accepted. It has a sense found in several other places in Shakespeare, that winds and waters, if an attempt is made to 'wound' them, merely close or repair 'piece' themselves again.

111 *That sings with piercing*: The whine of the bullets becomes a song sung by the air.

113 *forward*: Eagerly facing the enemy, in the van of the battle.

114 *caitiff*: Wretch.

117 *ravin*: Ravenous.

119 *owes*: Owns.

121–2 *Whence honour but of danger wins a scar, | As oft it loses all*: From the battlefield, where honour survives danger with nothing but a scar to show for it, and often does not survive danger at all.

126 *angels officed all*: All the work was done by angels.

127 *pitiful*: As taking pity on, being kind to Bertram.

128 *consolate*: Console.

129 *with the dark, poor thief, I'll steal away*: The last words
of this speech make an effective close to the first movement of the play.

III.3

0 *drum and trumpets*: That is, a drummer and trumpeters.
2 *Great in our hope*: With high hopes.
lay our best love and credence: Wager our love and faith
in you.
7 *helm*: Helmet.
9 *file*: Ranks, army.

III.4

4 *Saint Jaques*: *Jaques* is pronounced in two syllables. The
shrine referred to here (and as *Saint Jaques le Grand* at
III.5.33) is clearly that of Great St James at Compostella
in north-west Spain. Since Helena is starting out from
Rossillion in south-west France, it is something of a
surprise to meet her next in Florence, a city which
neither Shakespeare nor most of his audience can have
believed to be on any direct route from the one to the
other – even though the Widow, in III.5, shows no
surprise at the route. There is an element of mystery
here, as in the rumours of Helena's death propagated
by the rector of the shrine (IV.3.46–58). Possible
explan-ations are: Providence, chance, Helena's
contrivance, or combinations of any of these. It is also
possible that Shakespeare is using the romance mode
(where such things need no explanation) to move the
stress from the rational motivation or cause of events,
on to their fruits or effects. The mystery worries few
in the theatre.
5 *Ambitious love*: The phrase '*ambitiosus amor*' occurs in
Ovid's *Amores* (II.4.48) – though the consonance may
be accidental.
7 *sainted vow*: A vow to a saint.
9 *hie*: Hasten.
12 *His taken labours*: The labours he has undertaken.
13 *despiteful Juno*: Hostile Juno imposed on Hercules his
legendary twelve labours.
14 *From courtly friends, with camping foes to live*: 'Court'

and 'camp' were commonly linked at this period, usually in opposition.

17 *Whom I myself embrace to set him free*: *Whom* refers to death, *him* to Bertram; but, coming as it does as the last line of a sonnet, the line has an epigrammatic finality and paradoxical point that makes it sound as though Helena were also embracing Bertram to set him free – as, in a sense, she does.

19 *you did never lack advice so much*: You were never so ill-advised.

22 *prevented*: Forestalled.

23 *at overnight*: Last night, last evening.

27 *her prayers*: It is just possible that this is a reference to the intercessory prayers of the Virgin Mary, a Popish reference which, like Helena's pilgrimage, could be safely thrown into a play set in the world of feudal romance. But it is more likely that the Countess is referring to Helena, and making her sound like a saint interceding.

30 *this unworthy husband of his wife*: This husband unworthy of his wife.

III.5

0 *A tucket*: A trumpet-call signalling someone's approach.
her daughter Diana, and Mariana: F reads here *her daughter, Violenta and Mariana*. If there was ever a separate character called Violenta, she has nothing to say, and she has disappeared from the stage by line 96 of this scene, where there are only four characters present – Helena, Diana, the Widow and Mariana. It may be that the comma prefacing *Violenta* in F was an error, and the name was a first idea for the Widow's daughter, later cancelled; hence the curious stage direction at IV.2 in F, *Enter Bertram, and the Maide called Diana*. The name *Diana*, which was that of the goddess of chastity, has an obvious appropriateness to the girl's role in the play.

13 *honesty*: Chastity.

16–18 *a filthy officer he is in those suggestions for the young Earl*: This is ambiguous. It probably means 'he is a disgusting go-between who leads girls astray for the young Earl', but may mean, more simply, 'he is a horrible soldier who is always tempting the young Earl'.

19 *engines*: Tricks and traps.

20 *the things they go under*: What they seem to be.

21 *example*: Punctuation here follows Rowe in making the word a parenthetical insertion, meaning 'for example'.

23 *dissuade succession*: Prevent others from following in her footsteps.

23–4 *limed with the twigs that threatens them*: Caught by the trap waiting for them, like birds on twigs spread with bird-lime.

25 *grace*: Seemliness.

30 *lie*: Lodge.

34 *palmers*: Pilgrims. The word is here used in its ordinary loose sense; more precisely, the word describes a pilgrim coming from the Holy Land and bearing a palm leaf.

35 *the Saint Francis*: That is, an inn with Saint Francis for a sign.

port: City gate.

37–9 *Ay, marry, is't. Hark you, they come this way.* | *If you will tarry, holy pilgrim,* | *But till the troops come by*: The curious lineation here may be the effect of verse-speaking that is broken by stage business, noises off, etc. Or it may be evidence of revision in the text. Or it may be a compositor's misunderstanding of a somewhat overwritten and confused copy that should perhaps read

> Ay, marry, is't.
> Hark you, they come this way. Holy pilgrim,
> If you will tarry but till the troops come by . . .

42 *ample*: Well, fully. The Widow may be quibbling genially and also mean that the hostess and herself are 'liberal', 'generous of good things'.

50 *His face I know not*: Strictly speaking this is a lie and an unnecessary one. Shakespeare's intention is presumably to express Helena's desire to make a fresh start: it is *as if* she had never met Bertram.

50 *Whatsome'er*: Whatever.

51 *bravely taken*: Thought a very fine fellow.

54 *mere the truth*: Absolutely true, nothing but the truth.

56 *coarsely*: Slightingly, meanly.

58 *In argument of praise or to the worth*: If we are discussing her praiseworthiness or comparing it to the worth.

60–61 *all her deserving | Is a reservèd honesty*: Her only merit is a well-guarded chastity.

65 *I warrant*: F's *I write* has been much emended. *I warrant* is excellent sense, and is supported by the fact that 'warrant' is misprinted where it occurs elsewhere.

67 *shrewd*: Bad, nasty.

70 *brokes*: Bargains.

78 *honester*: Where Diana's 'honesty', discussed earlier in the scene, is her chastity, the range of meanings for the word in relation to Bertram is wider – encompassing honour, irreproachability and decency as well as sincerity.

81 *Yond's*: That one there is.

87 *Lose our drum*: Apart from the symbolic reference that Shakespeare gives to the drum by making it the particular attribute of Mars (see III.3.11), it had peculiar importance in carrying the colours of the regiment, so that the loss of the drum was a very signal loss of honour.

88 *shrewdly*: Intensely.

91 *courtesy*: Parolles has saluted the women. The words 'curtsy' (a bow or other salute, male or female) and 'courtesy' were not distinguished in spelling, so that Mariana may be speaking of the act of courtesy in the abstract or the concrete.

   ring-carrier: Bawd, go-between in seductions. Presumably the ring signifies the promise of marriage.

93 *host*: Lodge.

   enjoined penitents: Those bound by oath, like Helena, to undertake a pilgrimage as an act of penance.

97–8 *the charge and thanking | Shall be for me*: I shall pay for it, and thank you for coming.

99 *of*: On.

III.6

1 *put him to't*: Make him show himself up utterly.

3 *hilding*: Worthless fellow.

5 *bubble*: Something as pretty, empty and worthless as a bubble.

8–9 *as my kinsman*: Making the kind of allowances for him that I would for a kinsman.

11 *entertainment*: Patronage, attention, reception.

17 *fetch off*: Recapture, win back.

22 *hoodwink*: Cover, blindfold.

24 *leaguer*: Camp.

28 *intelligence*: Information.

35 *John Drum's entertainment*: A rough reception.

38–9 *in any hand*: In any case.

40–41 *sticks sorely in your disposition*: Vexes you a good deal.

42 *pox*: Plague (literally, syphilis).

45 *rend*: Split, tear apart, break up.

46–7 *in the command of the service*: On the orders given for the action.

50 *our success*: The way we came out of it.

57 *or hic jacet*: Or die in the attempt. '*Hic jacet*' ('here lies' in Latin) traditionally begins an epitaph.

58 *stomach*: Appetite, will.

59 *mystery*: Mastery, art, skill.

61 *magnanimious*: An alternative form of 'magnanimous'; here in the sense of 'great of spirit', 'great of heart'.

62 *speed*: Succeed, prosper.

65 *syllable*: Perhaps just metaphorical for 'minute quantity', perhaps an *ad hominem* joke referring to the name of Parolles.

68 *presently*: Immediately.

69 *dilemmas*: Arguments leading to a choice of two or more conclusions.

70 *my mortal preparation*: Preparation either for his own death, that is, making his will and so on, or for that of another, that is, arming himself.

74 *success*: Outcome.

76 *possibility*: Capability.

91 *probable*: Likely-sounding.

92   *embossed him*: Run him down (a term from hunting: 'to emboss' is to drive an animal to the point of exhaustion so great that its mouth foams).

96   *case*: Flay.

     smoked: Exposed, like a fox driven out of its earth by smoke. But the *first* also gives the word its other sense of 'suspected', 'got wind of'.

98   *sprat*: Small fish, here used as a term of contempt.

100   *twigs*: Trapping manoeuvres. Twigs spread with bird-lime were used for catching birds.

102   FIRST LORD: The speech-prefix here, and those at 104 and 110, are in reverse in F, so that Second Lord leaves the stage and First Lord stays with Bertram. But clearly they fulfil the opposite roles in what follows (First Lord directs the ambush of Parolles and Second Lord accompanies Bertram to Diana's house). It is therefore necessary to make such emendations in speech-prefixes here as will straighten out the confusion.

107   *have i'th'wind*: Have got scent of, are hunting down.

III.7

3   *But I shall lose the grounds I work upon*: Except by cutting the ground from under my own feet (that is, by revealing herself to Bertram).

7   *staining*: Disgraceful, dishonouring.

9   *sworn counsel*: Private ear, on the understanding of absolute secrecy.

11   *By*: In regard to, as to.

19   *carry*: Conquer, take by assault.

     in fine: Finally (or perhaps 'in short').

21   *important*: Importunate, demanding.

22   *County*: Count.

26   *choice*: Special estimation.

     idle fire: Mad or foolish passion.

27   *will*: Lust, object of appetite.

33   *In fine*: See note to 19.

35   *To marry her*: As a dowry to marry on.

37   *persever*: Accented on the second syllable.

39   *coherent*: Fitting, accordant.

41   *To her unworthiness*: The Widow seems to be showing

here the crisp rebuttal of romanticism that in the next
Act reveals itself as a characteristic of her astringent
daughter. Some editors, however, believe that the
meaning of this phrase is that Bertram's musical
performances are ruining Diana's reputation, and
making her 'unworthy'.

It nothing steads us: It's of no use to us at all.

44 *speed*: Succeed.

45 *meaning*: Intention.

45–7 *Is wicked meaning in a lawful deed . . . and yet a sinful
fact*: The first two lines of this riddle or charade deal
with each of the partners in the bed-trick singly, and
the last line takes them together. Bertram intends adultery and accomplishes it in lawful sexual intercourse
with his wife; Helena intends and accomplishes lawful
intercourse with her husband; both together succeed in
making innocent an act that could have been in fact
fornication or adultery.

IV.1

11 *linsey-woolsey*: A mixture of flax and wool; hence, a
medley of words, a mish-mash of language.

14–15 *strangers i'th'adversary's entertainment*: Foreign merce-
naries on the enemy's side.

15 *smack*: Smattering.

16–19 *we must every one be a man . . . to know straight our
purpose*: Every man must make up his own fantasy
language, so that we shan't know what we are saying
to each other – but to *seem* to understand each other
is what we are aiming at.

19 *choughs' language*: Jackdaw-chat.

21 *politic*: Shrewd and skilful.
couch: Get down.

26 *plausive*: Plausible.

27 *smoke*: Suspect.

39 *instance*: Evidence (so the phrase means 'where's the
evidence').

40 *butter-woman's*: Presumably dairywomen were loud and
frequent talkers.

41 *Bajazeth's mule*: Shakespeare elsewhere associates mules

with silence, and one might therefore furnish Parolles with the tongue he needs. Why it has to be *Bajazeth's* mule is a question so hard of solution as to have driven editors to frequent and various emendations of the whole phrase. It is possible that Parolles does not know either: words do not always act as he intends them to.

47 *afford you so*: Give you that much, let you off that easily.

48 *baring*: Shaving.

62 *Alarum*: Call to arms.

67 *Muskos*: Presumably the Muscovites.

71 *discover*: Reveal.

80 *hoodwinked*: Blindfolded.

81 *Haply*: Perhaps.

87 *A short alarum*: J. Dover Wilson in his edition suggests that this is an ironic drumroll.

89 *woodcock*: A bird noted for its stupidity.

91 *'A*: He.

IV.2

0 *Enter Bertram and Diana*: F reads *Enter Bertram, and the Maide called Diana*. See the second note to III.5.0.

1 *They told me that your name was Fontybell*: The attribution of this obtrusively romantic name to Diana suggests the callow or ingenuous nature of Bertram's romanticism.

3 *worth it, with addition*: You are worth further splendid titles also.

14 *vows*: Not to be a husband to Helena.

18 *our roses*: Our virginity.

19 *You barely leave our thorns*: You leave our thorns (of painful guilt and shame) bare and exposed to the view. There is perhaps a quibble, 'you leave us nothing but the thorns'.

21–31 *'Tis not the many oaths that makes the truth . . . At least in my opinion*: What Diana is saying here is important to the theme of the play as a whole, but the course of her close arguing is difficult at first sight. Bertram imagines himself (perhaps) to be passionately serious; Diana is trying to show him that real seriousness is a will-to-good-actions. She tells him first (21–2) that frequency in promises is less important than sincerity; then adds (23–9) that in any case sincerity is not the most important thing, if we mean by it only a subjective passionate conviction, for all men *take the highest to witness* at some time in that sense. The vital thing is to *vow true* by objective standards – to act out the love that is vowed, and to swear only the love that can be acted out.

25 *Love's*: F reads *Ioues*, with the 'I' and the 'u' that were normal usage for 'J' and 'v' at the time. The possibility of confusion between 'I' and 'l' will be obvious. When to this fact is added another, that at two earlier points where the text cites *love* as a divinity (II.3.74 and 84) a later Folio misread or emended the word to *Jove*, then it will be clear that the 'love'/'Jove' confusion suggests (what Johnson first conjectured): that the printer misread Shakespeare's 'Love' (or 'love'). To read *Love* here also clarifies a difficult argument, for Diana needs the verbal identity of the beloved and the sworn-by divinity for her case – that it is possible, in the name of Love, not to love one's love.

27 *love you ill*: Not love you, or love you with ill effect.

30 *poor conditions but unsealed*: A contract that is only a poor one so long as it remains one without legal ratification.

32 *holy-cruel*: Holy by being cruel, cruel by being holy (perhaps with a quibble on 'holy'/'wholly').

35 *my sick desires*: Bertram sees his *desires* detachedly, even coldly, as though they were a diseased acquaintance of his whom Diana must cure, as Helena cured the King.

36 *recovers*: An archaic third-person plural form (cf. I.1.103 above).

38 *I see that men make vows in such a flame*: F reads *I see that men make rope's in such a scarre*. Attempts have been made to defend this, but *some* degree of corruption has clearly taken place; and the line has been variously emended. The present reading adopts a nineteenth-century conjecture of *vows*. Diana must have some

words to indicate that she is (supposedly) melting, and
beginning to favour Bertram; and she does this by
speaking – seriously to Bertram, but ironically in the
understanding of the audience – the high love-language
of romance that he has just been talking about and in.
vows is a word very obviously relevant to its context
here. *flame* has occurred twice earlier in the play in the
sense of 'passionate love' (I.3.206, II.3.79) and once
in the sense of 'life' (I.2.59). In 'secretary' hand
(Shakespeare's probable script) it is possible to mistake
'vowes' for 'rope's' and 'flame' for 'scarre' – particularly since the latter word seems often to have been spelt
by Shakespeare 'scarre' (with the long-tailed 's' (ʃ)).

42 *honour*: An object to which honour is attached.

45 *honour*: Chastity.

49 *proper*: Personal.

56 *band*: Bond, obligation.

65 *though there my hope be done*: Though this succumbing
to you finishes my hopes of becoming a wife.

71 *had*: Would have.

73 *braid*: Of uncertain meaning: perhaps 'loose', 'licen-
tious', from Scots 'braid' meaning 'broad'; or perhaps
'deceitful', from the word 'braid' meaning 'plaited',
'twisted'.

75 *in this disguise*: In this game of deceiving.

76 *cozen*: Deceive.

IV.3

4 *he changed almost into another man*: If taken over-
literally this suggests something for which there is no
later evidence at all. The remark should probably be
taken as a high-wrought and courtly way of saying that
Bertram was at least shocked and shaken.

13 *perverted*: Seduced, corrupted.

15 *fleshes his will in the spoil*: The image is from hunting:
a hawk or hound was given a piece of the kill (*the spoil*)
to reward it and excite it with the prospect of further
occasions, and this was 'fleshing'. Bertram's lust (*will*)
was to be fleshed on Diana.

16 *monumental*: Serving as a memento.

16–17 *thinks himself made in the unchaste composition*: Thinks
       himself a made man by his dishonourable bargain.

   18 *delay*: Some editors have proposed emendations for F's
       delay: 'allay' and 'lay'. *delay* may have the sense
       'quench', or it may have the more frequent modern
       sense of 'postpone', with a colloquial idiom being used:
       'total moral reformation is too much to hope for, but
       an improvement for the next day or so might feasibly
       be petitioned'.

       rebellion: This word frequently carries, in Shakespeare,
       a subdued sexual reference: 'the rebellion of the flesh',
       'anarchic lust'.

   19 *ourselves*: In ourselves alone, without grace.

   20 *Merely*: Nothing but, absolutely.

20–24 *as in the common course of all treasons . . . in his proper
       stream o'erflows himself*: All traitors, all the way through
       their treacherous plots and enterprises and up to the
       achievement of their wicked ends, are expressing their
       own true treacherous natures; even so Bertram, here
       destroying his own honour, does it in a way charac-
       teristic of his own peculiar energies.

   25 *Is it not meant damnable*: Is it not intended to be a mortal
       sin.

 28–9 *dieted to his hour*: Limited to his one hour.

   31 *company anatomized*: Companion dissected and probed
       into.

 32–3 *wherein so curiously he had set this counterfeit*: In which
       he has given this false jewel so elaborate a setting.

 34–5 *him . . . he . . . his . . . the other*: Parolles . . . Bertram
       . . . Bertram's . . . Parolles.

   41 *higher*: Unclear: perhaps 'further'.

   43 *counsel*: The word plays on 'council'.

   47 *pretence*: Intention.

   49 *sanctimony*: Sanctity, holiness.

   53 *justified*: Proved, confirmed.

   57 *rector*: Probably 'priest', possibly 'ruler'.

   59 *intelligence*: Information, news.

   61 *to the full arming of the verity*: Fully and forcibly
       substantiating the truth of it.

71–3 *Our virtues would be proud . . . our virtues*: An elusive
and figurative passage, whose paradoxes are vital to the
play. The rough sense is: 'Our virtuous selves would
grow arrogant, were they not humiliated [into being
good?] by the sense of our faults; and our criminal
natures would give up hope, were they not aided and
abetted by all that is best in us.'

79–80 *They shall be no more . . . commend*: Even if they said
more than any letter of recommendation could, they
would still be no more than is needful (to reconcile the
King to Bertram).

85 *By an abstract of success*: Either 'to give a brief summary
of my successes', or 'to summarize briefly and in order
of events'.

86 *congied with*: Taken my leave of.

88 *entertained my convoy*: Hired my transport.

89 *parcels of dispatch*: Items to be settled.
nicer: More trivial (with a quibble on the sense 'wanton',
'lecherous').

95–6 *fearing to hear of it hereafter*: Since Diana may take him
at his word and claim him as her husband.

98 *counterfeit module*: Sham image.
has: Who has.

101 *gallant*: Showy, smart.

102–3 *His heels have deserved it in usurping his spurs*: It is what
he deserves, for being base when he should have been
chivalrous.

106 *shed*: Spilled.

115 *Muffled*: Blindfolded.

117–18 *Hush, hush! Hoodman comes*: These four words appear
to be a call from the old game of Blind Man's Buff;
Hoodman is another name for the Blind Man. F gives
the first two words to Bertram, who so little joins in
the playfulness of the two Lords as to make this seem
to need emendation.

135–6 *how and which way you will*: The exact significance of the
sacrament, and the manner of its administration and reception, were all of course matters crucial to the Reformation
and at this period gave rise to great debate and polemic.

Parolles refers helplessly here to the possibility of large
difference of opinion on the matter, especially since he
does not know the nationality of his captors, or whether,
if Christian, they are Protestant or Catholic.

137 *All's one to him*: F adds this to the end of the last remark
of Parolles. It is possible that *him* is a slip for 'me', on
the author's part rather than the compositor's. But most
editors have seen it as a mistake comparable to that at
117, and have given it to Bertram, as here.

141 *theoric*: Theory.

142 *chape*: Metal plate on a scabbard, covering the point of
the dagger.

150–51 *But I con him no thanks for't, in the nature he delivers it*:
But I refuse to thank him gratefully for it, when it is
such truth as he tells.

158 *live this*: Some editors emend this F reading to 'live but
this', 'leave this', or 'die this'. It is possible that Parolles
is, in his confused condition, conflating two statements:
'as I hope to live' (see 133 of this scene) and 'if I were
to die this present hour'.

159–63 *Spurio . . . Vaumond, Bentii*: Some of the names in this
passage are strange in their formation, and they make
an odd assortment as a whole. G. K. Hunter, in his edition,
suggests that Shakespeare is inventing odd names in order
to give the impression of an international force.

164 *muster-file*: List of those in an army or in a particular
division of it.

165 *poll*: Head.

166 *cassocks*: Military cloaks.

176 *well-weighing*: Heavy (but also quibbling on the sense
'influential').

182 *botcher*: Clumsy patcher (that is, tailor or cobbler
without much expertise).

184 *shrieve's fool*: The Crown had nominal charge of insane
persons – 'fools' or 'innocents' – but where their estate
was of no value their care was delegated to the sheriff
or *shrieve*.

187 *his brains are forfeit to the next tile that falls*: He's heading
straight for a sudden violent death.

198 *In good sadness*: Honestly, to be perfectly serious.

208 *advertisement*: Word of advice, piece of good counsel.
proper: Decent, respectable.

210 *ruttish*: Lustful (a derisive term: deer are 'in rut' in the
mating season).

216 *fry*: Small fish (swallowed in huge numbers by the whale).

219 *After he scores he never pays the score*: After he's hit the
mark (with sexual innuendo) he never pays the bill.

220 *Half-won is match well made; match, and well make it*:
If you get the terms of a bargain good and clear and
satisfactory, you're halfway to getting your money –
so draw up your terms, and make sure they're good.

221 *after-debts*: Bills remaining unpaid after the goods are
delivered.

223 *mell*: Be involved with (but with an obvious bawdy
sense here).

224 *For count of*: On account of.

231 *manifold linguist, and the armipotent soldier*: A mocking
echo of the earlier bombastic language of Parolles.
armipotent means 'mighty in arms'.

232 *cat*: Shylock in *The Merchant of Venice* speaks of 'Some
that are mad if they behold a cat' (IV.1.48).

244 *an egg out of a cloister*: Even the most trivial thing out
of even the most holy place.

245 *Nessus*: The centaur who attempted to rape Deianira,
the wife of Hercules. Centaurs were associated with lust.

251 *conditions*: Habits, characteristics.

259 *has*: He has.

259–60 *has led the drum before the English tragedians*: The
strolling players advertised themselves by processing
with a big drum at their head: and one such company,
so Parolles is affirming, had one of the Dumaines for
drummer.

262–3 *Mile-end*: Where the London citizen militia drilled,
often the subject of jokes. Cf., for example, *Henry IV,
Part II*, III.2.270 and Thomas Middleton and Thomas
Dekker's *The Roaring Girl*, II.1.190–91.

263 *doubling of files*: A simple drill exercise in which every
alternate man takes up position behind the next.

270 *cardecue*: Quarter of a crown or '*quart d'écu*' (old French silver coin of small value).

fee-simple: An estate held by its owner and his heirs absolutely and for ever.

271–3 *cut th'entail from all remainders, and a perpetual succession for it perpetually*: Make quite sure that his heir will not inherit the interest on the estate, nor his nor any heir for ever and ever.

281–2 *outruns any lackey*: A lackey at this time was a 'running footman' who went on errands and ran before the coach of his employer.

290–91 *beguile the supposition*: Gratify and fool the mind.

323 *thing*: When applied to human beings, this word usually means 'creature' in Shakespeare; though the meaning may extend here to cover 'object' as well.

328 *being fooled, by foolery thrive*: Since I have been made a fool of, I had better live and prosper by playing the fool.

IV.4

6 *which gratitude*: Gratitude for which.

7 *Tartar*: The racial group seen as least likely to feel tenderness.

9 *Marcellus*: That is, Marseilles. The spelling is one that probably records the pronunciation of 'Marseilles' at the time, and may be Shakespeare's own.

10 *convoy*: Transportation.

11 *breaking*: Disbanding, dispersing.

12 *hies him*: Hastens.

19 *brought me up*: Brought me to adulthood (or perhaps 'ennobled me', 'enriched my fortunes').

20 *motive*: Shakespeare is using the word here in a way which seems to be unique to him and which is paralleled in 'every joint and motive of her body' (*Troilus and Cressida*, IV.5.57); that is, to mean 'moving-agent', thing by which something moves.

23 *saucy trusting of the cozened thoughts*: Lecherous acceptance of the fantasies of the fooled mind.

25 *for that*: Taking it for that.

28–30 *Let death and honesty . . . Upon your will to suffer*: I am willing to endure any suffering, even death, upon your orders (*impositions*), so long as I retain my chastity.

30 *Yet*: Yet further, still more (suffering).

31 *But with the word the time will bring on summer*: This line has generally been regarded as a 'crux', and has been much emended. The major problem seems to have been the exact reference of the phrase *But with the word*: what word? It seems likely, however, that Helena refers to the word which she has just uttered twice – the word 'yet', with all its complex and quibbling senses. Helena is breaking it to Diana and the Widow, after their involvement in the bed-trick, that there is *yet* another ordeal for them still (*yet*) to suffer. *Yet* she has a comfort for them. Their journeyings and sufferings *will* bring them to a happy ending, just as *time*, saying *Yet* (both 'nevertheless' and 'yet a little longer to wait'), *brings on summer*, like the presenter leading on one of the characters in a Masque of the Seasons. It is in this sense that (as she says at 34) *time revives us*, making things new, and bringing hope.

34 *revives*: Refreshes (but also with its literal sense prominent: time 'gives life to us again').

35 *the fine's*: The end is.

36 *the renown*: The part that makes us famous.

IV.5

1–2 *snipped-taffeta*: Slashed-silk (a cut both at Parolles's fancifully pretty clothes and at his somewhat double personality).

2 *saffron*: Used as a starch at this time, hence the link with the clothes of Parolles; it was also used to colour pastry, hence the *unbaked and doughy youth* at 3.

6 *red-tailed humble-bee*: Noise and uncreativity make the point of the comparison between Parolles and a bumblebee.

10 *dearest*: Full of both love and pain.

13 *sallets*: Salads.

15 *herb of grace*: Rue.

16–17 *They are not herbs, you knave, they are nose-herbs*: The distinction here is between herbs for salad, called simply *herbs*, and sweet-scented plants, called *nose-herbs*.

18 *Nabuchadnezzar*: The King of Babylon who is said in his insanity to have eaten grass: Daniel 4:28–37.

19 *grass*: With a quibble on *grace*, which is what F reads at this point.

20 *Whether*: Which.

22 *service*: This word frequently gives occasion for a sexual innuendo, or for an actual bawdy quibble, and does so here.

28 *bauble*: Rod of office carried by a court fool (a bawdy quibble).

37 *name*: F reads *maine* here. It is just possible that this is correct and that the word means 'meinie', or 'household servants'. There is a stronger probability that *maine* was a misreading of the usual emendation of it, *name* – a probability supported by the wordplay which some find between *name* and *fisnomy* (fis*namy*) meaning 'physiognomy'.

38 *more hotter*: The Clown is playing with two ideas: that the Black Prince, who fought wars in France, was therefore more choleric and heated there; that he must also have had syphilis, 'the French disease'.

43 *suggest*: Tempt.

47 *the prince of the world*: Cf. 'Now is the judgement of this world: now shall the prince of this world be cast out' (John 12:31).

48–53 *I am for the house with the narrow gate . . . the broad gate and the great fire*: Cf. 'Enter in at the strait gate. For wide is the gate, and broad is the way, that leadeth to destruction, and many there be which go in thereat. Because, strait is the gate, and narrow is the way, which leadeth unto life . . .' (Matthew 7:13–14).

51 *chill and tender*: Faint-hearted and fond of comfort, cool and sensitive.

59 *jades' tricks*: The Clown's joke depends on a simultaneous reference to the literal and metaphorical usage of this phrase, which then comes to mean 'the kind of

vicious practices you expect from ill-tempered, broken-down nags, or from clowns'.

61 *A shrewd knave and an unhappy*: A sharp-tongued, discontented fellow. Some editors understand *unhappy* to mean 'mischievous' and would gloss *shrewd* with a harsher word than 'sharp-tongued'; but there seems no linguistic evidence for this.

65 *pace*: The temperate, obedient movement of a trained horse.

71 *self-gracious remembrance*: An act of recollection owed to his own gracious self (and not to someone's reminder).

78 *post*: At express speed.

81 *intelligence*: Information, news.

83–90 *I shall beseech your lordship to remain with me . . . I thank my God, it holds yet*: In a mannered, courtly diction which utilizes legal metaphors (*privilege*, *charter*), and with the utmost politeness, the Countess is inviting Lafew to stay at her castle until the meeting of the King and her son, and Lafew is pleased to accept.

91–2 *patch of velvet*: Such as might cover either a battle-scar or the marks of surgery for syphilis.

95 *is worn bare*: Has no patch on it, reveals bare skin.

98 *carbonadoed*: Slashed (with cuts by a surgeon, treating syphilitic ulcers).

V.1

1 *exceeding posting*: Extreme haste.

4 *wear*: Tire.

5 *bold*: Confident.
requital: Debt.

6 *Enter a Gentleman, Astringer to the King*: F's stage direction, *Enter a gentle Astringer*, has been emended by editors to '*Enter a Gentleman*', '*Enter a Gentleman Usher*' and '*Enter a Gentleman, a stranger*' (in the last of these, the presumption is that Shakespeare is reminding himself or others that this 'Gentleman' is not one of those who have appeared earlier). The main difficulty about F's *Astringer* is the question of how his profession, that of a keeper of hawks – for that is what the term means – could have been made clear to an audi-

ence. The opening stage direction of *Henry VI, Part II*, II.1, contains '*falconers halloing*', but their occupation is explained by the dialogue which follows. Otherwise, there is no intrinsic unlikelihood of Shakespeare's so denominating a minor character in this courtly and often socially realistic play.

In happy time: Just at the right moment.

15 *Which lay nice manners by*: Which cause us to put aside delicate politeness.

26 *adverse*: Accented on the second syllable.

35 *Our means will make us means*: Our resources will allow us.

V.2

1 *Lavatch*: There seem to be various discrediting suggestions behind Lavatch's name. One is '*la vache*', 'cow', but colloquially meaning something like 'trollop'; another is *lavage* (or the Italian form of the same word, *lavaccio*) meaning 'slop'.

4 *muddied in Fortune's mood*: *mood* means 'anger', 'displeasure'. The word carries a quibble that explains the lengthy lavatorial wordplay that follows. *muddied* and *mood* echo the now obsolete word 'mute', which is the correct term for an animal's or more specifically a bird's droppings. Once Parolles, with his high-flown phrase, has fallen into this trap, the Clown eagerly continues the references to bad smells in *close-stool* (17; an early form of lavatory), *pur* (19; meaning 'animal excrement') and *unclean fishpond* (20).

8–9 *allow the wind*: Go down-wind.

19 *pur*: Apart from the sense referred to in the note to 4 above, this word quibbles on 'purr', hence the transition to *Fortune's cat*. The word has a third sense, that of the knave in a card game of the time, and this sense is picked up in Lafew's next speech (30–31).

20 *not a musk-cat*: A type, not of cat but of deer, from which the scent musk is obtained. The Clown means that Parolles is far from sweetly scented.

21 *withal*: With it.

22 *carp*: A last lavatorial insult, as carp are, it seems, bred

in manured fish-ponds; with a quibble also on the word for a 'carper', or 'talking fellow'.

23 *ingenious*: This word, the reading of F, has a somewhat random appearance in the Clown's list. It has been explained as meaning 'un-genious', that is, stupid, on the analogy of Shakespeare's use elsewhere of 'illustrious' to mean 'unlustrous'; it has also been emended by editors to 'ingenerous' and 'ingenuous'. The Clown is perhaps merely using the word ironically, as 'clever' might well be used now.

24 *similes of comfort*: F reads *smiles of comfort*, which may just be correct, and mean 'invigorating, fortifying jokes'. There are, however, two separate points which support emendation. The first is that *similes* picks up the wordplay with *metaphor* at 12 and 13. The second is that the phrase 'similes, comfortable and profitable' occurs elsewhere in this period, the word 'similes' in it appearing to mean 'instructive sayings or parables', and such a meaning may be present here.

33 *justices*: After 1601 Justices of the Peace were in charge of the very poor and could relieve those who they felt deserved it.

40 *more than 'word' then*: He refers to the name 'Parolles', or 'words'.
   Cox my passion: An oath produced by euphemistic distortion from 'God's my passion', that is, 'by the suffering of God'.

42–3 *found me*: This and Lafew's *lost thee* in the next line repeat the wordplay of II.3.204–5, by which *found* quibbles on 'found out', and 'lost' contains the meanings 'dropped' and 'forgot'.

V.3

1 *of*: In.
   esteem: Value in absolute terms, worth (repeated in *estimation*, 4).

4 *home*: To the heart, fully.

5 *make it*: Consider it.

6 *blade*: The green part of a plant before the ear appears. The word is emended to 'blaze' by some editors,

because of the felt lack of congruence with the 'oil' metaphor; but this is unnecessary.

10 *high bent*: Fully, strongly bent, like a taut bow.

12 *first I beg my pardon*: With nervous punctiliousness Lafew, the true courtier, apologizes for being about to express a different opinion from the King's. Cf. his equally nervous apology for bringing a new doctor to the King at II.1.61.

17 *richest*: Most experienced.

21–2 *kill | All repetition*: Put an end to any discussion of the past.

23 *The nature of his great offence is dead*: The essence of his offence is dead now that Helena herself is dead.

25 *incensing relics*: Memories arousing anger.

29 *hath reference to*: Exists only in relation to.

32 *not a day of season*: Not seasonable (meaning 'not conforming to the conventional idea of a summer day, that is all sunshine, or a winter day, that is all hail').

35 *Distracted*: Playing on the two meanings of 'divided' and 'troubled'.

36 *high-repented blames*: Bitterly repented faults, sins.

37 *All is whole*: All is well.

38 *consumèd*: Past.

39 *take the instant by the forward top*: Take time by the forelock.

45–52 *ere my heart . . . To a most hideous object*: Bertram's language is so abstract and generalized here that it is impossible to know whether he is talking about Helena or the lady later named as Maudlin. The main current of meaning seems to be that he fell in love with Maudlin *At first*, but did not dare to propose to her, or did not dare to tell the King and company that he had fallen in love with her; once his eye was fixed on her, he felt *Contempt* for every other face, especially Helena's. But he may mean that he loved Maudlin before that moment when he spoke all too boldly to the King, and when contempt fixed his eye and made Helena seem hideous.

48 *perspective*: An optical instrument or device that distorts (accented on the first syllable).

49 *favour*: Face.

57 *the great compt*: The great reckoning. The phrase sounds
   as though it must mean 'the day of judgement', but may
   mean only 'the long account of your sins in this matter'.

58 *remorseful*: The word may mean 'compassionate', or
   may reflect more on Bertram's situation than on its own
   metaphorical context, and carry its more modern
   meaning of 'guilty', 'regretful', 'sorry'.

59 *turns a sour offence*: Like milk sent too dilatorily to a
   starving man: it turns sour, and is merely offensive, and
   is seen as merely offensive by the would-be-great sender.

66 *shameful hate sleeps out the afternoon*: To our shame,
   hatred sleeps a sweet after-dinner sleep without regrets
   (having *Destroyed our friends* and left torpid love to
   wake and weep them uselessly).

68 *Maudlin*: The name may well be yet another of the
   play's significant proper names. It is a common
   English form of (Mary) Magdalen, the Saint of
   Penitence ('the Weeper'). Maudlin's name suggests
   that she is a proper match for a young man who is
   nominally penitent.

71–2 *Which better than the first, O dear heaven, bless!* | *Or,
   ere they meet, in me, O nature, cesse*: F assigns these two
   lines to the King, but they are clearly more appropriate
   to the Countess, and are usually so assigned. The
   Countess expresses the hope that she herself may die
   (nature cease (*cesse*) in her) before the second marriage
   comes to resemble (*meet*) the first.

74 *digested*: Swallowed up.
   favour: Token, present.

75–6 *To sparkle in the spirits of my daughter,* | *That she may
   quickly come*: That the jewel may give its own brilliant
   brightness to my daughter's present thoughts of you,
   and make her come to you happily and soon.

79 *The last that e'er I took her leave at court*: The last time
   I ever took leave of her at court.

85 *Necessitied*: In need of.

86 *reave*: Rob, deprive.

87 *stead*: Help, benefit.

96 *ingaged*: The word may mean 'engaged', in which case
the sense is that the maiden perceives Bertram as bound
to her by picking up and keeping her ring, or 'ungaged',
in the sense of not promised to anyone else.

96–7 *subscribed | To*: Admitted, acknowledged.

100 *In heavy satisfaction*: In sad acceptance of the facts.

101 *Plutus*: The god of wealth and gold. Logically enough,
he is shown here as the greatest of alchemists, having
huge *science* or expertise in *nature's mystery*, the art of
turning base metals into gold and multiplying gold
itself, by means of the *tinct* or 'elixir'.

105–7 *then if you know . . . Confess 'twas hers*: This is somewhat obscure, but the King seems to mean 'admit it
was hers, a truth which is as clear as the fact that you
know you are yourself'.

115–20 *If it should prove . . . More than to see this ring*: The
disjointed movement of this sentence echoes the
disturbed, wretched, and finally conclusive movement
of the King's mind.

121–3 *My fore-past proofs . . . feared too little*: However the
affair turns out, the proofs which have already accu-
mulated show that my fears are anything but vain; the
vanity or folly has rather been in fearing too little.

131–2 *Who hath for four or five removes . . . herself*: Who has
tried to catch up with you (to present her petition
herself) but has just missed doing so, on the last four
or five stages of your journey from one stopping-place
to the next (*removes*).

136 *importing*: Full of significance (or perhaps 'urgent').

137 *verbal brief*: A summary by word of mouth.

148–9 *toll for this*: Enter this one as 'for sale' in the toll-book
of a market.

151 *suitors*: Petitioners.

156 *as you swear them lordship*: As soon as you swear to be
their lord and marry them.

157 *Enter the Widow and Diana*: F brings on Parolles with
the Widow and Diana here, although there is a separate entry for him at 230.

164 *both shall cease*: Both her ageing life and her honour

will come to an end with grief and shame if Bertram
is not made to marry Diana.

170 *this hand*: She presumably points to Bertram's left hand.

178 *fond*: Foolish.

183 *them; fairer*: F reads *them fairer.*, which has been
emended by editors to the punctuation as here given.

188 *gamester*: Prostitute.

192 *high respect and rich validity*: Great honour and high
value.

195 *'tis hit*: She has got him there, she has hit the mark.
Some editors emend to ''tis it', on the ground that *hit*
in F represents merely the old emphatic form of 'it'
and should therefore be modernized.

197 *sequent issue*: Next heir.

198 *owed*: Owned.

199–200 *Methought you said | You saw one here in court could
witness it*: Diana has not in fact said this so far. Either
Shakespeare is using a dramatic shorthand to cut down
tedious complications, or this is a rewriting of the
possible earlier idea for this scene in which Diana and
Parolles entered in company (see note for stage direction at 157).

205 *quoted for*: Regarded as, spoken of as.

206 *With all the spots o'th'world taxed and debauched*:
Accused (*taxed*) of being corrupted with all the
disgraceful crimes in the world.

208 *Am I or that or this for what he'll utter*: Am I to be written
down a 'this' or a 'that' on *his* evidence.

211 *boarded*: Accosted.

212 *She knew her distance*: She knew how to keep just far
enough off (to madden and attract me more).

214–15 *in fancy's course | Are motives of more fancy*: In the way
of passionate desire only serve to increase that desire.

215 *in fine*: 'At last' or 'to be brief'.

216 *Her infinite cunning with her modern grace*: Her immense,
timeless artfulness and her commonplace charm. F
reads *insuite comming* for the first phrase. It is just
possible that *insuite* is correct and is an anglicization
of a Latin word for 'unusual'; but orthographical

evidence strongly supports the supposition of mis-reading.

217 *rate*: Price.

221 *diet me*: Restrain me, limit my pleasures.

232 *boggle shrewdly*: Startle and shy away from things violently.

    every feather starts you: A mere feather makes you jump. This remark, like that which immediately precedes it, is of course ironical; it has taken a good deal of battering to make Bertram admit this much.

237 *By him and by this woman*: Concerning him and this woman.

245–6 *as a gentleman loves a woman*: The social difference in these two terms makes the point of the answer here.

248 *He loved her, sir, and loved her not*: He loved her person, but not *her*.

249–50 *equivocal companion*: Equivocating, quibbling fellow.

253 *He's a good drum, my lord, but a naughty orator*: Lafew's surface meaning is that Parolles is a good drummer but a poor – or wicked – orator; but he uses *drum* quibblingly so that an apparently kind and even protective remark becomes rather harsher, and means, 'He's good at making noise when beaten, and can boom out notes invented by someone better than himself, but as more than a mere instrument he's worthless or worse.'

262 *other motions*: Proposals, offers (but probably with a bawdy quibble).

266 *fine*: Subtle.

284 *customer*: Prostitute.

294 *owes*: Owns.

297 *quit*: The main sense here is 'acquit', but there is also a wordplay, on the sense 'am quits with, have my revenge on', and also 'leave'.

301 *quick*: Alive (but also with a quibble on 'pregnant').

302 *exorcist*: One who summons and lays spirits.

303 *truer office*: That is, to see real things.

305 *shadow*: A word whose many meanings contribute much to the moment: a *shadow* may be a ghost, an image or imitation, a reflection, or an actor.

307 *like*: In the place of.

308 *kind*: In Shakespeare's day this word held more, and more complex, meanings than it does now. Helena's intended meaning is 'kind' in the modern sense: Bertram has been humane and generous. But the whole situation to which she alludes reminds a reader of the rich ground for irony and double meaning which the potentially disparate other senses of the word afforded. A major sense at this period was 'natural': a 'kind' person is one who acts after his 'kind' or his nature. A subordinate sense was 'sexually responsive, willing to make love'. It is Helena's triumph that she has achieved, even if only momentarily, the unification of these meanings, and is able to suggest that Bertram's sexual instincts are not only natural but humane and generous.

310–11 *When from my finger you can get this ring . . . And is by me with child*: Cf. the earlier form of the letter, at III.2.56–9.

323 *even*: Exact, precise.

329 *Resolvèdly*: So that uncertainty is removed.

EPILOGUE

1 *a beggar*: In asking for applause; and in being only the 'shadow' of a king, until the audience confirm him by applause.

4 *strife*: Striving.

5 *Ours be your patience then and yours our parts*: We shall patiently wait while you 'act out' applause as you patiently waited while we acted out the play.

6 *Your gentle hands lend us and take our hearts*: Your kind and civilized applause will win our love.

The National: three theatres and so much more...

www.nationaltheatre.org.uk

In its three theatres on London's South Bank, the National presents an eclectic mix of new plays and classics, with seven or eight shows in repertory at any one time.

And there's more. Step inside and enjoy free exhibitions, backstage tours, talks and readings, a great theatre bookshop and plenty of places to eat and drink.

Sign-up as an e-member at www.nationaltheatre.org.uk/join and we'll keep you up-to-date with everything that's going on.

NATIONAL THEATRE
SOUTH BANK
LONDON SE1 9PX

PENGUIN SHAKESPEARE

AS YOU LIKE IT
WILLIAM SHAKESPEARE

WWW.PENGUINSHAKESPEARE.COM

When Rosalind is banished by her uncle, who has usurped her father's throne, she flees to the Forest of Arden where her exiled father holds court. There, dressed as a boy to avoid discovery, she encounters the man she loves – now a fellow exile – and resolves to remain in disguise to test his feelings for her. A gloriously sunny comedy, *As You Like It* is an exuberant combination of concealed identities and verbal jousting, reconciliations and multiple weddings.

This book includes a general introduction to Shakespeare's life and the Elizabethan theatre, a separate introduction to *As You Like It*, a chronology of his works, suggestions for further reading, an essay discussing performance options on both stage and screen, and a commentary.

Edited by H. J. Oliver

With an introduction by Katherine Duncan-Jones

General Editor: Stanley Wells

PENGUIN SHAKESPEARE

A MIDSUMMER NIGHT'S DREAM
WILLIAM SHAKESPEARE

WWW.PENGUINSHAKESPEARE.COM

A young woman flees Athens with her lover, only to be pursued by her would-be husband and by her best friend. Unwittingly, all four find themselves in an enchanted forest where fairies and sprites soon take an interest in human affairs, dispensing magical love potions and casting mischievous spells. In this dazzling comedy, confusion ends in harmony, as love is transformed, misplaced, and – ultimately – restored.

This book includes a general introduction to Shakespeare's life and the Elizabethan theatre, a separate introduction to *A Midsummer Night's Dream*, a chronology of his works, suggestions for further reading, an essay discussing performance options on both stage and screen, and a commentary.

Edited by Stanley Wells

With an introduction by Helen Hackett

General Editor: Stanley Wells

PENGUIN SHAKESPEARE

A MIDSUMMER NIGHT'S DREAM
WILLIAM SHAKESPEARE

WWW.PENGUINSHAKESPEARE.COM

A young woman flees Athens with her lover, only to be pursued by her would-be husband and by her best friend. Unwittingly, all four find themselves in an enchanted forest where fairies and sprites soon take an interest in human affairs, dispensing magical love potions and casting mischievous spells. In this dazzling comedy, confusion ends in harmony, as love is transformed, misplaced, and – ultimately – restored.

This book includes a general introduction to Shakespeare's life and the Elizabethan theatre, a separate introduction to *A Midsummer Night's Dream*, a chronology of his works, suggestions for further reading, an essay discussing performance options on both stage and screen, and a commentary.

Edited by Stanley Wells

With an introduction by Helen Hackett

General Editor: Stanley Wells

PENGUIN SHAKESPEARE

MUCH ADO ABOUT NOTHING
WILLIAM SHAKESPEARE

WWW.PENGUINSHAKESPEARE.COM

A vivacious woman and a high-spirited man both claim that they are
determined never to marry. But when their friends trick them into
believing that each harbours secret feelings for the other, they begin to
question whether their witty banter and sharp-tongued repartee
conceals something deeper. Schemes abound, misunderstandings
proliferate and matches are eventually made in this sparkling and
irresistible comedy.

This book includes a general introduction to Shakespeare's life and the
Elizabethan theatre, a separate introduction to *Much Ado About
Nothing*, a chronology of his works, suggestions for further reading, an
essay discussing performance options on both stage and screen, and a
commentary.

Edited by R. A. Foakes

With an introduction by Janette Dillon

General Editor: Stanley Wells

PENGUIN SHAKESPEARE

TWELFTH NIGHT
WILLIAM SHAKESPEARE

WWW.PENGUINSHAKESPEARE.COM

Separated from her twin brother Sebastian after a shipwreck, Viola disguises herself as a boy to serve the Duke of Illyria. Wooing a countess on his behalf, she is stunned to find herself the object of his beloved's affections. With the arrival of Viola's brother, and a trick played upon the countess's steward, confusion reigns in this romantic comedy of mistaken identity.

This book includes a general introduction to Shakespeare's life and the Elizabethan theatre, a separate introduction to *Twelfth Night*, a chronology of his works, suggestions for further reading, an essay discussing performance options on both stage and screen, and a commentary.

Edited by M. M. Mahood

With an introduction by Michael Dobson

General Editor: Stanley Wells

PENGUIN SHAKESPEARE

TIMON OF ATHENS
WILLIAM SHAKESPEARE

WWW.PENGUINSHAKESPEARE.COM

After squandering his wealth with prodigal generosity, a rich Athenian gentleman finds himself deep in debt. Unshaken by the prospect of bankruptcy, he is certain that the friends he has helped so often will come to his aid. But when they learn his wealth is gone, he quickly finds that their promises fall away to nothing in this tragic exploration of power, greed, and loyalty betrayed.

This book includes a general introduction to Shakespeare's life and the Elizabethan theatre, a separate introduction to *Timon of Athens*, a chronology of his works, suggestions for further reading, an essay discussing performance options on both stage and screen, and a commentary.

Edited by G. R. Hibbard

With an introduction by Nicholas Walton

General Editor: Stanley Wells

PENGUIN SHAKESPEARE

THE WINTER'S TALE
WILLIAM SHAKESPEARE

WWW.PENGUINSHAKESPEARE.COM

The jealous King of Sicily becomes convinced that his wife is carrying the child of his best friend. Imprisoned and put on trial, the Queen collapses when the King refuses to accept the divine confirmation of her innocence. The child is abandoned to die on the coast of Bohemia. But when she is found and raised by a shepherd, it seems redemption may be possible.

This book includes a general introduction to Shakespeare's life and the Elizabethan theatre, a separate introduction to *The Winter's Tale*, a chronology of his works, suggestions for further reading, an essay discussing performance options on both stage and screen by Paul Edmondson, and a commentary.

Edited by Ernest Schanzer

With an introduction by Russ McDonald

General Editor: Stanley Wells

Read more in Penguin

PENGUIN SHAKESPEARE

All's Well That Ends Well
Antony and Cleopatra
As You Like It
The Comedy of Errors
Coriolanus
Cymbeline
Hamlet
Henry IV, Part I
Henry IV, Part II
Henry V
Henry VI, P...
Henry VI, Pa...
Henry VI, Pa...
Henry VIII
Julius Caesar
King John
King Lear
Love's Labour's L...
Macbeth
Measure for Measur...
The Merchant of Veni...

The Merry Wives of
  Windsor
A Midsummer Night's
  Dream
Much Ado About Nothing
Othello
Pericles
Richard II...

...A Lover's

...Shrew

...Two Noble Kinsmen
The Winter's Tale